Partners of Zaynab

STUDIES IN COMPARATIVE RELIGION
Frederick M. Denny, Series Editor

Partners of Zaynab

A Gendered Perspective of Shia Muslim Faith

Diane D'Souza

The University of South Carolina Press

Published by the University of South Carolina Press
Columbia, South Carolina 29208

www.sc.edu/uscpress

Manufactured in the United States of America

23 22 21 20 19 18 17 16 15 14   10 9 8 7 6 5 4 3 2 1

Library of Congress Cataloging-in-Publication Data

D'Souza, Diane, 1960–
Partners of Zaynab : a gendered perspective of Shia Muslim faith / Diane D'Souza.
pages cm. — (Studies in comparative religion)
Includes bibliographical references and index.
ISBN 978-1-61117-377-2 (hardbound : alk. paper) — ISBN 978-1-61117-378-9 (ebook)
1. Shi'ah—Customs and practices. 2. Shi'ah—Doctrines. 3. Women in Islam.
4. Women—Religious aspects—Islam. I. Title.
BP194.2.D755 2013
297.8'2082—dc23

2014007289

This book was printed on recycled paper with 30 percent postconsumer waste content.

To the Shia community in Hyderabad, and especially its women,
for sharing their lives and faith with me

CONTENTS

ILLUSTRATIONS

SERIES EDITOR'S PREFACE

Diane D'Souza's study is a major contribution to scholarship on Shi'ite Islam in general, as well as a revealing study of ways in which both Shi'ite men and modern western scholars have traditionally failed to consider Shi'ite women as significant players in Shi'ite communal and cultural life anywhere in the culturally, ethnically and socially diverse Muslim world. The author lived for many years in Hyderabad, India, and became deeply immersed in Shi'ite women's ways of belief and community leadership in that important region of Shi'ite presence and influence in India. The study thoughtfully and respectfully addresses not only the stresses that Shi'ites--both male and female--often experience within Sunni Muslim majorities in the Muslim world but also the difficulties that Shi'ite women often have encountered within their own sectarian boundaries.

In addition to the project's high level of formal scholarly integrity and field-based originality of data is the fact that it is a good read and should find a wide generally educated as well as academic readers market including comparative religion, Islamic studies, gender and women's studies, cultural/social/ethnic studies, and ritual studies. The book will also significantly contribute to sorely needed data-gathering and understanding of Shi'ite Islam in general as well as Muslim women in particular in the contemporary Indian subcontinent. The project is full of new and substantial religious and cultural data made interesting and intelligible by sophisticated and assertively argued critical/theoretical analysis and interpretation.

This series has in recent years published important new studies on religion in South Asian contexts: Fred Clothey, *Ritualizing on the Boundaries: Continuity and Innovation in the Tamil Diaspora* (2006); Kelly Pemberton, *Women Mystics and Sufi Shrines in India* (2010); and Guy L. Beck, *Sonic Liturgy: Ritual and Music in Hindu Tradition* (2012). Diane D'Souza's *Partners of Zaynab: A Gendered Perspective of Shia Muslim Faith* is a strong addition to this list.

Frederick M. Denny

PREFACE

I first encountered the religion of Islam through interactions with Muslims in the South Indian city of Hyderabad. I had moved there from Canada in 1985 with a six-month-old son and an Indian husband. My husband's work at the Henry Martyn Institute, an institution with a focus on Christian-Muslim relations and interreligious dialogue, brought me into contact with Muslims in a city known for its vibrant Islamic culture and heritage. Fortunately I left North America before today's era of stereotypes about Muslims, for it allowed me to begin my relationship with a people and their religion without the baggage of preconceived ideas. Initially what I learned about Muslim faith came from local encounters in a thriving metropolis where the call to prayer was a melodious backdrop to the bustle of the city. I gradually got to know fruit sellers and shop owners, neighbors and teachers, housewives and domestic workers. My interest in and connections to people further expanded as I visited local religious sites and met with Muslims from across the socioeconomic spectrum. I and my young children spent a good deal of time in female company when we visited people's homes, as was the local custom especially in conservative circles. Being a "foreigner," however, I was given greater latitude than most Indian women and often was invited into the formal parlor or meeting place of men, as well as into the bedrooms, kitchens, and living areas where women and children tended to congregate.

My interest in the Muslim community thus began as part of nearly twenty years of life spent in India. Part of my identity there included being a rare white foreigner among the six million people who identified Hyderabad as home, the mother of three engaging children, the wife of a Christian Islamic scholar, and a researcher whose interests in gender and psychology led me to teach and write about Muslim women's lives. As my social networks deepened and my engagement with Muslim communities grew, I drew increasingly upon published writings to further my interest in Islam's foundations, history, and practices. Although this information was at times useful, it was also occasionally very unsatisfying. For example, I was fascinated by the vibrant local observances surrounding *Shab-e-Barat,* the "Night of Mercy" (D'Souza 2004), when the faithful remember those who have died and affirm that life and death are in God's hands. Muslim neighborhoods are lit up and active long into the night as the devout engage in rituals of personal and communal piety. In stunning contrast, scholarly sources barely mention this hugely popular event. Even specialist encyclopedias confine it to the margins of Muslim experience.

As my research continued, I eventually grew frustrated by the pejorative ways in which women's spiritual lives were overlooked, glossed over, or devalued in the writings of many male religious leaders and religious studies scholars. This was particularly true when women's rituals or activities fell outside the established pillars of Islamic practice: daily prayer, fasting during Ramzan, pilgrimage to Mecca once in a lifetime, regular tithing for those whose economic situation allows it, and affirming one's faith through a straightforward formulaic recitation. Although I saw women doing all these things, I saw them faithfully doing much more: being generous to the poor, praying for their personal needs and for the intercession of powerful spiritual figures, engaging in simple or elaborate rituals with deep layers of meaning. The unsatisfying gap between what women named or practiced as important to their religious lives and what male scholars and religious leaders defined as central motivated me to conduct research that could accurately and respectfully portray female devotional lives. I chose an empirical process rather than a historical one in order to provide women with a chance to define and describe for themselves their religious perceptions and experiences.

An issue which has further galvanized my writing has been the persistent bifurcation of religious practice into normative and popular categories. One notices this tendency in the religious and Islamic studies fields, but it also surfaces among anthropologists and other social scientists who study Muslim cultures. *Normative* refers to standard doctrines and behaviors, the "established religion," while *popular* indicates rituals, actions, and beliefs that self-identified Muslims practice but that fall outside the established religion. Scholars thus distinguish between universal and local religion or, in a flurry of binaries, between official and unofficial, orthodox and heterodox, central and peripheral, or Great and Little traditions. The actual terms are less important than the dichotomy they suggest or the accompanying presumption that universal, official, orthodox practices and beliefs are of a higher or purer form than local, unofficial, or heterodox ones. By privileging certain types of religious behavior Muslim women's devotional expressions are often marginalized. An unexamined gender bias tends to channel many female practices into the latter devalued category, profoundly weakening our understanding of religion.

In this book, then, I offer a glimpse into what religiosity means for a group of devout Shia women in the South Asian urban context. I do not give an overview of the entirety of women's devotional lives but focus on uniquely Shia rituals that women perform collectively. This allows me to dispel their relative scholarly neglect and delve more deeply into a significant set of religious practices. By this choice I do not mean to imply that rituals shared with Sunnis, such as fasting or the pilgrimage to Mecca, or those enacted individually—personal prayer, for example—are insignificant in female lives. Rather my aim is to provide a detailed look at a group of rituals that profoundly influences the lives of devout women in the religious mainstream and to see how an analysis of gendered ritual practice enlarges our understanding of Shia Muslim faith.

I conducted most of the research for this book during a six-year period from 1994 to 2000, although my interest in Shia religiosity started a decade earlier upon first witnessing the main Shia mourning procession make its impressive way through the crowded Old City streets of Hyderabad. Over the years I took part in hundreds of ritual events in Muslim homes, shrines, and gathering places—the majority being in all-women environments. At the start of my research a well-respected professor and Shia preacher whom I knew directed me to seek out a popular and highly regarded female preacher. The relationship proved to be invaluable, for this influential female religious leader gave me not only information and encouragement but also patronage. Through her, for example, I first gained entry to Yadgar Husayni, a unique all-women *ashurkhana,* or assembly building cum shrine. Her wide network of friends, followers, and acquaintances graciously welcomed me into female devotional spaces and responded to my questions. This circle of contacts expanded as women introduced me to relatives and friends, putting me in touch with an ever-widening cross section of devout Hyderabad Shias from many different walks of life, including a few who settled abroad but return to the city to visit their extended families. My emphasis has been on women who participate in religious activities; thus this book describes the religious behavior of a not-so-unusual group of practicing believers within the Indian Shia community. To protect people's privacy, pseudonyms have been used for all involved.

The women whom I studied were all religiously active but varied widely by age, education, economic situation, class, and social status. Most were from the urban middle class, which I define as being part of families that use motorcycles or scooters for transport, have household goods such as televisions and fans, spend more than a bare minimum on their children's education, and often own their own homes. Low-income families have few durable goods and clothing and tend to receive education and healthcare through government-run schools and hospitals. The wealthy, in contrast, have large homes, multiple servants, own high-end consumer products such as new cars and electronics, and often have memberships in exclusive private schools and clubs. As far as living arrangements are concerned, most Shia women are part of joint or extended families, although there is considerable variability in what that means: some homes consisted of a number of siblings and their families; in others married families live with one or more elderly parents or grandparents. The majority of young women with whom I spoke expected to join their husband's household at the time of marriage, although this traditional practice is changing as increasing numbers of families choose to create independent households.

Few of the women whom I met sought paying jobs or worked outside the home. Working-class women were the main exception: they struggled to increase their livelihood by sewing piecework clothing or goods, cooking and selling specialized food items, or earning income as servants in the homes of middle- and upper-class families. Most other women embraced their role within the joint household as full-time caretakers for their families, although a few had careers as doctors, teachers, lawyers, professors, and business women.

Among the many devout women with whom I interacted over the years, there were a dozen with whom I developed deep relationships and spoke at length about their experiences of faith. These women were all educated middle-aged or older women who were respected by their peers; I came to meet many of them through the recommendations of others. Most of the women had been educated outside the home, with two having achieved their doctorates and one her legal degree. Half were from well-known and respected extended families in Hyderabad and thus shared with them an elevated social status. Several played leading roles in ritual events outside their own family networks. Almost all had been married, a few were widowed, and nearly all had children. Unlike the majority of Shia women, half of this circle of informants had been or continued to be employed outside the home, most in the education field. Nearly all were connected in some way to the Shia diaspora through children, siblings, or members of the extended family living abroad. In Hyderabad this is not unusual: almost all families have some relative who is either working or settled abroad and the higher the class and education level, the greater number of relations who are part of the international Shia community. For some of the women their family's economic position was demonstrably strengthened by this network of support. Approximately half lived in Hyderabad's Old City, a few in small dwellings with restricted economic circumstances, most in spacious ancestral homes that served as a symbol of the family's elevated social status before Indian independence. The other half dozen women lived in various newer parts of the city: all had relatively new homes or flats built within the last fifteen to twenty-five years, demonstrating a strong degree of financial stability and cash flow in their families.

Over the course of my research I repeatedly had to explain to women the reasons for my interest in their devotional lives. On the whole, people were supportive, patient, and gracious, although occasionally a woman expressed confusion or suspicion about my intent. I usually explained my work by describing the lack of useful books or materials to help outsiders like me understand the faith and practices of Shias—particularly from women's points of view. This explanation was helpful for women who had some exposure to systems of formal education but proved to be incomprehensible to women for whom books held limited meaning. Once, for example, an older woman saw me writing up detailed field notes at Yadgar Husayni and sat down next to me to ask about the person with whom I was corresponding. Even after I explained that I was writing a book to help others understand the stories and personalities that are precious to Shia believers, she remained puzzled about my aim and purpose. On another occasion in Yadgar Husayni an elderly ritual leader demanded to know why I kept coming back to spend time writing at the shrine. Although several weeks earlier we had talked about my research and the reasons for it, on this occasion she brushed aside my words and expressed angry suspicion: What more did I need to know? I had already heard everything, so why was I still hanging around?

Part of the explanation for the suspicion I infrequently encountered is rooted in the minority position of Shias within the larger Muslim community. A tremendous amount of persecution has taken place during the roughly fourteen centuries of Shia existence. At one point in history the situation became so dire that leaders propounded a concept of assimilation (*taqiyya*), encouraging Shias to conceal their identity when it came to choosing between affirming one's religious belief and protecting one's life or livelihood. Shias in Hyderabad have their own history of persecution, the low point being three hundred years ago in the wake of an invasion by Sunni Mughal rulers from North India. Although Shia intellectuals have tended to describe Hyderabad's history as one of positive coexistence between Sunnis and Shias, the situation seems to be more complex. For example, some Shia families still face discrimination when trying to rent homes in Sunni localities. With most Shias being aware of these historic and practical challenges, it is not surprising to encounter people's occasional suspicion of outsiders as an expression of concern for the safety of their community.

In general, women gave me the benefit of the doubt and trusted my intention, perceiving me as someone who was trying to understand what they believed to be the true religious path. When women asked about my religious affiliation, I openly admitted to my Christian background, which most accepted with equanimity. A good number seemed to expect that as I learned about Shia truths, I would eventually come to embrace their beliefs. This undoubtedly influenced some women to spend time explaining their spiritual lives to me. Women sometimes commented on my participation in different rituals, pointing out to others how I joined in reciting lamentation choruses or performing the rhythmic chest beating (*matam*). This was done with appreciation and pride—at least when I overheard the remarks, as I was no doubt meant to. The women seemed to feel that my participation clearly demonstrated a love and respect for the venerated family of the Prophet and was a further testimony to the inherent greatness of these holy personages. I did my best to conform to women's expectations of me out of respect for the beliefs of the community and the sanctity of ritual moments, places, and actions, as well as to ensure my continued acceptance by the community. I did not participate in religious events for which I was not qualified (involving the recitation of Arabic, for example) or did not feel comfortable. For instance, I did not perform the ritual prayer (*namaz*) or partake in the collective reciting of litanies for vows. I used my own judgment on what was appropriate and allowed women to guide and advise me. Most women were both helpful and discreet in passing along instructions which they felt were crucial, especially surrounding issues of purity and the handling of sacred objects.

I feel it was inevitable that my presence as an observer influenced people's behavior to at least some degree—if only by inspiring ritual participants to perform well before the outsider in their midst. Although I did not attempt to draw attention to myself, I could be easily noticed in smaller gatherings, the sole white-skinned foreigner in a crowd. Yet I did not get a sense that the passion and dedication with which women engaged in devotional rituals—whether mourning gatherings, fervent prayers for healing, or celebratory events—was manufactured or staged on my account. The dynamics of devotional activities (including socializing) seemed fully to occupy most participants; I never got the feeling that women were doing things markedly different because I was there. Especially in events where fifty, a hundred, or several hundred women gathered, my presence seemed to be of little interest or importance compared with women's own concerns and engagements.

This book would not exist without the encouragement and support of many people. My deepest thanks goes to the Muslim community in Hyderabad for all the warmth and gracious hospitality. I am indebted to Shia friends, acquaintances, and strangers for welcoming this ever-inquiring outsider in their midst. In particular, I am grateful to Zakia Sultana for her gift of time and her unswerving patience. My thanks to Miriam Banu, Riyaz Fatima, Mehoor Ali Abbas, Sirtaj Bahdur Ali, Ameena Naqvi, Tahira Naqvi, Rabap Patel, Tasneem Husayn, Sabiha, Ismat, Atiya Ahsan, Sayyida Jafari, Maryam Naqvi, Sakina Hasan, and their families for welcoming me into their homes with great kindness and trust. I am thankful to Mawlana Syed Ghulam Husayn Raza Agha for his input on Shia life and practice in Hyderabad and to Sadiq Naqvi for his encouragement and unfailing delight in knowledge. The members of the Shia community went to great lengths to help me understand their beliefs and practices, and I have tried my best to honor their patience and trust. Any shortcomings in this book spring from my own limitations and misunderstandings.

I have benefited greatly from the challenge and support of the international academic community. My first thanks goes to Anton Wessels and Nelly Van Doorn-Harder for advising and accompanying me through various stages of this work. Andreas D'Souza encouraged me in my research and read many early drafts of my research. Kari Vogt and Johan ter Haar gave wonderful feedback on my initial manuscript, and Susan Sered offered wise advice about shortening and consolidating the text. I also received valuable input from Toby Howarth, Robert Schick, Jorgen Nielsen, Willy Jansen, Stella van de Wetering, Imtiaz Ahmed, Joyce Flueckiger, Yoginder Sikand, Mary Hegland, and the late Omar Khalidi. My thanks goes to Fred Denny, Jim Denton, and the team of editors and readers associated with University of South Carolina Press for pushing me to make this book sharper and more focused.

I am deeply indebted to the staff and faculty at the Henry Martyn Institute for their assistance on matters large and small and their willingness to support me in my research and writing. Other institutions that deserve special thanks are Vrije University, Suffolk University, and the Massachusetts Institute of Technology. I am grateful to the many partners of the Henry Martyn Institute who helped support my writing and travel costs over the years, including the United Church of Canada, the Reformed Churches in the Netherlands, the Church of Sweden, the Church of Scotland, the Evangelical Lutheran Church in America, and the Church of Our Saviour in Milton, Massachusetts. I hope these institutions succeed in their commitment to building a world in which people of all faiths are equally respected and appreciated.

Finally, my thanks go to the family and friends whom I hold closest in my heart. To Noel, Tara, and Mira D'Souza for their patience over many years with a mother who gets swallowed up by research and writing and for their delight in having me complete this work. To Art Weingarten, for the happiness and laughter he has brought into my life. To the late Mildred Christian, Robert Diener, and the late Preston W. Smith Jr. for their presence and encouragement. To Lalita Iyer, Lakshmi Raman, Jeanne Dooley, Kate Zilla-ba, and other friends who have offered the right words at the right time, especially when things have been difficult. To Rizwana Anees for her trust, friendship, and home in the Old City and to Carolyn Pogue and Jasmin Nordien for their whoops of laughter and unswerving, affectionate devotion.

NOTES ON TRANSLITERATION AND TRANSLATION

This book springs from the South Indian Shia Muslim experience and thus contains a good bit of Urdu vocabulary, as well as some Arabic and Persian words. In choosing a transliteration system for words that cannot be translated into English, I have been guided by two desires: to reflect the local Urdu-speaking context and to ensure the readability of the text by nonspecialists.

When it comes to the local context, I have used Urdu transliterations as much as possible, even when the word has Arabic or Persian origins. To give just a few examples, when translating "blessing," I use the Urdu *barakat* rather than the Arabic *barakah;* in speaking of the family of Prophet Muhammad, I use *Ahl-e-Bayt* rather than *Ahl al-Bayt;* in writing about the Muslim month of fasting, I use *Ramzan* rather than *Ramadan*; and in describing the ritual prayer I use *namaz* rather than *salat.* I believe that such choices help to capture a bit of the flavor of the language as it is spoken in Hyderabad, which situates the study firmly within its South Indian context.

As far as the book's readability is concerned, I have based my transliteration on the system adopted by the American Library Association / Library of Congress but have dropped all diacritical marks (including those indicating *hamza* and *ayn*), and occasionally have made spellings more intuitive (representing the letter *chim* as "ch" rather than "c," for example). I have made these choices with two audiences in mind: the community whose lives I chronicle and readers whose interests or research specialties lie outside the Islamic studies field. I have found that both groups struggle at times with opaque transliteration systems that render familiar words unfamiliar or make pronunciation confusing. For instance, a female orator in Hyderabad Shia circles is known as a *zakira.* When the word is written locally using the Latin alphabet, it is spelled just that way. Yet scholars who use formal transliteration systems based on Arabic most commonly write it as *dhakîra,* using *dh* to indicate a particular Urdu letter of the several which give the sound of *z.* Although such formal systems are undoubtedly useful, allowing specialists faithfully to reconstruct the word's spelling in its original language, in this case it results in a word that is distanced from the very people whose lives it describes; it leads as well to suggest to those not familiar with transliteration codes to imagine that the word starts with the sound of *d* (as I have been embarrassed to see happen at one very public academic event).

As with any transliteration system, there are some exceptions and irregularities that require additional explanation. First, I use *Shia* to indicate both the noun *Shia* and the adjective *Shi'i*, as seems to be increasingly common today. Second, I do not italicize Urdu, Arabic, or Persian proper names (for example, Ali, Hyderabad, Ramzan) or words that have entered the English language (for example, Quran or imam). Third, in those Persian-origin words where the letter *wao* is silent, I have elected to drop it in the transliteration; for example, *dastarkhan* and *rawzah-khan* rather than *dastarkhwan* and *rawzah-khwan.* Fourth, there are a few words for which a particular romanized spelling has become standard but that spelling does not follow the transliteration system I have adopted. The spelling of the word *hadith* (tradition) is so common among those familiar with Muslim studies that I have not forced it to conform to the book's transliteration system, where it would be rendered *hadis.* I have bowed to the popular rendering of *Mecca* and *Madina,* rather than *Makkah* and *Madinah.* All other exceptions come from accepted local spellings (keeping in mind that India's declining Urdu literacy has resulted in a greater use of the Roman script in Urdu communications) and involve the long form of a vowel where *ee* replaces î, and *oo* replaces û. These are: *shalwar kameez, durood, masumeen,* and *mumineen,* which I would otherwise render as *shalwar kamiz, durud, masumin,* and *muminin.* My choice has been to respect the popularly recognized form. Finally I have used the English convention of making plurals by adding *s* to the singular form of the Urdu word rather than using the "broken" plural form of the original language—a practice which local speakers tend to adopt when using Urdu words in English. I therefore write *ashurkhanas, zaris,* and *jeshns,* for example, instead of *ashurkhane, zarian,* and *jeshnha.* A few exceptions are *ulama* (the plural of *alim*) since it has already entered popular usage in English, *majalis* (plural of *majlis*) since it seems awkward to follow English rules and add an *es,* and the examples above of *masumeen* (pl. of *masum*) and *mumineen* (pl. of *mumin*). I trust that the glossary at the end of the book will help make new vocabulary more comprehensible to the non-Urdu-speaking audience.

Finally, unless noted otherwise all Quranic references and translations are from the monumental translation and commentary by S. V. Mir Ahmed Ali (1997), *The Holy Quran: With English Translation of the Arabic Text and Commentary according to the Version of the Holy Ahlul-Bait.* I have chosen this version of the Muslim scripture for two reasons. First, it is an edition translated with a Shia mind and heart and draws upon Shia commentary in explaining the text. Second, the translator, commentator, and compiler is a South Indian and thus comes from a background and context shared by the community studied in this book. Ali's version of the Quran is widely available at Shia bookshops in Hyderabad's Old City and has gained visibility and respect within the local English-speaking Shia community.

Introduction

This book examines the gendered expressions of Shia Muslim faith. My main interest is to understand how women from the majority Ithna Ashari, or Twelver, Shia community construct and experience their religious lives. To do so I take female stories and understandings as my starting point, drawing primarily on the lived experiences of women in one of the largest Shia communities in India, in the southern city of Hyderabad. The book is thus an ethnographic account of Muslim ritual that also makes use of textual material such as poetry, sermons, hagiography, and historical texts to analyze how gender impacts understanding of Shia faith and practice. This gendered lens is key, for most research and writing on Shia faith, whether by Muslim religious scholars or academics in religion or social science fields, implicitly or explicitly reflects male expressions and beliefs.

My aim is to answer three questions. First and most important, how do pious Shia women nurture and sustain their devotional lives within a patriarchal culture? In exploring this question five key entry points into female religiosity are identified—religious narrative, sacred space, ritual performance, female leadership, and iconic symbols—along with factors for each which impact women's piety. My second question interrogates this primary material to ask what new insights into Shia faith are gained through a more complete grasp of the gendering of religious practice. Finally, I investigate how unexamined gender assumptions complicate the scholarly dichotomy between normative and popular religion and ask what alternatives might be considered for conceptualizing the diversity of religious behavior.

Defining Religion and Ritual

My initial encounters with Islam came through personal contact with Muslims, particularly women. It was only later that I began to make use of published writings to supplement what I learned. This pathway to knowledge was crucial in shaping my thinking. I recall learning, for example, from a friend who murmured a Quranic verse over a glass of water before giving it to her sick child to drink. She hardly thought about her action and struggled to articulate what she believed when she gently recited those memorized words. Our conversations helped me understand the power of sacred words that go beyond their revelatory meaning, and a supreme being who listens to one's heartfelt cry and acts in compassion—if it is God's will. I was frustrated, however, when I looked to published resources to deepen my understanding of this important aspect of my friend's faith. In the relatively small body of literature addressing people's religious expressions, academicians and Muslim scholars alike tended to focus on what they identified as the "pillars" of Islam. Most classified ritual behavior falling outside those "fundamental" beliefs and practices as popular or folk religion, clearly distinguishing it from normative Islam. The tone was often pejorative, with many female religious behaviors condescendingly devalued or dismissed as superstition or magic.

Part of my frustration in dealing with the gaps between women's practices and academic treatises on Islam was that women explained their faith-filled actions as part of a well-connected whole. My friend who called God's presence into the intimacy of her relationship with her sick child also performed daily prayers, observed the annual month of fasting, and hoped to one day perform the pilgrimage to Mecca—these latter actions being part of what scholars define as the established requirements of Muslim faith. She and her sisters frequently joined their father in voluntarily teaching Arabic to neighborhood children, and most nights she gave away whatever was left from her family's evening meal to people who came to her door to beg for food. My friend explained all these actions—and many more—as integral to being a Muslim. In contrast, I found most scholarly texts much less holistic. The absence of nuance, as well as a tendency to separate normative from popular practices, set up boundaries that seemed to obscure rather than clarify how actual people see and understand the world, their lives, and their relationship with the cosmos. As Nancy Tapper and Richard Tapper (1987, 83) argued in their study of Turkish celebrations of the Prophet's birthday, it is extremely misleading to dismiss these important ritual behaviors as peripheral to the lives of Muslims.

Central to this dichotomy between textual representations and practical spirituality is the question of how we define, and therefore approach, religion. My own experience of Muslim women's religious lives is that their faith embodies many forms and expressions—some of which established religion names as primary, some of which it does not. I therefore see religion as a fairly open-ended construct defining a dynamic set of symbols, beliefs, and activities that people use to help give structure and meaning to their lives. To look at religion in this way, as personal, experiential (individually or collectively), and consequently somewhat plural, contrasts with the dominant scholarly tendency to posit religion as a cumulative tradition, the expressions and beliefs of which are defined and bounded by institutional structures and hierarchies. Wilfred Cantwell Smith highlighted this contrast in his seminal work *The Meaning and End of Religion* (1991,

131) by noting that "the participant is concerned with God; the observer has been concerned with 'religion.'" My interest is thus focused on Islam as faith-inspired Muslims describe and practice it.

To understand religious faith through the beliefs and actions of adherents is especially important when working with people who are marginalized from the defining of religion. In the Muslim context, excluded voices include women, the economically disadvantaged, people in rural or village areas, and communities outside the geographic mainstream of the Arab Middle East or the sectarian mainstream of Sunni Islam. For such groups religious ritual becomes a central mode for expressing theology and worldview. In fact, we might best describe such ritual as embodied belief, for it is more about doing something than saying something—even when spoken words are involved. It is through ritual that people are initiated into the meanings, customs, and values of a given culture, and ritual also helps to shape those meanings, customs, and values. Ritual draws communities together, mediates between the past and the present, forms identities, and teaches ethical norms for human behavior. It gives people opportunities to express or channel emotions, transforms individual psyches, expresses complex realities, and accesses power. It also offers means of communicating between individuals, among groups, and between people and a higher reality. Not every ritual does all of these things, but many do at least some of them.

James C. Livingston (1989, 98) describes religious ritual as "an agreed-on and formalized pattern of ceremonial movements and verbal expressions carried out in a sacred context." The emphasis on sacred context is important, for it reminds us of the role of place, space and time, as well as the intention and perception of the performer. However, Livingston's insistence on "agreed-upon" and "formalized" gives preeminence to behaviors that are recognized by established, authoritative powers. Such a definition ignores rituals practiced by marginalized groups (such as women) or those that are in the process of developing; in both cases a religious hierarchy may refuse to acknowledge a given ritual's legitimacy. Hence I see religious ritual as a pattern of ceremonial movements and verbalizations carried out in a sacred context and having a somewhat fixed, recognizable, and repeatable sequence or cluster of behaviors. The meaning and function of any single ritual is intimately tied to its context, including the desires and actions of the performers, the symbolism associated with the rite, and the circumstances under which it is performed.

An Imperfect Dichotomy

From the beginning of the Western study of Islam, researchers have drawn upon two distinct sources of information: texts and direct contact with Muslim cultures and peoples. Nineteenth- and early-twentieth-century orientalists, fueled by Christian missionary agendas or an interest in comparative religions, focused on authoritative texts. Early Islamicists visited Muslim countries mainly to gather or consult manuscripts; these, they felt, provided the key to the religion of Islam. Determining Islam's core truths was crucial in order to compare it with Christianity or other world religions, often with the aim of proving it wrong. At the same time researchers affiliated with colonial powers and operating largely outside of university systems described Islam as they saw it lived by "natives" in the "colonies." Most of these men had little familiarity with Muslim authoritative texts or the development of Muslim theology, doctrines, or laws. For them official Islam was a set of religious ideals propounded by remote theologians or jurists; Muslims around them provided a window into the local practice of religion. These two early sources of knowledge combined to frame Islam as a formalized, bounded category which local Muslims followed imperfectly.

This outlook mirrored the views of many Muslim religious scholars (*ulama*) who functioned as a source of authority for enquiring non-Muslims. As spokesmen who defined the scope of official religion, the *ulama* articulated a belief in a unified Islam and generally attributed any discrepancy between actual practices and official norms to people's ignorance, illiteracy, and superstition. Hence the theological assertions of recognized religious leaders supported orientalists in conceptualizing a definitive and unitary Islam.

Today the term *normative* is used to refer to standard, prescribed practices of the established religion, while *popular* indicates rituals, actions, and beliefs that self-identified Muslims practice but that fall outside the defined norms. This basic division is expressed in different fields and contexts through various binaries: *universal* and *local, official* and *unofficial, establishment* and *folk, orthodox* and *heterodox, Great* and *Little.* The actual terms are less important than the dichotomy they suggest and the presumption that universal, official, orthodox Islam is a higher or more correct form than local, folk, or popular Islam is.

Looking at this dichotomy with an eye to gender we find that women's religious behaviors are most often associated with the popular or folk category, while normative or orthodox religion most predictably encompasses the perspectives and activities of men. This circumstance is linked to the fact that religious authorities and textual sources have been largely a male domain. In other words the power to define what is and is not religion generally rests with elite men who have tended to downplay, ignore, or even dismiss as illegitimate many aspects of female spiritual expression. A gendered explanation of human nature is used to support this position, with religious scholars asserting that God created females with a weaker, more emotional nature than that of the stronger, more rational males. Men are therefore inherently superior to women, including in their knowledge about and practice of religion.

Associating women with marginal or incomplete religious activity has justified a lack of Western scholarly interest in female religious lives, since orientalists saw the study of women, like research on the beliefs and practices of illiterates, peasants, and other nondominant groups, as being of only limited use in advancing an understanding of the religion of Islam. Thus, for example, J. Spencer Trimingham ([1959] 1970, 86) in his authoritative book on Islam in West Africa noted that many pilgrims still walked the route to Mecca "accompanied by women and children." The fact that this renowned scholar completely overlooked the female pilgrim right before his eyes demonstrates how the emphasis on men as the sole normative actors in a male-defined religious world made it difficult even to acknowledge that women had religious lives—let alone independent ones worthy of study.

Over the years criticism has grown of this way of conceptualizing religion. Some social scientists and religious studies scholars have questioned whether an unchanging "official" Islam actually exists and whether the paradigm of a simplified dichotomy obscures rather than clarifies religious identities and interactions. An early effort at a more nuanced view came from Jacques D. Waardenburg (1979), who first proposed the term *normative* to replace less subjective words such as *official.* According to Waardenburg, "normative Islam" consists of those doctrines and beliefs that establish the norms for Muslim life and are therefore pursued by those who seek to regulate and order personal and community religious expression. He affirms that this is not a singular or unified category, for there are competing normatives that each offer their own particular interpretation of Islam. These he considers "alternative" in nonhierarchal relation to each other. For example, from the Shia normative perspective Sunnis follow an alternative form of Islam since a number of their practices or beliefs contradict those of Shias. When one speaks from the normative point of view of Sunnis, however, Shias are the alternative group.

Although he acknowledges diverse visions of Islam, Waardenburg limits them to Sunni, Shia, and Sufi forms and distinguishes these from popular expressions. He notes that at the level of lived religion people's practices and beliefs may or may not encompass Islam as it is articulated by acknowledged religious leaders. However, even when practitioners have little in common with the normative claims of the religious elite, in Waardenburg's view they still tend to regard them as the ideal. This is what distinguishes popular practices from alternative ones. Another difference is the involvement of recognized religious authorities. Popular Islam does not have a spokesman in the way normative forms of Sunni, Shia, or Sufi Islam do. According to Waardenburg, ordinary people's religiosity lacks a "more or less 'official' religious stamp" (370) and does not get expressed in ways comparable to the articulations of religious scholars.

In conceptualizations like Waardenburg's, normative or alternative Islam is the product of a dominant group in society, while popular Islam is expressed by people who have only limited ability to name something as a defining norm. It is the dynamics of hierarchy, power, and control, therefore, that determine whose views are privileged in a given society. Similar dynamics are at work in academic inquiry, for researchers choose whom to identify as a religious authority. In Waardenburg's case the normative ideal is voiced by the religiously educated scholar who formulates his vision in the accepted traditional scholarly fashion. Women's visions, authority, and sources of knowledge are often expressed outside such conventionally recognized establishments. Does this limit the power or resonance of their vision? Or does it limit our ability to see or acknowledge it? Are normative and popular categories simply reflections of our own vision of dominance and subordination? Certainly the very prevalence of popular forms of piety suggests that people's devout practices and beliefs are shaped by more than just the vision of religious elites.

The attempt to dichotomize religious behavior presents another challenge, for one cannot always distinguish a popular action from a normative one. For instance, a person may perform the pilgrimage to Mecca as part of a vow she has taken to seek intercession on a vexing problem. Or a group may mark the death anniversary of a family member by reciting the whole Quran. Even if one were able to classify either of these devout, complex actions as conclusively popular or normative, the focus on trying to determine their category rather misses the point of how they have meaning for the believer. Moreover, we may discover in trying to categorize individuals that people's values and beliefs are sometimes a surprising mixture of normative and popular elements. I think of a Hyderabad Muslim known staunchly to oppose the "cult of the saints" who was seen at a local shrine by one of my colleagues. This conservative stalwart held in his hands the flowers and ritual items that are popularly offered at such sites and was nonplussed by the encounter. He begged my colleague not to mention it to other people, explaining that a death anniversary necessitated his visit. The ritual life of this man, who stressed the simplicity of "pure Islam" in interreligious gatherings of Muslims, Hindus, and Christians, was actually much more complex than he chose to communicate in those public meetings. Religious identities are many-layered, and people's internal belief systems can defy easy classification into normative or popular categories.

The anthropologist Abdul Hamid el-Zein (1977) argued that diversities in Muslim belief and practice are so numerous and complex that it is arbitrary and unhelpful to speak of a unified, autonomous normative that expresses religion for everyone. How should one proceed to articulate Islamic fundamentals when Muslims in a Turkish town honor the birthday of the Prophet with special poetry recitals, while those in Saudi Arabia treat the day as completely ordinary? Or when Moroccan Muslims observe the tenth of Muharram with fasting and the presentation of gifts to children, while Iranian townspeople perform a tragic passion play to reenact the martyrdom of Husayn? El-Zein argues that the starting point must be the diverse viewpoints of faith-inspired Muslims rather than a predetermined set of hierarchical ideals. In other words, instead of speaking about a unitary Islam, it is more correct to speak about "islams."

Some Muslim and non-Muslim scholars vigorously refuted el-Zein's point, insisting that Islam has an irreducible set of core principles. The Muslim intellectual Fazlur Rahman (1985, 197), for example, argued that positing a multiplicity of islams was misleading and "incurably relativistic" and would lead to a "free for all" Islam. He asserted that Islam has a "normative anchoring point" found in the Quran and the Prophet's definitive conduct, since "all Muslims agree" that these are the only essential criteria for judging belief and action. Divergences simply reflect that members of a religious community do not understand their religion fully.

The argument that Islam is unitary rather than variable is a powerful and sincere theological statement that has been articulated for centuries by Muslim philosophers and theologians. Thus, in Fazlur Rahman's assertions, we find a respected religious studies scholar speaking in large part as a believer—for it is from the faith perspective that boundaries signal the division between right and wrong or belief and unbelief. Unlike a social scientist who might speak of diversity, a religious adherent tends to frame variability as truth or untruth. Part of the impetus, then, for preserving a distinction between normative and popular comes from attempts to convey the unified vision of Islam expressed by many Muslims. The actual problem, as Ronald A. Lukens-Bull (1999, 10) has observed, is the comingling of the theoretical question "What is Islam?" with the theological question "What is Islam?" Or, as Andrew Rippin (2007, 13) has asked, "How do we reconcile what we are told about the religion by insiders with what we might observe as historians or sociologists?" At issue is one's methodological approach: is it beneficial to use a presumed normative Islam to help us understand what Muslims believe and practice? If so, what shape does it take when the religious lives of marginalized believers such as Shia women are placed at the center?

Gender and Shia Ritual

The fact that Shia piety has received relatively less academic attention than Sunni beliefs and practices is not simply because Shias are only 10 to 13 percent of

Muslims worldwide.* Western research on Islam began to acknowledge Shia religious behaviors as legitimate only in the latter part of the twentieth century. Up until that point academics tended to focus almost exclusively on Sunni expressions, partly because Western societies had more contact with Sunnis and also because orientalists had tended to adopt the majority community's dismissive polemical perceptions of Shias. As Seyyed Hossein Nasr ([1975] 1981a, 3) noted, scholars of comparative religion rarely acknowledged Shia Islam, but when they did, it was usually to relegate it to a "secondary and peripheral status of a religio-political 'sect,' a heterodoxy or even a heresy." Despite the work of a few sensitive scholars, Louis Massignon and Henry Corbin among them, much of Shia belief and practice remained a closed book. It is only in recent decades that Western scholarship has accepted Shia faith as a religious expression in its own right. Interest has been catalyzed by the emergence of a Shia Islamic state in Iran and the escalation of sectarian divisions in the wake of the U.S. invasion and occupation of Iraq and Afghanistan.

This relative scholarly neglect is one of the reasons I have chosen in the present book to focus in depth on two sets of collective Shia rituals. A more comprehensive presentation of female piety in Hyderabad might offer an overview of the entirety of women's devotional lives, from ritualized daily prayer (*namaz*) to fasting during the month of Ramzan, from tithing and the giving of alms to reciting the Quran, from pilgrimage to Mecca or the tombs of the family of the Prophet to offering litanies of prayer through the night, from rituals that sanctify life-cycle events such as marriage or death to practices that commemorate special annual festival days. While such an approach might be more comprehensive, it would also, of necessity, be more superficial. My preference is to provide an in-depth look at a select group of rituals that profoundly influence the lives of devout women in the religious mainstream and to see how a gendered analysis of ritual practice enlarges our understanding of Shia Muslim faith. To start it is useful to clarify the basic concept of gender.

Like class, race, caste, or ethnicity, gender is an organizational category that helps us understand, analyze, and explain the structure and functioning of a society. While *sex* refers to biological differences between men and women, *gender* refers to the meanings that societies and cultures assign to these differences. In

*This percentage is taken from "Mapping the Global Muslim Population: A Report on the Size and Distribution of the World's Muslim Population," 7 October 2009, posted on the website of the Pew Forum on Religion and Public Life, a project of the Pew Research Center; http://www.pewforum.org/Muslim/Mapping-the-Global-Muslim-Population(6).aspx (accessed 1 June 2012).

other words gender shapes how a society perceives, evaluates, and expects males and females to behave (King 1995, 5). Unlike sex, it is a humanly constructed category that varies across cultures. Less variable is how societies have used it to justify sexual inequality in thought, language, and social institutions, a practice known as patriarchy. I follow Zillah Eisenstein (1984, 90) and Asma Barlas (2002, 12) in broadly defining patriarchy as a politics of sexual differentiation that privileges males by transforming biological sex into politicized gender, prioritizing the male while making the female different (unequal), less than, or the "other." One can accurately describe many societies as patriarchal, and the Muslim Shia community is one of these.

Saba Mahmood (2005, 154–88), in an effort better to grasp how gender impacts female spiritual expressions within a patriarchal context, moved beyond assumptions of passivity or confrontation to a more nuanced understanding of women's agency and male-female dynamics. In her analysis of the women's mosque movement in Egypt, she describes women who participated in mosque-based teaching and discussion circles as active agents in cultivating an embodied practice of personal piety, which she argues is best understood in the context of the threat of Western-inspired secularism. Mahmood makes the point that female agency—the capacity for self-direction exercised on one's own behalf—can develop capacities and skills to undertake particular kinds of moral actions, including pious passivity. It need not be automatically linked to resisting domination, whether patriarchy or other forms of oppression.

The concept of agency is indeed valuable in expressing women's power and possibility in shaping meaningful religious expression, and Mahmood's warning to set aside assumptions about patriarchal dynamics is to the point. Muslim males and females are not, by definition, oppositionally aligned. As Elizabeth Warnock Fernea and Basima Q. Bezirgan (2005, 236–37) point out in the Iranian Shia context, men and women often have instrumental roles in rituals conducted by the other. For example, it may be men who, under the instruction of women, purchase food for a women-only ritual or drive a vehicle to transport a group of women to a local sacred site. Similarly, women may prepare the setting and food for male-led rituals. Thus, while focusing on gender-divided performance, it is important also to recall that there are ongoing interactions between men and women that enrich these activities and enable them to take place.

When we look at Shia devotional practices through a gender lens, we notice women-only rituals, men-only rituals, and those in which both genders participate—separately or together. Of central importance to the vast majority of Shia women and men are gatherings to honor members of the family of the Prophet, commemorating their births, deaths, and other key events in their lives. The most widely observed in India and worldwide is the *majlis* (lit. "sitting"; pl. *majalis*), known as *rawdah* in Iran and *qiraya* in southern Iraq. This is a gathering to remember and mourn the martyrdom of Imam Husayn, the grandson of Prophet Muhammad, and his family and followers. Somewhat less popular but also widely prevalent is the *jeshn* (lit. "jubilee" or "rejoicing"), a gathering very similar to the *majlis* but which marks birth anniversaries and other happy occasions in Shia history. Men as well as women organize and attend these gatherings, following an annual cycle of tragic and joyous remembrance days that are well known in most Shia households. Individual families organize a *majlis* or *jeshn* at home or in a neighborhood *ashurkhana* to commemorate days of special meaning. These ritualized events are held on an annual, weekly, or daily basis during the annual two-month mourning period; they are also sponsored at major life-cycle ceremonies such as weddings, funerals, and death anniversaries.

Women participate in almost every male-directed remembrance gathering, although it is men who assume leadership when there are male and female participants. Women usually sit in an area separated from the main performance space by a screen, curtain, or wall. In other places they may sit or stand in a marginalized position relative to the male performers, separated by virtue of their modest dress (*hijab*). Women also organize, lead, and take part in exclusively female gatherings. In fact, in Hyderabad women-organized assemblies outnumber those organized by men (Howarth 2001, 78). In such gatherings women perform all leadership roles that their male counterparts play in mixed gender rituals. Men are only infrequently present during such events and sometimes listen to the proceedings in a separate room through a special audio transmission.

Women, and probably to a lesser extent men, also engage in a variety of rituals to seek divine intervention in solving personal problems. Making a vow (*mannat, nazr*) is the most popular and occurs in many forms: reciting a litany of prayers (*amal;* lit. "practice") or the entire Quran; making a sacrifice or offering (*sarka*); preparing, sanctifying, and consuming food in the name of members of the Prophet's family (*niyaz;* lit. "petition"); and relating miracle stories about one or more of the holy revered members of the Prophet Muhammad's family. Two forms of these supplication rituals are *amal* and *dastarkhan.*

There is, in short, a broad universe of religious meaning and action that Shia women and men share and that is reflected in community teaching, preaching and ritual. Yet ritual roles are also highly gendered: in Hyderabad it is men alone who perform the rhythmic self-flagellation (*matam*) involving swords, knives, and blades; and only men go to the mosque or conduct mourning or celebratory processions in the streets (with one noteworthy exception). It is only women who mark the fulfillment of a vow with a *dastarkhan* (lit. "meal cloth"; known as *sofreh* in Iran), a ritual meal to which men are not allowed. In addition it is usually women who play key leadership roles during most home-based supplication rites, even when men participate in them. Thus gender profoundly influences the type of religious experiences to which men and women have access.

Part of this has to do with gender-dictated areas of authority. When men and women come together to honor the Prophet's family at a remembrance gathering, all participants assume that men will lead the proceedings. In the absence of men, women assume the role of leaders. Both of these scenarios are supported by the community's religio-historical memory and by the way in which Shia society genders male-female characteristics and roles. For example, Shia interpreters use Imam Husayn's battleground comment that "It is not for women to fight" to justify men having the sole right to shed blood ritually in memory of the martyrs. While women can and do engage in the physically taxing practice of self-flagellation or *matam,* they do so without the use of swords or blades. The result is that the message of *matam* is a gendered one: for women it expresses a solidarity with the grieving women who survived the massacre at Karbala; for men it communicates one's willingness to stand alongside the martyrs and give one's life.

Inquiring into the gendering of religious experience, whether the creation of religious space, the use of icons, or the leadership of ritual events, offers information about women's vivid religious lives and the impact of ritual on the wider community; it also facilitates a more complete understanding of how Shia faith has meaning. Before delving into this inquiry, however, it is important to contextualize people's religious identities with a brief look at the historical and cultural background of Hyderabad.

Religious Identity and the Hyderabad Context

What does it mean to be Shia in Hyderabad? From an Indian political perspective, one is first and foremost a minority within a minority. According to the 2011 census, 41 percent of Hyderabad's nearly seven million people are Muslim (compared to 13 percent of the national population). Shias are estimated to be 10 percent of that group, or somewhere near 270,000 people (exact figures are hard to verify since the Indian census does not collect information about religious sect, and Shias sometimes conceal their identity in situations of discrimination or perceived threat). The double minority status means that Shias define themselves in dynamic relationship to Hindus on one hand and Sunnis on another. These relationships have been shaped through a rich history that includes two Muslim dynasties, the Qutb Shah (1518–1687 C.E.) and the Asaf Jah (1724–1948 C.E.), and the emergence of India as an independent nation in 1947.

The Qutb Shah rulers were among the first in India to adopt the Shia faith as a state religion. They patronized public devotional ceremonies, modeled devout behavior, and built and supported religious structures. Popular history recalls that both the founder of Hyderabad Muhammad Quli Qutb (r. 1580–1612 C.E.) and his father Ibrahim Quli Qutb Shah (r. 1550–1580 C.E.) had especially close ties with Hindu leaders and subjects and were patrons of local Telugu (Hindu) literature and culture. Indeed the stories of religious amity under Shia reign has contributed to the common characterization of Hyderabad as a city of "composite culture" where people from different groups live in "communal harmony." Thus, for example, one of the main themes of a popular tourist attraction, the sound and light show at Golconda Fort, is the history of Hyderabad as a peaceful mingling of Muslims and Hindus.

The Shia gaze finds a wealth of meaning in a city dotted by buildings and monuments from this period. The most prominent is Charminar, an impressive Old City landmark and the quintessential symbol of Hyderabad. A popular legend about this graceful four-storied structure is that Muhammad Quli Qutb Shah had it constructed in 1591 C.E. to honor a vow he made during a deadly plague. Yet the Shia eye sees much more: its shape is that of the *zari* or *taziya*, the iconic tomb of a member of the Prophet's family (*Ahl-e-Bayt*); and images of *alams* (emblematic crests or "standards" associated with the *Ahl-e-Bayt*) adorn the building's façade. These details, unremarkable to casual observers and ignored in most tourist materials, give the site profound meaning for devout Shias. In their eyes the structure is not only a reminder of political ascendancy, but a powerful symbol of Shia faith as well.

Shia collective memory also includes a dramatic fall from political power. In 1687 C.E. an invasion by the Mughal emperor Aurangzeb ended more than a century and a half of Qutb Shah reign, the attack having been motivated in part by the Sunni ruler's condemnation of Shia beliefs and practices. This ushered in the lowest point in the history of Hyderabad's Shia community, with the persecution of prominent Shias, the migration of religious leaders and other eminent persons, an abrupt curtailment of public expressions of religiosity, and the eventual emergence of an independent Sunni state. Through these dark times local Shias became part of a larger troubled history of Sunni-Shia relations worldwide. Indeed, at a fairly early point in Muslim history, experiences of persecution led Shia leaders to promote a theological concept of dissimilation (*taqiyya*), justifying the concealment of one's religious identity to protect one's life or livelihood. It seems clear that at least some of Hyderabad's Shias chose to conceal their faith in order to survive these times.

Within several generations of Aurangzeb's invasion, however, Shia rituals and structures began to regain public visibility under Sunni rule. The Asaf Jah monarchs, known as the nizams, started to bear the expenses for the repair and upkeep of certain Shia shrines, as well as the costs of public processions (Rizvi 1986, 1:307–8; 2:341–46). Hyderabad's most opulent Shia gathering place and shrine, Aza Khana-e-Zehra, was built in the 1930s with the patronage of the seventh nizam Mir Osman Ali Khan, who dedicated it to the memory of his Shia mother Amtul Zehra Begum. The nizam even paid for certain Shias to pursue their religious studies in Iran. In fact, it is symptomatic of the sometimes porous boundaries between Sunnis and Shias that people often speculated that the nizam was a Shia who hid his true religious identity.

More than four centuries of Muslim rule came to an end with the birth of modern India. Following the withdrawal of British colonial forces, the seventh nizam asserted his sovereignty but was quickly defeated by the Indian army. Eight years later the Indian government redrew the geographical borders of the former nizam's dominions, making Hyderabad the capital of the new secular state of Andhra Pradesh. This curtailed Muslim political dominance and plunged Hyderabad's ruling class and those who depended on them—both of whom included many Shia families—into less privileged social and economic positions. The collapse of the pre-1948 feudal system and fears of Hindu-Muslim violence in the wake of India's partition into Muslim-majority Pakistan and Hindu-majority India catalyzed an exodus of Muslims from the rural districts and into the capital city. This increased the unskilled or semiskilled labor force within an urban community already reeling from unemployment, accelerating a collective spiral to poverty which affected a good portion of Hyderabad's Muslim community—Sunni as well as Shia. Many of those who had the economic means to leave did so. From 1951 to 1961, for example, the reported Shia population in the Old City dropped astoundingly from 22 to 6 percent (Naidu 1990, 26). Initially many Shias immigrated to Pakistan, spurred by fears of life in a Hindu-dominated democracy and hopes that a Muslim majority state would offer new opportunities. As economic insecurity continued through the 1970s others sought new beginnings in Europe, North America, the Middle East, and Australia, giving birth to a vibrant and widespread diaspora (Leonard 2007, 33–55; Akbar S. Ahmed 1988, 158–71).

Hyderabad's Muslim community began to enjoy a measure of economic recovery starting in the 1980s as both transient and permanently settled diaspora men and women began remitting funds to their families. Those in India also advanced in their careers and businesses. The local economy began providing additional jobs and resources as Hyderabad developed as an international site for information technology and commerce, particularly under the initiative and leadership of Chief Minister Chandrababu Naidu (1995 to 2004). Still, many Shias continued to remain impoverished, as did a sizeable proportion of Indian Muslims generally (Sachar et al. 2006). Those who experienced greater economic success often chose to leave traditional neighborhoods in the crowded Old City area and move to more modern and spacious dwellings in newer localities in Hyderabad.

The double minority status of Indian Shias motivates an urge to accentuate commonalities with Sunni Muslims. One only occasionally hears references to

Sunni-Shia tensions, for example, when a person speculates on how participants at a neighboring Sunni mosque perceive Shia mourning gatherings or when someone notes the difficulty families face in trying to rent homes in some Sunni localities. Occasionally religious leaders are more overt, such as when, following the 11 September 2001 attacks in the United States, a religious orator (*zakir*) linked that act of aggression with Sunni-sponsored hostility against Shias in Iraq and Pakistan, enforcing caricatures of Sunni violence in contrast to ideals of peace-loving Shias (Hyder 2006, 91–92). In general, however, religious leaders tend not to exacerbate divisions between local Muslims. This seems to be a critical difference in climate between South India and Pakistan, as Toby M. Howarth (2005, 54–55) has noted.

In fact, India's Shias seem to be generally less affected by currents that seek to manipulate a distinct Shia identity. Unlike the situation in Lebanon, Iran, Pakistan, or Uzbekistan, for example, there is no strong Shia Islamicist movement, nor are there attempts to mobilize a Shia religious identity for political capital or modernization purposes. Such forces can exert pressure, particularly on women, to conform to idealized identities or to confine religious behaviors to narrow definitions of orthodox practices.

In part, a shared perception of attack unites Shias and Sunnis in India. Hindu nationalist groups, which became more articulate in the postindependence era and assumed national leadership from 1998 to 2004, have challenged Muslims' very identity as Indians. One can observe certain aspects of this Hindu-Muslim dynamic played out in Hyderabad. For decades politicians neglected the upkeep and development of the Old City in favor of the "new city" across the Musi River, where Hyderabad's current centers of economic, political, and social power reside. Although the Old City area was once the splendid center of the capital, being the site of political and social power, and dotted with palaces, fine shops, and markets, it was equated with Muslim rule and continued to have the highest concentration of Muslims in the city. There was little political will to develop or maintain Old City infrastructure, and it has remained run-down, crowded, and with a higher density of low-income families in comparison to most other parts of Hyderabad.

The clear shift from Muslim to Hindu power is perhaps conveyed most tellingly by a small Hindu temple which was constructed years ago at the base of the Charminar, despite the fact that several temples already existed within a stone's throw of the monument. From its simple makeshift beginnings, this shrine to Lakshmi continues to grow more prominent and more popular each year, transforming but not replacing an aging symbol of Muslim power. Being an Indian Muslim increasingly means being part of a community that certain groups of Hindus distrust or revile. The rise of anti-Muslim sentiments in the West has further exacerbated feelings of vulnerability and persecution.

It would be a mistake, however, to categorize Hindu-Muslim relationships and perceptions as simply confrontational. Although the city has witnessed several rounds of what newspapers tend to label Hindu-Muslim rioting, local Muslims (and many Hindus) generally describe such events as politically motivated rather than as indications of a deep divide between the communities. This point of view is confirmed by studies that suggest that Hyderabad riots have their roots in competition between political parties and intraparty factionalism (Varshney 2002, 205–9; Agraharkar 2005). Such explanations fit easily within a Shia worldview in which the corruption of political leaders and the battle between good and evil are familiar themes. By identifying the causes of violence as the actions of corrupt officials or people from outside the city, Hyderabad Shias safeguard their image of a composite and harmonious culture. Many are well aware of and take pride in the fact that Hindus participate in annual rituals including public processions and mourning gatherings. The commemoration of the Prophet's family during Muharram and other Shia practices had become popular staples in local Hindu culture by the early nineteenth century (Wink 1993, 221), just as they were in other parts of India (Jones 2011, 94–101). Thus, as Peter Gottschalk has wisely cautioned in his book *Beyond Hindu and Muslim* (2000), one should not assume that people's religious affiliations are their sole or even primary identity, for boundaries between groups are often blurred, and people's ties to place, to rituals, and to communities or groups complicate our sometimes simplistic attempts at categorization.

In this book we meet women who identify themselves as part of the complicated network of identities and alliances that make up Hyderabad's Shia community. Their female perspective on religious expression not only gives us new insights into Shia faith as a whole, but also helps us better understand how we frame what is central and marginal to Muslim belief.

· CHAPTER 1 ·

Foundations of Shia Faith

To understand how devout Shia women construct and experience their religious lives, one must first grasp what they "know." By this is meant not just the normative essentials of faith but also the rich world of familiar stories, personalities, and ideas that form the basis for religious meaning. To introduce this foundational knowledge, two pivotal moments in religious history serve well as orienting points: the leadership struggle following the death of Prophet Muhammad and the martyrdoms and other happenings associated with the battle of Karbala.

In my quest to encounter women at the center rather than on the margins of faith, I draw upon a wide range of Shia sources, including prayers, poetry, hagiographic accounts, and the reflections of women preachers and others. While these informal narratives are meant to supplement the usual male-dominated texts, academic treatises, and religious literature, it is also true that they are at least as central to the religious lives of Hyderabad women as the more formally recognized texts. The possibility that some of these stories and traditions are embellished at the cost of historical accuracy is a point of contention among Shias, with reformers stressing the need for factual accountability. My own interest lies not in debating historical provenance but in highlighting narratives that illuminate the character and qualities of personalities who are central to Shia faith, providing a window into the everyday stories and beliefs that shape women's spiritual lives. I thus follow Mahmud Ayoub (1978, 180) who, in relating a dramatic and moving poem recited in a Shia remembrance gathering (*majlis*), notes: "Perhaps the poet knows, as well as his audience, that the picture presented is not the actual story. Yet, while the . . . *majlis* lasts, myth transcends itself; for the moment it becomes history."

The Rightful Successors to the Prophet

To have a sense of Shia faith, we need to start at its heart with the belief in a prophet of God who came to bring people back to the "right path." Like other Muslims, Shias know that Prophet Muhammad struggled and suffered to spread the message he divinely received. He overcame the indifference and attacks of his enemies and founded a community based on the revealed word. Contributing to this success were the guidance, revelation, and blessing of God, as well as his own strengths and qualities of leadership. With the Prophet's death, however, the survival and growth of the community became uncertain. Shias are clear that the Messenger of God intended his cousin and son-in-law Ali to be his successor and that political maneuvering prevented the Prophet's will from being followed. In fact, it is from Ali that the term *Shia* arose. Muslims who affirmed Ali's right to leadership of the community against those elected by a select consensus came to be known as Shiat (party or supporters [of]) Ali. For Shias the fact that Ali did not assume leadership for twenty-five years—then was assassinated after ruling for less than five—is the result of actions taken by members of the Muslim community whose concern for power led them astray from the teachings and example of the Prophet. As Moojan Momen (1985, 18–19) notes in his introductory book on Shia Islam, the division began at the time of Muhammad's unexpected death in 632 C.E. (11 A.H.): "When Muhammad died, his daughter, Fatima, her husband, Ali, and the rest of the family of Hashim, gathered around the body preparing it for burial. Unbeknown to them, two other groups were gathering in the city." Shias recall how the immediate family—including Fatima and Ali—were consumed by grief and did all they could to attend properly to Muhammad's remains. Meanwhile, however, certain clan leaders seemed poised to withdraw from their former alliances with Muhammad, splintering the young Muslim community into factions and precipitating a political crisis. The quick action, skillful strategies, and clever oration of Abu Bakr overcame this immediate threat and resulted in his being accepted as the first caliph. Ali and those closest to him, however, were absent from the leadership negotiations. Knowing that the son-in-law of the Prophet also had claims to leadership, Abu Bakr and Umar (who eventually became the second caliph) decided to meet the matter head on. They sent a summons for Ali and his followers to come to the mosque to give their vows of allegiance to the new caliph. The group refused, implicitly denying the legitimacy of Abu Bakr's command. The historian S. Husain M. Jafri has described what happened next in his retelling of the origins and development of Shia Islam (1979, 50–51):

> Umar, with his cut-and-thrust policy, advised Abu Bakr to act promptly before it was too late. The two men marched to Ali's house with an armed party, surrounded the house, and threatened to set it on fire if Ali and his supporters would not come out and pay homage to the elected caliph. Ali came out and attempted to remonstrate, putting forward his own claims and rights and refusing to honour Abu Bakr and Umar's demands. The scene soon grew violent, the swords flashed from their scabbards, and Umar with his band tried to pass on through the gate. Suddenly Fatima appeared before

> them in a furious temper and reproachfully cried: "You have left the body of the Apostle of God with us and you have decided among yourselves without consulting us, and without respecting our rights. Before God, I say, either you get out of here at once, or with my hair disheveled I will make my appeal to God." This made the situation most critical, and Abu Bakr's band was obliged to leave the house without securing Ali's homage.

In this narrative, and in Momen's earlier description, we encounter Fatima: passionate, devoted, and furiously loyal to the Prophet. As the mother of Hasan and Husayn, her place in the young community is especially important—given that Muhammad had no surviving sons and lived in a society that placed great value on the contribution and continuation of the male line. In Jafri's recounting we see Fatima full of rage, grief, and bitterness. She does not hesitate to speak out, confronting the men who have not respected the rights of the immediate family of the Prophet and now threaten to attack her husband, her home, and those who remain loyal to her family. She shames the attackers, drawing on her power as a woman whose disheveled hair signals severe emotional pain and turmoil. Her threat to take her appeal before God escalates the situation, for it would be a serious matter to have such a powerful entreaty made by the still grieving daughter of God's prophet. Fatima's intervention defuses a situation of escalating violence, for Abu Bakr and Umar feel obliged to retreat. According to most Shia accounts, Ali did not recognize Abu Bakr as caliph until six months later, after Fatima had died. We return to the story of Fatima in more depth below.

There are many stories that testify to Shias that Ali was the Prophet Muhammad's intended successor. These include tales of his courage and leadership, his prowess on the battlefield, and his deep loyalty to the Prophet. Shias know the Prophet often appointed his cousin and son-in-law to be his standard bearer when he and his followers entered into battle. He called Ali his brother and remarked that if he himself were the city of knowledge, Ali was surely the gate to that city. At one point the Prophet likened his relationship with Ali to the one between Moses and Aaron; on another occasion he affirmed, "I am from Ali and Ali is from me." Of prime importance for Shias in demonstrating Ali's special status is the speech given at the oasis of Ghadir-e-Khumm, where the Prophet Muhammad addressed his followers upon returning from a final pilgrimage to Mecca. After summarizing the essentials of faith the Prophet declared: "To whomsoever I am the *mawla* [the patron, master, leader, friend], this Ali is his *mawla.* O God, be Thou a friend to him who is a friend to him (Ali), and be Thou an enemy to him who is enemy to him" (Ali 1999, 493, note 703). When the Prophet finished this affirmation, God sent a revelation: "This day have I perfected for you your religion and have completed My favour on you, and chosen for you ISLAM [to be] the Religion" (5:3).

This revelation is important, for Shias see the perfecting of religion as embodied by two essentials: the commands of God about faith, practice, and belief and the designation of Ali as leader of the Muslim community. Ali's succession is not just the will of the Prophet but also the intention of God. Shias know, however, that not all people heard and adhered to these instructions. Some Muslims—including those who would eventually lead the community following the death of the Prophet—deviated from the divinely ordained course. In the words of the Quran these are Muslims whose "faith has not yet entered [their] hearts" (49:14) and who are to be clearly distinguished from the community of the true and faithful who remained steadfast to God's word.

The story of succession does not stop with Ali, however, for Shias see God's relationship with the community of believers as direct and ongoing. Although Muhammad is the last of the prophets, something of his divinely inspired nature or prophetic light is carried through his bloodline, giving rise to a chain of leaders with political and religious authority. These infallible male leaders known as imams (the first of whom is Ali) are the temporal and spiritual guides of the community. They are defined and elevated by three characteristics: being divinely chosen, descended from the Prophet, and without sin. These qualities set them apart from ordinary believers and ensure their status just below the rank of prophet. Indeed their importance as a source of guidance is second only to the Quran and God's Messenger, for the imams illuminate the community's understanding of the Quran. As a popular Shia tradition testifies, the imam is the "speaking Quran," and the Quran is the "silent imam." While this chain of divinely inspired leaders came to an end with the Twelfth Imam, his occultation ensures that the imam's invisible guiding presence remains ever available. Like the sun, which gives light and warmth even when it is concealed by clouds, the Twelfth Imam's unseen presence helps sustain the world until his return on the Day of Judgment. He speaks to faithful believers through the words and actions of religious leaders and through inner guidance along individual spiritual paths.

In many introductory texts on Shia Islam, a discussion of the key issue of succession concludes with a description of the twelve imams. Yet, the story of those who followed the Prophet is more complex. Henry Corbin (1988, 169) explains, for example, that when he refers to "the Imam" in his descriptions of Shia spirituality, he is actually indicating two things simultaneously: each individual imam and the collective fourteen "pure" or "sinless" ones (*masumeen;* from *masum* or "purity"): Muhammad, Fatima, and the twelve imams. From a metaphysical point of view, Corbin writes, "each one is equivalent to all the others" in "the unity of their essence." To put it more simply, the imams cannot be considered in isolation from the Prophet and Fatima. The Shia philosopher and scholar Seyyed Hossein Nasr (1988, 103) also elaborates on this point. He notes that Muhammad had two distinct powers as the leader of the Muslim community: prophecy and spiritual leadership. The power of prophecy is unique to prophets. But the power of spiritual leadership is passed on: being transmitted from Prophet Muhammad to Fatima and Ali, then through them to their sons and on to the remaining nine imams.

The Family of the Prophet

For most Shias there are three distinct groupings of elevated persons within religious belief. The first is known in the Indian subcontinent as the *panjatan-e-pak,* or "the five pure ones": Prophet Muhammad, Fatima, Ali, Hasan, and Husayn. These are not just exemplary people but beings whom God created first and loved best. The second is the *masumeen,* which expands the initial circle to fourteen by including the remaining nine imams. Finally, there is the *Ahl-e-Bayt,* literally, "the people of the house[hold]," that is, the people of the Prophet's house or family. Some Shia scholars use this term to refer only to Muhammad, Ali, Fatima, Hasan, and Husayn (the *panjatan*); others to the holy fourteen, the *masumeen.* Most often, however, and especially at the contemporary popular level, the term encompasses a larger group of special men and women within the family of the Prophet.

It is not uncommon for Shias to use metaphysical terms to emphasize the primacy of the Prophet's immediate family. A common story concerns the light (*nur*) that God created before bringing the universe into being. The following version of this popular *hadith* is taken from a biography of Fatima (Sayyid 1981, 1–2) and is credited to the Prophet's uncle Abbas who once asked Muhammad to explain the truth about his "real self." "As soon as Allah willed to create our 'essence and spirit,' He decreed two 'words,' one after another. The first 'word' created the light, the second created the soul. The light was joined with the soul to create me, Ali, Fatima, Hasan and Husayn. We praised Him when there was no one to praise Him, we worshipped Him when there was no one to worship Him."

The *panjatan,* then, are pre-eternal embodiments of light and soul who were present before God created the world.* They praised and worshiped the creator and were the first to know and be known by God. The whole creation affirmed this, with nature, the prophets, and the sages all recognizing these special souls and having knowledge of the heartrending sacrifices they would eventually make in order to follow the path of God.

Numerous traditions uphold the central and primary place of the holy five. One commonly cited story concerns the incident of the "*Mubahila,*" a spiritual contest where the two disputing parties were to settle their disagreement by evoking

*Although this narration is familiar to many Shias, the story is told with many variations depending on the beliefs and emphasis of the person who relates the account: in some it is Ali and the Prophet alone who are born from the first light; in others it is the Prophet, Fatima, and all twelve imams.

God's curse upon those speaking untruth. The Quran (3:60–63) briefly records the theological dispute between a group of Christians and the Prophet, the occasion prompting a revelation that directed Muhammad to invoke divine action to determine who stands on the side of truth: "And unto him who disputeth with thee therein after the knowledge hath come unto thee, Say! [O' Our Apostle Muhammad! Unto them] 'come ye, let us summon our sons, and [ye summon] your sons, and [we summon] our women and [ye] your women, and [we summon] our selves and [ye] your selves and then let us invoke and lay the curse of God on the liars!'" (3:61) Muhammad follows the direction from God and the challenge is accepted. He and the Christians of Najran agree to bring their sons and women together at an appointed time and place to evoke a divine curse. The matter is serious for at risk is a twofold tragedy for the erring side: the striking down of the young men who, according to Arab culture and society, are the legacy of a community, and the annihilation of the mothers, sisters, and daughters who bear and nurture the succeeding generations. We take up the story from when the two sides meet for the contest, drawing upon the Quranic commentary of the religious leader Ayatullah Allama Agha Mirza Mahdi Pooya Yazdi:

> At the appointed hour the Christians witnessed the Holy Prophet entering the field with Husain in his lap, Hasan holding his finger and walking beside him, Lady Fatema following him with Ali behind her. The Holy Prophet reaching the appointed spot stationed himself with his daughter, her two sons and her husband, raising his hands to [the] heavens said . . . Lord these are the people of my house [*Ahl-e-Bayt*]. At the appearance of these godly souls with the hallow [*sic*] of the divine light radiating from their holy faces, the chief Monk who had brought the selected group of the Christians, began to gaze at the faces and exclaimed, "By God! I see the faces which, if they pray to God for mountains to move from their places, the mountains will immediately move." (Ali 1997, 302)

The monk enquires about the holy ones whose halos are so visible. After Prophet Muhammad explains who they are, the Christian leader encourages his people to withdraw from the contest, telling them that they will be wiped eternally out of existence if "these godly souls" curse them. The capitulation is a victory of truth for the Muslims. For Shias it is something more: a testimony to the spiritual purity and the holiness of the *Ahl-e-Bayt.* It also confirms the primacy of the *panjatan,* for although the Prophet could have brought many others to the fateful contest—including his wives—he chose only four: his daughter, her husband, and their two sons. These, say Shias, are the closest family to the Prophet.

The second tradition that confirms the special place of this select group of five is *Hadith-e-Kisa,* the "Tradition of the Cloak." Within Sunni and Sufi traditions, the Prophet's cloak has a long and rich history, most often symbolizing protection and even something of the soul of the Prophet (Stetkevych 2010, 62–66). Among Shias the Tradition of the Cloak uses this powerful symbol to underscore the centrality of the *panjatan.* The devout believe the recitation of this story brings great blessing, and it is a well-known staple in many Hyderabad rituals. For this reason it is useful to analyze it in detail and, to give a flavor of the text, to reproduce a portion of its English translation from the Arabic as it appears in a popular widely available book on the life of Fatima (Sayyid 1981, 41–45).*

> One day her [Fatima's] father came in. He was not feeling well. She brought a Yameeni blanket [that is, a heavy cloak or shawl from Yemen] and spread it on him. Her son, Imam Hasan (A.S.),† walked in. "*Assalaamu Alaykum* [peace be with you] mother," he said.
>
> "*Wa Alaykumus Salaam* [and peace be with you], my dearest darling."
>
> "Mother! Where is my grandfather? I feel his nearness."
>
> "He is under the blanket, my son."
>
> "*Assalaamu Alaykum* grandfather. May I come in with you under the blanket?"
>
> "*Wa Alaykumus Salaam* my son. Yes, join me." Imam Hasan (A.S.) went inside the blanket.

The tradition continues with a repeating pattern: first Husayn, then Ali, enters their home; they respectfully, lovingly greet and are greeted by Fatima; sense the presence of the Prophet and ask Fatima about it; greet Muhammad, ask his permission to join him under the cloak, and are lovingly welcomed. When her two sons and husband have joined the Prophet under the cloak, Fatima also approaches:

> "O my father, do you allow me to be with you?"
>
> "My dearest darling daughter, I welcome you." So she too went inside the blanket.
>
> Then the Holy Prophet raised his hands towards the heaven and said: "O Allah! These are my *Ahl-e-Bayt,* my own flesh and blood, my protectors and my inheritors. I am unhappy if they are disturbed. Their enemies are

*In using Sayyid's translation I have taken the liberty of modifying the spelling of names and titles so that they conform with the spellings used in this book; for example, Gabriel for "Gibraa-eel," Ahl-e-Bayt for "Ahlul Bait," and so on.

†*Al-salam*: a contraction formed from the abbreviation of *salla allah alaihi wa salam,* "may God bless him and grant him peace," a blessing that is commonly recited (or, in this case, written) following the mention of the name of the Prophet or other revered figures.

> my enemies. I love their friends. Indeed they are me and I am them. Take away whatever human uncleanliness there is and purify them with absolute purification."
>
> The Almighty Allah addressed the Angels. "Verily I have not created the heavens and the earth, the resplendent sun and the bright stars, the rotating cosmic systems, the universe, the flowing seas, the sailing ships, but for the sake of and in love of the Five Souls lying underneath the vestment, in the house of Fatima. Do you know Gabriel who they are? Fatima, her father, her husband and her sons."
>
> The Archangel submissively asked, "O my Lord. May I go and join them?"
>
> "Yes. Go and give my message of peace and what I have said, and convey the verse of purification."

With four beloved family members gathered around him under the cloak, the Prophet witnesses to God that these are "my own flesh and blood, my protectors and my inheritors." The words describe more than a group inheriting the legacy of a patriarch; these are also souls who contribute to the Prophet's protection—not just personally but by guarding as well the divine message he himself received. Muhammad's relationship to them is intimate: "I am unhappy if they are disturbed. Their enemies are my enemies. I love their friends." Through this avowal the Prophet proclaims "they are me and I am them," then beseeches God to grant them absolute purification. God, who looks with approval on the scene, tells the angels that he brought all creation to life for the sake and love of the five souls now gathered in Fatima's house. Angel Gabriel, the messenger of God and part of a heavenly cloud of witnesses, is attracted by the light emanating from these holy figures. Receiving God's permission to join them, he comes before the *panjatan* with a divine message:

> Gabriel came down and stood in front of the Holy Prophet (A.S.). "*As-salaamu Alaykum* O *Ahl-e-Bayt.* Allah has sent me to reveal the verse of purification. 'Verily Allah intends but to keep off from you (every kind of) uncleanliness, O you the people of the House, and purify you (with) a thorough purification.' (The Holy Quran, 33:33). Allah has allowed me to ask your permission to be with you, under the vestment. May I?"
>
> "*Wa Alaykumus Salaam,* O Gabriel. Join us," replied the Holy Prophet (A.S.).

Hadith-e-Kisa not only testifies to the primacy of this circle of souls; it also provides the context for an important Quranic verse affirming their freedom from sin. God's gift of "thorough purification" implies a purity of intention, action, belief, and faith—to be without error in every aspect of thought and behavior. Thus the revelation of this verse and its tie to divinely selected members of the Prophet's progeny is an essential component in Shia belief about who is the right and true guide for the Muslim community. *Hadith-e-Kisa* also affirms Muhammad's primacy as a divinely ordained leader, with each family member—and Angel Gabriel—deferring to him. The image of the archangel humbly seeking permission from Muhammad to join him and his family under the cloak underscores the Prophet's position and authority. The imams and Fatima can never replace Muhammad in his preeminence in this world and the hereafter.

Yet it is also true that in this popular account each member of the family is defined through their relationship with Fatima—even the Prophet himself. It is Fatima who brings the cloak and covers her ailing father. Her sons and husband greet her first when each arrives at home. And it is Fatima whom they ask to direct them to the Prophet. When God draws the attention of the angels to the presence of the five holy souls, it is to Fatima's—not Ali's—house that he points. The Tradition of the Cloak is unimaginable without the presence of Fatima, for she is the hinge on which the event turns. Despite this centrality, however, most academic summaries of the tradition eliminate the special active role of Fatima and focus instead upon the actions of the Prophet. The story is then reduced to a singular male action: the Prophet wraps his cloak around the family, declares them to be his beloved progeny, and asks for a blessing from God. Presenting the story in this way collapses the more nuanced meanings that are part of what Shia believers hear and know. It eliminates Fatima's agency in attending to her sick father and directing others to him, the agency of the imams who sought the Prophet out, and the respect and love so clearly expressed between them. Finally, the narrative not only communicates Fatima's traditional "feminine" qualities such as her loving intimacy with her father and her nurturing concern for her family; it also implicitly upholds her singular place among the five. Though she is neither prophet, imam, nor angel, she has a unique power and presence among those most beloved by God.

In both the *Mubahila* and *Hadith-e-Kisa,* the main characters are the *panjatan.* However, the term which the texts use to refer to these five is *Ahl-e-Bayt,* the "people of the House [of the Prophet]." This expression is central to two other well-known traditions, here recounted by Ayatollah Sayyid Kamal Faghih Imani (1999, 10–11), that uphold the primacy of the family of the Prophet.

> The Messenger of God said: "It is probable that I be called soon and I will respond. Then, I leave behind me among you two weighty (very worthy and important) things: the Book of God (i.e. the Quran), which is a stretched string from the heaven to the earth, and my progeny, my Ahl-e-Bayt; for

verily God, The Merciful, the Aware, informed me that never, never, will these two get separated from each other until they meet me at the Houd of Kauthar (the Pond of Abundance [in Paradise]). . . ."

The parable [likeness] of my Ahl-e-Bayt is similar to that of Noah's Ark. Whosoever embarks it certainly will get rescued, but the one who opposes the boarding of it, surely gets drowned.

As these traditions explain, God gifted humanity with two inseparably entwined sources of guidance: the revealed word and the progeny of the Prophet. To know one is to know the other; to draw closer to or be guided by one is to draw closer and be guided by the other. The *Ahl-e-Bayt* are humanity's refuge—like Noah's ark, whoever takes their help will be saved, whoever refuses it will perish. But who exactly are included in the *Ahl-e-Bayt*? Is it, as in the first two traditions, only the central holy five? Shia scholars have devoted much energy to discussing this point, in large part to show that the Quranic reference (33:33) does not include the wives of the Prophet, as Sunni scholars have claimed. Although the phrase may have been used at one time to indicate only the Prophet, Ali, Fatima, Hasan, and Husayn, it later widened to include a larger group, in particular the twelve imams. The practice seems to have changed further as rulers and others sought to widen the scope of those who had a direct holy link with the Prophet and were thus specially blessed by God. The Abbasid caliphs (750–969 C.E.), for example, based their legitimacy on their ties to the Prophet's family through his uncle Abbas and stood to benefit from an extension of the term. As Quranic exegesis debated the point down through the centuries, the general consensus emerged that *Ahl-e-Bayt* refers to a larger part of the extended family of the Prophet than just the imams and Fatima. For most Shias, however, simply being of the bloodline of the Prophet is not enough. Abida,* an articulate Indian woman now living in Canada as an expatriate, explains:

You know that the *masumeen* are not the only sinless ones; the prophets are all *masum* [without sin]. But the *masumeen* are the appointed ones to guide, and since the revelation and guidance are final, their knowledge supercedes that of the other prophets. We believe that Adam and Eve chose the lesser path; they were misled by Satan, but they did not mislead others. Otherwise how could we regard them as prophets? It would be out of character with God's justice if sinners were messengers. For the *Ahl-e-Bayt* there is a fairly specific meaning. It is not just anyone who is a *sayyid* [a person related by blood to the Prophet]. Just because I am of the family of a

*I use pseudonyms throughout the book to protect the privacy of the women I interview.

> *sayyid* I am not *Ahl-e-Bayt* [she laughs]. It's not just about DNA. The *Ahl-e-Bayt* includes Zaynab, all the children and wives and mothers of the imams; it is the very close family who lived their lives in character with the *masumeen.* So, for example, the second imam's wife, she poisoned him, so we don't count her. Besides, she was from a different family, a different people. There were others too. So it is important that they are in keeping with the character of women like Fatima, Zaynab, Khadijah. (Interview, Toronto, 6 April 2001)

The *Ahl-e-Bayt,* then, are defined by a number of clear characteristics. They are family members of the line of the Prophet, including, for example, children, wives, and mothers of the imams. Yet a close blood tie is not all. The members of the *Ahl-e-Bayt* are men and women who have lived their lives in character with the sinless divinely appointed guides (*masumeen*). They include people of exemplary character, such as Zaynab, the sister of Hasan and Husayn, or Khadijah, the Prophet's first wife and the mother of Fatima. Thus sanctity is not the sole preserve of the *panjatan* or the imams but includes certain others having blood ties with the Prophet—people such as Abbas, the step-brother of the third imam who courageously gave his life for Husayn in the battle of Karbala, and Fatima bint Asad, the kind and faithful mother of Imam Ali who also loved the Prophet as her own child, helping, along with her husband Abu Talib, the Prophet's uncle and guardian, to raise him. It is these souls, these holy ones favored by God, whose lives are also exemplary for ordinary Shias.

The *Ahl-e-Bayt* as it is popularly understood, then, broadens the universe of holy souls whose lives are celebrated and elevated by a community of faith. It thus provides Shias with a revered category to which significant numbers of women belong, their lives and personalities being recognized as inseparable from Islam's formative history. To understand in more detail how these feminine personalities have meaning within the worldviews of Shia women, it is important to know more about Fatima, the only woman who is part of the *Ahl-e-Bayt,* the *masumeen,* and the *panjatan.*

Fatima: The Chosen and Blessed

In her excellent book *Chosen among Women: Mary and Fatima in Medieval Christianity and Shi'ite Islam* (2007) Mary F. Thurlkill argues that stories about Fatima are a rhetorical tool in a complex discourse of identity and orthodoxy. She traces the origin of Fatima traditions and the glorification of the *Ahl-e-Bayt* to impulses to fashion a communal identity—whether by sectarian leaders for political purposes or by orthodox Shias against extremist ideologies. In analyzing how Shias have created meaning, Thurlkill demonstrates that this symbol of the holy has been shaped by male speakers to fit their own rhetorical strategies. Thus, for example, medieval theologians and hagiographers limit Fatima's miraculous action and existence to domestic spheres. Or the Iranian reformist Ali Shariati fashions a picture of Fatima that subsumes her life under those of her husband and father in a way that he feels offers an alternative to women tempted by the empty "freedoms" of the West. Thurlkill reminds us that in hearing the stories and interpretations of Fatima's life, we often learn more about the position of the writer or speaker than about Fatima herself.

My purpose here, and indeed in the portrayals of Hind and Zaynab, is to give the reader a sense of some of the stories that exist in the religious lore of contemporary Hyderabad women. Some of these narratives might be contested by those who seek a more rigorous historical view; the aim here is not to provide a historically verifiable picture of the daughter of the Prophet but to capture glimpses of the Fatima who inhabits the minds and hearts of contemporary Shias and to provide a sense of the stories and meanings that are part of the taken-for-granted world of devout Shias.

As we have already seen, Fatima is an integral part of Shia history and cosmology. She is among the few select souls first created by God and is intimately tied to the Prophet and the twelve imams. She brought a cloak to warm her father, then joined him, her husband, and her sons under it, being visited by an angel and blessed and purified by God. She was at the Prophet's side as he brought a small family group to face the Christians of Najran in a divine test. She passionately resisted attempts to force her family's acceptance of new leadership after the Prophet's death, speaking out against what she saw as political opportunism. These and other accounts help bring the figure of Fatima to life, giving birth to a host of qualities and characteristics that Shias associate with the daughter of Khadijah and Muhammad.

Before all else, Fatima is the beloved companion of the Prophet. While still a child, she comforted and supported him during the difficult days of ostracism, isolation, and persecution in Mecca. One well-known story is how, when the Prophet was prostrating in prayer at the ancient *Masjid al-haram* (sacred mosque), unbelievers dumped the entrails of a slaughtered sheep on him. It was Fatima who helped him remove the bloody filth and return home. Her nurture and care was of even greater importance after her mother's death. In the face of the tragic loss of Khadijah, father and daughter gained comfort from each other. The young girl's presence and loving care during a time of escalating personal and communal pressures caused the Prophet to give her the title "the mother of her father" (*Umm Abiha*).

As a young married woman in Madina, Fatima lived most of her life close to her father, and it was often her home to which he first returned after journeys or battles. Ayesha, the Prophet's youngest wife, acknowledged the great love the Prophet had for his daughter and described the loving respect that existed between them: "I had not seen any one who was more resembling the Messenger of God in his speech, conduct and manners than Fatima: when she used to enter [his house] he would stand up for her, take her hand and kiss it and make her sit in his sitting place; and when he used to enter [her house] she would stand up for him, take his hand and kiss it and make him sit in her sitting place."* This tradition (*hadith*) testifies not just to the affectionate and respectful behavior between Fatima and her father but also to the deep resemblance uniting them. The Prophet conveyed this link most simply when he affirmed that "Fatima is part of me. Whatever pleases her pleases me and whatever angers her angers me."†

The Prophet once said that Fatima was among the four women certain of a place in Paradise, being among "the best women in all the world" (the other three are the Prophet's wife Khadijah; Asiya, the wife of pharaoh; and Mary, the mother of Jesus). Even among these saintly four, she is preeminent, being known as "the *Sayyidah* (mistress, lady, chief) of the women of this world and the next." One of the qualities associated with Fatima's elevated status is her compassionate generosity. She responded to people in need, giving whatever she could from her own limited possessions and resources. During the lean years in Madina, for example, when her family occasionally struggled to have enough to eat, Fatima would sometimes give away food to hungry people who came to the door begging for help. Another oft-repeated story relates how, on Fatima's wedding day, a poor woman appeared who was in need of clothes. Fatima had only two dresses: the new one set aside for the day and an old one. The compassionate bride chose to give away her wedding dress.

Fatima's generosity is also a source of blessing. One story describes how an old man, weak from hunger, came to the Prophet asking for food and clothing. Since the Prophet had nothing with him, he sent the man to his daughter's house. When Fatima saw the elderly man's state and heard his request, she gave him a necklace. The man returned to the mosque and showed it to the Prophet. Sell it, the Prophet advised, and God will answer your problems. One of the Prophet's companions asked permission to buy the necklace and paid handsomely for it. He then gave it to his slave to carry to the Prophet, instructing him to inform Muhammad that both the necklace and the slave were gifts. When the Prophet heard the message, he directed the slave to go to Fatima's house, returning the necklace and saying

* *Ayan al-Shia,* Sayyid Muhsin al-Amin al-Amily, compiler (Beirut: Dar al-Ta'aruf), 1:307; quoted in Fadlullah (2002, n.p.).

† *Sahih al-Bukhari,* commentary by Shams al-Din al-Karmani, 15:5; quoted in Fadlullah (2002, n.p.).

that he wished her to have the slave. Fatima received the necklace and the message, then gave the slave his freedom. At this, the slave laughed. When Fatima asked why, he explained: "I was thinking of the abundance put in this necklace—it fed a hungry man, freed a slave and has returned now to its original owner" (Hameem n.d., n.p.).

Thus Fatima is *al-mubaraka,* "the blessed one," through whom people receive an abundance of God's gifts. This is not a surprise, for she—and her progeny—are the heirs of the man known as the "mercy of the worlds" (Quran 21:107). Fatima is also the daughter of Khadijah, the successful businesswoman who supported Muhammad emotionally and financially and whose wealth assisted the fledgling Muslim community in Mecca. As one of Fatima's biographers notes of Khadijah, "[her] fortune also found the right channel, the homes where it was needed most" (Sayyid 1981, 36). Like both her mother and father, then, Fatima is part of an ongoing stream of blessing. "From their house [the house of the Prophet and Khadijah, Fatima and her children] comes out everything, material and spiritual, like an ever-flowing river of generosity, which overfills every land, which does not dry out at any time" (37). Fatima and other blessed members of her family bring an abundance of material and spiritual gifts to the community of believers.

Being a source of blessing implies a divine connection. One way believers see this link manifested is through miracles, and many are associated with Fatima's life. While still in the womb, for example, she spoke to and comforted Khadijah, who was spurned by the women of her tribe because of her marriage to Muhammad.* At Fatima's birth, when the usual midwives refused to come, four beautiful women appeared to help: Asiya, the wife of pharaoh; Mary, the mother of Jesus; Kalthum, the sister of Moses; and Eve, the mother of all humanity.† God thus assured that Fatima's entrance into the world was heralded and assisted by exemplary women from across the ages. As the child was born she fell to the ground in a position of prayer, and at that moment "the brightness and brilliance of her face illuminated the skies from east to west" (Hameem n.d., n.p.), earning her the name al-Zahra, "the resplendent."

The varied and numerous miracle stories linked to Fatima's life are united by a common underlying theme: Fatima is the beloved and chosen of God and has a special status. Unlike other women, for example, she neither menstruated nor bled in childbirth, being known as "the pure one" (*al-Batul*) because of her freedom from "impure" blood. Her marriage to Ali also set her apart, for there was

*Muhammad Baqir Majlisi, *Gala al-uyun* (Tehran: Kitab-furushi-ye-Islamiya, 1348), 2:126–27; quoted in McAuliffe (1981, 6).

†Accounts vary as to who the women are; see, for example, Stowasser (1994, 80, note 115).

divine involvement in the selection of her husband and partner. Men from the tribe of Muhammad reportedly complained to him that although many respected companions asked for Fatima's hand in marriage, the Prophet never accepted them, choosing instead the relatively poor Ali. The father of Fatima swore that it was not he who was responsible for the choice. It was Angel Gabriel, he said, who had brought the news, informing him that if God had not created Ali there would have been no match for Fatima on the Earth.* All these stories and beliefs elevate Fatima beyond the realm of ordinary women, arguably making her a holy figure whom believers love and revere rather than a role model whom they emulate.

Fatima: The Emotional and Powerful

It is not only the compassionate, generous, nurturing or miraculous side of Fatima with which Shias are familiar, however. She is also well known as the woman rocked by grief and rage, whose anger and sorrow did not melt away into easy acceptance and forgiveness. This more passionate and emotional Fatima comes to the fore when faced with injustice, particularly with the events surrounding and following her father's death.

The whole Muslim community was shocked by the sickness and death of the Prophet. Fatima was among those who remained close by his side in the few short weeks of his decline. She was devastated to see her father lying ill in weakness and pain. On one occasion, when Fatima embraced him he turned his head and whispered something in her ear. At his words she began to cry, tears streaming down her face. A moment later he whispered to her once more, but this time she smiled, her face radiant. After this intimate exchange Ayesha—in whose room the Prophet lay—asked Fatima what had caused her quick shift from sorrow to happiness. She refused to answer, saying she would not divulge the Messenger of God's words while he lived. After his death, however, when asked again about this curious incident, she explained what had happened: "He whispered in my ear first that he was going to meet his Lord and that his soul was announced to him (his death), so I wept; then he whispered again in my ear that I was going to be the first of his family to go after him, so I smiled." This popular narrative underscores once again the unique love between father and daughter: it was Fatima alone to whom the Prophet confided the news of his upcoming death. It also testifies to the foreknowledge of the Prophet, for Fatima died within six months of his own passing. Even more powerfully, it affirms Fatima's choice to follow the Prophet into death rather than to continue a life without him.

Although many mourned the Prophet's passing, Fatima grieved for him in a way that was singular and immense. "Eight days after the Prophet's death Fatima

*Muhammad Baqir al-Majlisi, *Bihar al-Anwar* (43:141); quoted in Fadlullah (2002).

went to the mosque. While crying she said, "Oh! Father: Oh! My sincere friend: Oh! Abu Al-Qasim: Oh! The helper of the widowed and the orphans: who do we have for the Kaaba and the Mosque and who does your saddened and grieved daughter have?" Fatima then walked to the tomb of the Prophet: she had difficulties walking, as she could not see that well because her tears covered her eyes" (Hameem n.d.). We see in this popular description a woman blinded by sorrow, doubly grieving. On one hand she despairs for the community that has lost an incomparable leader, a person who helped widows and orphans and stood powerfully and humbly before God in the most sacred of places. On the other hand she laments the loss of a father and sincere friend, feeling the ache of being orphaned in the world. Many stories elaborate on the extent of Fatima's grief. The inhabitants of Madina reportedly voiced their concerns (or complaints) that her weeping was excessive, continuing for months after the Prophet's death. Her face never again bore a smile, and she spent so much time in the cemetery praying and mourning that Ali built a structure there to protect her from the elements (Sayyid 1981, 61).

Yet Fatima's grief was more than sadness at personal and community loss. It encompassed a deep anger at a series of injustices. First, that political wrangling among her father's companions and allies deprived her husband of his rightful succession as leader of the community—against what she knew to be the Prophet's clear wishes. Second, that Abu Bakr, in his new position as caliph, disallowed her inheritance of the property of Fadak, which she and her immediate family knew the Prophet had intended for her. The biggest issue in this latter controversy was not the land but the lack of respect given to Fatima and the family of the Prophet in resolving its ownership. In making his decision that Fatima was not entitled to Fadak, Abu Bakr gave greater weight to his memory of Muhammad's comment that prophets do not have heirs (which he alone heard the Prophet say) than he gave to the testimonies of the daughter and son-in-law of God's Messenger. By doing so he implicitly contested the long-held reputation of Fatima and her husband for supreme truthfulness. Thus Muhammad's death seemed to have lessened respect for the family of the Prophet. This is evident to Shias in the way in which Abu Bakr and Umar came to demand the allegiance of Ali and his followers. Umar did not recognize or respect the sanctity of Fatima's home but came prepared to burn down the house—even if Fatima was inside. According to popular understanding, when the future caliph succeeded in forcing his way inside, he inadvertently crushed Fatima behind a door, breaking her rib and causing her to miscarry a son—injuries that contributed to her untimely death.

Fatima's anger thus reflects a central theme of Shia identity: that after the death of Muhammad the community chose a course that led people away from the "straight path" established through divine will and prophetic leadership. Fatima was particularly bold among the Prophet's followers in stating this. She presented her position clearly before Abu Bakr and the community in a discourse delivered at the mosque to argue for her rightful ownership of Fadak. Fatima began her speech by praising God and stressing her father's role as God's Messenger. She summarized the main teachings of Islam, then upbraided people for throwing to the wind "every law and command" while choosing a caliph, usurping the rightful claim of the true and intended leader. She quoted parts of the divine revelation to demonstrate that people were ignoring its message in trying to deny her the right to inherit from her father. Finally she challenged the crowd: "Where are you heading to? This is the Book of Allah in the midst of you. With clear commands, with well-exposed instructions, with well-defined prohibitions, with precise obligations, and you have turned to a topsy-turvy outlook, tossing back that which taught you everything. You are drawing out contrary policies, in league with the incompatible, to mutilate the fundamental. Severe is the punishment for those who go astray" (Sayyid 1981, 77).

Here we see Fatima standing alone and courageous as a witness to truth. She is the "conscience of the nation," as the religious leader and scholar Ayatollah Sayyid Muhammad Husayn Fadlullah (2002, n.p.) puts it. This role of witness is a singularly important task. Fadlullah explains it to be an even greater occupation than that of martyr for it describes God's role ("He is a witness over all things"; Quran 41:53) and the role of God's prophets ("We shall bring forth from every people a witness"; Quran 4:41). Thus in being a witness Fatima joins the prophets in boldly naming the truth before the people. She takes on a task that has echoes in the divine, refusing to accept actions that she saw as going against the word of God and the intentions of God's Messenger. Her protest is so steadfast and uncompromising that it even continued after her death. Fatima made her husband promise to bury her at night, in limited company, without the participation or knowledge of those who had opposed her. Through this final act, she would leave the world making a clear and strong protest against injustice, refusing to concede to political leadership which had gone astray.

Most Shias believe that Fatima's sorrow and anger encompassed more than the events of her own lifetime. They also included future tragedies about which she had foreknowledge—particularly the massacre at Karbala. One popular story among those that demonstrate this knowledge of things to come describes Fatima on her deathbed telling her daughter about the sufferings that lie ahead. When Fatima finishes her narration six-year-old Zaynab asks if all this could possibly take place, for the tragedy is vast and incomprehensible. Fatima assures her that it will and encourages her to endure it with great patience. The child solemnly promises to do this and agrees to look after her brothers through it all. But with innocence and a pure heart she asks one thing of her mother: "Will you promise that when that time comes, and I call on you for help, you will come?" Fatima, the eternal mother, the miraculous, compassionate friend of God, reassures the child that she always will be there: "Whenever a terrible event happens to you, and you call upon me, I will come to you."* To this day believers share the faith of Zaynab and take Fatima at her word; they know that in the face of any tragedy, experienced or remembered, she is present.

Fatima's sorrow and anger combine to make a powerful force that did not die with her as she passed from Earth but accompanied her to Paradise where it transformed into a flaming fire. There it remains a source of grief and anger for all celestial beings. It also incites the wrath of God who, out of love for Fatima and a desire to avenge those who wronged her, gave her the power to judge all Earth's creatures. Fatima is thus the Mistress of the Day of Judgment. On the Day of Resurrection she will stand in all her glory at the gates of Hell as believer (*mumin*) is divided from unbeliever (*kafir*) and those whose sins are too many are ordered into hellfire. Not only will Fatima be vindicated by seeing punished those who wronged her family; she will also uphold those who truly loved them, interceding with God on their behalf. As the religious studies scholar Mahmud Ayoub (1978, 214) noted in his seminal study of the Shia concept of redemption, Fatima has the God-given authority—unique among all creatures—to counteract even divine judgment. "She does not intercede on the behalf of a believer that his punishment may be lightened [as might happen with the intercession of prophets or friends of God, when coupled with divine mercy], but rather saves a sinner from the torment of hell altogether. Of special interest in this . . . is the conscious identification of the love for *ahl al-bayt* with faith."

Thus, even if a believer's sins far outweigh her good deeds, her soul will be spared on the Day of Judgment if she sincerely loved the family of the Prophet. Although faithful Muslims stand for justice, follow the revealed word of God, and love and honor the family of the Prophet, it is this last quality that is the definitive mark of a true believer. Fatima, as the ultimate intercessor on the Day of Judgment, holds the gift of redemption for all those who love her family.

The Tragedy of Karbala

After the issue of succession, the second most important historical/religious moment for Shia believers is the martyrdom of Husayn and his followers on a desolate plain near the Euphrates River in 680 C.E. (61 A.H.). The events at Karbala were actually the culmination of a struggle for power which had begun several decades earlier when the powerful Syrian governor Muawiya ibn Abu Sufyan contested

*As related by Mawlana Reza Aga, a prominent Hyderabad religious leader; quoted in Howarth (2005, 239).

the choice of Ali as the fourth caliph. Muawiya refused to acknowledge Ali's leadership, and after the first imam was killed five years later he seized power. Although Ali had specified in his will that his eldest son Hasan was to succeed him, Muawiya forced Hasan to abdicate, backed by a strong and loyal army that he had built up over the years. Shias know that Hasan capitulated to Muawiya only after reaching an agreement that his family and followers would not be persecuted and that Hasan would succeed Muawiya as caliph. However, the second imam was killed by poison (an act committed by Hasan's wife but which Shias know was instigated by Muawiya), and the way was clear for the caliph to promote his son Yazid as successor. Thus when Muawiya died after twenty years of rule, Yazid became the new leader of the Muslim empire, continuing the Umayyad dynasty (661–750 C.E.). Like his father before him, Yazid knew that the presence of the family of the Prophet was a potentially destabilizing force in his realm, for it held out a viable alternative to his leadership. He therefore insisted that the sole surviving grandson of the Prophet publicly proclaim his allegiance to him as caliph. Husayn's refusal to do so lies at the heart of the Karbala story.

The events of Karbala can be outlined briefly. While in Madina, Husayn was informed that Yazid required him to swear an oath of allegiance before the local governor. He managed to avoid doing so and immediately set out for Mecca with a small entourage of family and supporters. About four months later, just before the annual pilgrimage, Husayn and his followers left the sacred city, having heard that Yazid had dispatched assassins to Mecca to capture or murder Husayn. The group headed toward Kufa, the former capital of the Islamic empire (under Ali's rule). For years Husayn had received pledges of support from Kufans who were dissatisfied with Umayyad leadership. Their entreaties increased following the ascent of Yazid, with many urging Husayn to assume his rightful place of authority by drawing on the backing of loyal Muslims in Kufa. One of Husayn's first actions when he arrived in Mecca, was to send to Kufa his trusted cousin—Muslim ibn Aqil—as an emissary to gauge the strength and sincerity of people's support. However, the newly appointed local governor Ubaydallah ibn Ziyad squashed the simmering movement when he took over from a previous less confrontational governor. Ibn Ziyad commanded his soldiers to capture Ibn Aqil, then killed him along with others who were vocal in their loyalty to the grandson of the Prophet. The governor next sent an army to intercept Husayn, with orders to halt his caravan on a dry plain, cut off from access to water. Three days of crippling thirst did not change Husayn's position: he refused to give allegiance to a monarch he believed would ruin Islam. The battles thus began, with approximately seventy men and boys facing thousands of soldiers loyal to Yazid. The outcome was as predictable as it was tragic: the martyring of the seventy-two, the taking of their heads, and the despoiling of their bodies; the capture of women and children; the looting of possessions from the dead, the women and the caravan tents; and the return of the army with the captives and symbols of victory to the governor at Kufa.

In his traditional recounting of the events of Karbala, the Shia philosopher and theologian Allamah Tabataba'i ([1975] 1981, 199) noted that, following the martyrdom of Husayn and his followers, the soldiers of Yazid "plundered the *haram* [lit.,the "forbidden" or "prohibited"; that is, the women's quarters] of the Imam and burned his tents." The soldiers then "moved the members of the haram, all of whom were helpless women and girls, along with the heads of the martyrs to Kufa." Tabataba'i notes that three men were captured along with the women, and gives their names, details about their ages and how they escaped the fate of the other men. He does not provide similar information about the lives and circumstances of the women captives. For this highly respected Shia leader, it is men who are the active figures in the Karbala story. His references to women and children are framed first in terms of possessions of Imam Husayn (*his* haram is plundered, *his* tents are burned), then as being helpless, passive objects to be moved to Kufa along with the martyrs' heads. A single exception is Tabataba'i's brief mention of Zaynab, the sister of Husayn: "The event of Karbala, the capture of the women and children of the Household of the Prophet, their being taken as prisoners from town to town and the speeches made by the daughter to Ali, Zaynab, and the fourth Imam who were among the prisoners, disgraced the Umayyads" (200). Although Tabataba'i names Zaynab, he limits his comment to the shame her speech brought upon the Umayyads. In tune with his earlier reference to women as helpless victims, the purpose in mentioning her is to demonstrate the inhumanity and injustice of the enemy.

It is important to note that we could present Husayn and the other Karbala martyrs in the same light as Tabataba'i portrays the women: as victims who are helpless in the face of tyranny. Yet the Shia community does not choose to cultivate this image. Rather the popular understanding is that the seventy-two martyrs actively embraced their fate, being faithful believers committed to the cause of justice. When we frame the story of Karbala as a tale of martyrdom—defining bravery as the choice to give one's life on the battlefield—women automatically fall on the periphery. After all, as Imam Husayn said to a woman who wanted to die by the side of one of his soldiers, "It is not for women to fight" (Abu Mikhnaf, as quoted in Tabari 1997, 19:131). We might quickly note, however, that that very woman, Umm Wahab bint Abdullah, the wife of Abdullah ibn Omayr al Kalbi, did die on the Karbala battlefield when she went out to embrace her dying husband and was clubbed to death by the enemy (Tabari 1990, 19:129–31, 141). Still, in the male narrative a woman's role in the Karbala drama is mainly to be a foil to the central story: they bewail the fall of the heroes, then assume their place as the defenseless prisoners of an unjust, cruel, and impious ruler. After the excruciating loss of brothers, husbands, sons, and fathers, their main suffering (according to male accounts) is the humiliation and shame of being exposed unveiled in public. However, if we shift the frame and move women's actions and perceptions from the periphery to the center, we begin to notice that, like the men, the women traveling with Husayn and residing in the wider society were actively engaged in making decisions and taking action. They, too, had key roles to play in events connected to Karbala.

Most devout Shias have been exposed all their lives to the events and characters involved in the Karbala scenario. They know, for example, about Abbas, the fierce and courageous warrior and half-brother of Husayn who sacrificed his life trying to bring back water for the besieged children in the camp. They know about the moment when Hur, one of the army commanders, changed sides to fight with Husayn rather than against him. Familiar also are many stories of women whose lives were deeply entwined with Karbala. Two of these are Hind or Hinda, the wife of the despot ruler Yazid, and Zaynab, the granddaughter of Prophet Muhammad, both popular figures often portrayed by faithful Shias as having actively shaped events.

Hind: The Faith-Filled Wife of Yazid

Although Hind bint Abdullah ibn Amir ibn Kurayz, the wife of the caliph Yazid, is a minor character in the Karbala drama, her story has been part of the Shia devotional landscape for centuries. The seventeenth-century religious scholar Muhammad Baqir al-Majlisi records one account in *Oceans of Light (Bihar al-Anwar)*, his encyclopedic collection of history and faith-based narratives. According to this story, Hind had a dream in which she saw a light shining from the severed head of Husayn. A large number of angels were coming down from heaven, weeping and saluting the head, and the Prophet lay prostrate over it, crying that they had killed Husayn without understanding who he was. Confused, Hind searches out Yazid and relates to him her dream. The frightened and despairing caliph then frees the captives, sending them back to Madina with rich gifts (45:196; quoted in Ayoub 1978, 130).

In other accounts Hind hears rumor of the slaughter of the family of the Prophet and immediately rushes to her husband to discover the truth, veiling herself for a public appearance in the court rather than waiting to see him in more private quarters (Tabari 1990, 19:175–76). In all the narratives Hind hears of the tragic events indirectly—through rumor or dream—implying that she does not have direct access to her husband's political decisions. She is deeply troubled by the information; her reverence for the family of the Prophet marks her as a devout, rightly guided Muslim, even while she is married to the evil Yazid. Moreover, her action precipitates a positive change. In Majlisi's account her confrontation of her husband motivates him to free the captives and to attempt, through the giving of gifts, to treat them with respect and honor.

Contemporary popular stories give a more detailed picture of Hind's character and actions, stressing her shock and horror as she learns of the tragedy and describing her active role in intervening to free the captives. We find a good example of this type of narrative in the popular and much reprinted *Tears and Tributes* (1980), a literary work written under the pseudonym Zakir that recounts the Karbala story in an engaging easy-to-read style. The character in the account is named Queen Hinda, not Queen Hind, most likely to distance this heroic figure from Hind bint Utbah, Yazid's grandmother whom Shias remember as one of the Prophet's most bitter enemies.

The narration begins with the news that Queen Hinda has decided to visit the dungeon where Zaynab and the other survivors of Karbala reside. It is the first time she has ever ventured inside a prison.

> With ushers announcing her arrival, Hinda entered the cell accompanied by a few of her ladies-in-waiting. When her eyes got accustomed to the darkness of the dungeon, she saw some ladies sitting with their heads bowed and faces covered with their tresses. She also saw in one corner the emaciated figure of Ali Zainal Abedeen [the son of Husayn], with heavy chains and manacles, engaged in prayers. For a few minutes Hinda was perplexed to see a grave in one corner of the cell and one lady resting her head on it. She instinctively went over to the lady and put her hand gently on her head and whispered to her: "My good lady, tell me who you are, to what family you belong and whose grave it is on which you are leaning. I can see from your face that you have suffered untold agonies. For God's sake let me know what is the cause of all your sufferings." (111)

There is a sharp contrast between the queen with her entourage, kindly manners, and power to move with respect in the state's prison and the dark dungeon in which the suffering family of the Prophet resides. Hind is moved by the agony she witnesses but is clearly ignorant about what has taken place at Karbala. She confesses that her husband has been evading her inquiries, telling her to leave to him the affairs of government. Intuiting that Zaynab is the group's leader, she recalls that she had glimpsed her a few weeks previously in the courts of the palace. Even in passing, the woman's defiant courage and strength of character had made an impression. Now, however, she is silent. The queen continues to probe, recounting her recent disturbing dreams:

> I see my Lady Fatima, daughter of our beloved Prophet. She comes to me wailing and wringing her hands and telling me, "Hinda, you are not aware of what has been done to my son Husain and what has befallen my daughters Zainab and Kulsum and the other ladies and children of our family. You are living in the lap of luxury whilst my children and grand-children are undergoing tortures and torments beyond human endurance." . . . It has dawned on me now that, perhaps, My Lady's coming and bewailing in my dreams had some connection with your incarceration, though I wonder how it could be possible for the family of the Prophet to have anything in common with you all. (112)

Hind speaks as someone personally acquainted with the family of the Prophet. During the days when Ali was caliph, Zaynab was respected in her own right as a learned and gracious personage, and Hind had been her constant companion—much as the queen's present ladies-in-waiting are to her now. Hind's memory has not dimmed, but the events of Karbala have so dramatically altered the family of the Prophet that the family members are unrecognizable even to those who knew them. Yet the queen senses something familiar and, sitting before the woman, gently parts the hair covering her face. She is shocked by the woman's resemblance to Zaynab, and, wondering if her memory is playing a cruel trick, cries out, "O lady, I am at the moment becoming demented by the thought that I see before me the family of the Prophet of Islam, though this very idea is so absurd, so ridiculous and so revolting to me that I consider it almost a blasphemy to entertain it even for a moment" (113). With Hind's deep love for the members of the Prophet's family, she cannot imagine them reduced to such a lowly state. Sobbing, she confides that she has been longing for years to see Zaynab and, suspecting that the woman before her is somehow related, pleads for news of Zaynab's various female relatives, asking after each of their children as well. It is Hind's act of remembering the children, reminiscing that they must now be of marriageable age, that finally undoes the mutely suffering Zaynab. Despairing, she cries out: "Hinda, forget Zainab about whom you are talking—that Zainab died on the plains of Karbala with her brother and the youths of the family who were martyred with her brother Husain. Hinda, you see before you the shadow of that Zainab whom neither you, nor any other person can recognise or care to recognise" (114). Zaynab weeps bitterly as Hind falls prostrate at her feet. The queen begs forgiveness for "not probing deeper, when my suspicions were aroused on the day of your presentation in my husband's court." She inquires after the small child she saw clinging to Zaynab that day and learns that Husayn's daughter Sakina died and is buried here in the cell. This news ignites a storm of weeping among the captives and their visitors, the first occasion on which the imprisoned family members can grieve with and receive the comfort and condolences of those who share the pain of their loss. The author draws attention to the balm this is for Zaynab and the other survivors, lightening the burden of their "emotion-packed" hearts.

Having made the choice to visit the prison, Hind now makes her second important decision. She leaves her beloved companions and returns to the palace fired with determination to free the prisoners and restore their honor. She summons her son Muawiya, the only male issue of Yazid, and tells him all that she has learned. The son, having "inherited many of her good qualities," is aghast and agrees to join her in confronting Yazid. In a disheveled state they rush to the caliph's private quarters and find him agitated and regretful, plagued by dreams in which the Prophet upbraids him for his actions. Hind immediately relates all that she learned, starting with the dreams that led her to visit the prison. Shaking with grief and rage, she ignores the consequences of her husband's wrath and tells him that she and her son have decided that, unless the Prophet's family is set free that very day, they will no longer live in the palace and will denounce him as a tyrant, even if their actions bring imprisonment, torture, or beheading.

Yazid is stupefied by this "bold and dauntless" outburst from his usually soft-spoken wife. Muawiya quickly endorses his mother's words, demanding his father's immediate action and calling on God to forgive their failure to alleviate the sufferings of the family of the Prophet. Yazid realizes that it may be advantageous to concede to the demands, for in the city news of the death of Sakina and the treatment of the Prophet's family are causing rising consternation. Women taunt their husbands, brothers, and sons for their cowardice in not attempting to free the captives, and men talk among themselves, questioning Yazid's actions. Conceding to his wife's wishes could stem this ferment, and so Yazid makes the decision to convene the court immediately and announce his release of the prisoners. However, the caliph scolds Hind and Muawiya for the shocking way in which they made their request. Now, he says, they can rest in peace while he recovers from their untoward behavior. Hind is unrepentant: "Peace did you say? . . . Can you think that I, or my son, can ever have peace in this life after knowing what you did to the grandson of Prophet Muhammad and his family, in furtherance of your diabolical designs? Are the things you did, even after the massacre of Karbala, not enough to make us hang our heads in shame and fill our hearts with remorse and contrition? Would to God that I had not lived to see this day" (119). Hind then demands that Yazid make amends for the evil he has done "for the sake of Allah and His Prophet," offering full restitution for all who were killed. Securing Yazid's vow that he will act according to her wishes, Hind finally leaves. Ultimately the caliph does all that she has stipulated, releasing the captives, offering them restitution (which they angrily reject), and seeing that they travel back to Madina via Karbala, as they desire.

This faith-filled portrait of Hind, with its wealth of detail and emotion, offers a glimpse of a women whom many Shias see as playing a small but important role in the Karbala drama. Hind is one of several minor female characters in the story whose actions reveal their great love for the family of the Prophet. Indeed Hind risks her life to try to change the circumstances of the survivors. She skillfully strategizes the best way to catalyze the release and restoration of honor of the survivors. Choosing to stand with her husband's only son as her ally, she confronts Yazid with the most powerful threat she can muster—that they will abandon the palace and publicly denounce him if he fails to act—and neutralizes his power to coerce her by stating at the outset that they are willing to be imprisoned or killed for making their demand. The weapons Hind chooses to wield are weak but carefully selected. Her husband could easily kill or imprison her, for wives are numerous and no one can question the actions of a caliph. A public denunciation would have only limited impact in a society where a woman's testimony is questionable, even when one is the wife of the ruler. Yet Hind identifies a weakness in Yazid's affection for their son, named after the caliph's father. Still, the success of her confrontation is linked to her husband's awareness of a simmering unrest among the populace and his willingness to use the occasion to placate public opinion. Thus Hind's story not only portrays a woman acting courageously; it also highlights women's isolation from political awareness and their circumscribed arena of power in the face of male dominance—a picture that echoes the experience of many Shia women today.

Also important is Hind's role in helping to meet the emotional needs of the grieving family of the Prophet. Along with her small coterie of companions, Hind is willing to listen, to remember, and to mourn, displaying her great love for Zaynab and her family. She and the women of her court offer the first opportunity for Zaynab and the other survivors to tell their stories to compassionate listeners. Their joint grieving embraces not just the loss of the martyrs, but also the sufferings of the whole family which has endured pain, imprisonment, and the recent death of Sakina. If Zaynab is the first to narrate the sufferings of the Prophet's family at Karbala—laying the foundation for subsequent rituals of mourning and commemoration—Hind co-creates the space by being a fully present listener, receiving and holding the painful stories of the survivors. She thus provides a feminine model of loyalty and courage for the whole community of believers who seek to stand beside the family of the Prophet in an expression of immense, timeless grief.

Zaynab: The Partner of Husayn

The second woman worthy of focus is Zaynab—by far the best-known woman involved in the tragedies of Karbala. Already we have had glimpses of the sister of Husayn in the interchange with Hind in the Damascus prison; as a child at her mother's deathbed listening to Fatima's foretelling of events and promising to look after her brothers; and in references to her speeches as a captive before the Umayyad court. Stories about how Zaynab acted, what she did and what she said, are an inseparable part of the narrative of Shia religious gatherings. Only Fatima is more represented in faith-inspired poetry and Shia hagiographic literature. Zaynab's story is inseparable from the events at Karbala, and, arguably, without her the story would not live on today in the hearts of Shias. As the editors of the Iranian women's magazine *Mahjubah* observed in an article on Zaynab (anonymous 1996, 29): "The history of Karbala is based on two pillars: the rising of Imam Hussein (a.s) and the rising of Zainab (a.s.)."

Stories about Zaynab highlight many saintly attributes. She is a "pillar of strength," a problem solver, a learned teacher. Her compassion and kindness are vividly conveyed through tales of her patient care of her fellow captives. One story highlights the post-massacre march from Karbala to Kufa when Zaynab's nephew Ali ibn Husayn, popularly known as Zayn al-Abidin, is in chains. The young man had fallen sick before the caravan halted at Karbala and was unable to take part in the fighting. He is now the sole surviving son of Husayn and the fourth Imam. As the merciless sun heats his shackles to an unbearable temperature, Zaynab bends over him so that her shadow shields him from the sun's rays. Eventually, after performing this mercy hour after hour, day after day, she can no longer completely straighten her back. Another account begins with Zayn al-Abidin noticing that his aunt is sitting while doing her prayers rather than performing them in the usual way: standing, bowing, and prostrating. When the surprised young man asks Zaynab why she does not follow the prescribed formula, he learns that since the prison food is rationed and people are hungry, Zaynab has been giving her own food to Sakina and others and is now too weak to stand.

Stories like these color and shape Shia perceptions of Zaynab and, like the stories of Fatima and Hind, continually evolve as they are narrated for generations in formal and informal settings. To get a sense of how Zaynab is viewed in the contemporary Hyderabad setting, I asked a popular woman preacher (*zakira*) to help me understand Zaynab's role in the development of Shia Islam. Dr. Jamila Jafri (not her real name) has been preaching publicly in remembrance gatherings (*majalis*) since she was a young woman, and although she does not speak for all Shias—nor for all women or even all preachers—her views are respected in her community and contribute to the understanding and interpretations of those who hear her.

The meaning of the word *Zaynab,* Jamila noted at the beginning of the interview, is derived from *zinat,* meaning adornment or ornament, and *ab,* meaning father. Thus Zaynab is the beautiful embellishment of the first imam, whom Shias revere for his fine character, strength, and devotion. Zaynab's name was not given through human favor or design, according to Jamila; it came from God. Upon the birth of each of her sons, Fatima took the infant to her father to be named. On both occasions the Prophet Muhammad responded by saying that not he but God would name the child. Angel Jibrail then came down with the names: Hasan for the firstborn, Husayn for the second. "Zaynab's importance starts here," Jamila explained, "for Fatima also brought her daughter to the Prophet. Once again he said, 'Not I but God will name the child.' You see, Hasan and Husayn were Imams, so it is expected or right that they receive their names in this way. But Zaynab was a woman, and women at that time were given less importance. Yet, through this act, the Prophet demonstrated her equality with Hasan and Husayn" (interview, Hyderabad, 30 September 1996).

Zaynab's special position is also underlined in Fatima's dying wish that Zaynab "take care of Husayn and Hasan." This wish is profoundly important, notes Jamila, for Hasan and Husayn were imams. One might expect that, given their spiritual and temporal position, they would be given charge of Zaynab; instead she is asked to look after them. Ali extracted the same promise from Zaynab many years later. Before he died the first imam not only entrusted his daughter with the care of her brothers; he also foretold the trip to Karbala and made Zaynab promise that she would travel with Husayn.

Jamila's points are interesting. We have already seen how the *panjatan-e-pak*—the Prophet, Ali, Fatima, Hasan, and Husayn—have unique status as pre-eternal souls, blessed and purified by God. However, in Jamila's account, Zaynab, like her brothers, also was named by God. And although one might expect those who are in God's special favor to be the source of strength, comfort,t and security for others, it is Zaynab who is entrusted to care for them.

Jamila also pointed out that among the many names given to Zaynab, two especially reflect her importance. Each one links Zaynab to other revered figures in the *panjatan,* deepening the name's meaning for the faithful. The first is *Sani-e-Zahra,* "the second Fatima" or "the match of Fatima" (referring to the popular title *al-Zahra,* "the shining one"). This name brings associations of the beloved daughter of the Prophet, a light to others, who has a special place in heaven and who precedes all women in God's favor. Despite the uniqueness of Fatima's place within the Shia community, some believers, like the poet in the following Urdu couplet, have hinted that Zaynab's place is even greater: "After Zahra [Fatima] we met the Second Zahra [that is, Zaynab] but / After Zaynab, we don't find a second Zaynab."* In other words, as great as Fatima was, there followed her a soul

*Related to me in the women's shrine Yadgar Husayni in September 1996 by an anonymous Shia woman.

whose light and grace were comparable to her own. For Zaynab, however, there were subsequent souls to whom she can be compared—her character and her role among the faithful are singular and unique. This formulation is somewhat reminiscent of the Muslim view of Prophet Muhammad as the "Seal of the prophets," an epithet that points to his position as the last of God's messengers, a soul who is matchless before all who follow him.

A second name for Zaynab emphasizes her closeness to her brother, the third imam. According to Jamila, "There was no sacrifice which was enough for her. That is why we call her *Sharikat al-Husayn* which means 'the partner of Husayn.' She is what Husayn is. Wherever Husayn is, Zaynab is. And where Husayn left off, Zaynab took over. The episode of Karbala would not be complete without Zaynab." For Jamila evidence of this partnership is found in many of Husayn's choices and actions. For example, when Yazid demanded that the third imam pledge his loyalty to the caliph, Husayn decided to leave Madina. It was Zaynab whom he first informed about this act of resistance, and it was she who made arrangements for the caravan and its provisions. By choosing to confide in her before speaking to his advisors or other close family members, Husayn demonstrated his intimate tie to Zaynab.

Later, while traveling to Mecca and then on toward Kufa, Zaynab was greatly worried that the followers of Husayn were so few. Her very awareness and concern, according to Jamila, demonstrate her central participation in the "whole process." And since "when Zaynab was strong the whole group would be at peace," Husayn tried his best to pacify her, telling her that it was not the number of people with him but their quality that was important. Here the emphasis for Jamila is on the centrality of Zaynab—not only was she the first to learn of Husayn's decision to leave Madina; she is also intimately aware of those who stand with Husayn and the implications of having too few people in the caravan. Moreover, her influence on her family and those who support them is such that her strength and resolve can reassure the whole group.

When the battle of Karbala was about to start on the tenth of Muharram, Husayn asked his sister who should bear his standard. It was she, in Jamila's account, who suggested the indomitable Abbas. Moreover, it was from her tent, from her comforting presence, that each of the seventy-two martyrs went out to battle. Finally, when Husayn was martyred, it was Zaynab who gave the *shahadat* ("evidence," "testimony"; here, the act of bearing witness before God to the deed of martyrdom). Following the death of each brave man or boy on the battlefield, Imam Husayn held the dead body and voiced the intention, "O God, I offer this person as a sacrifice on your path." When Husayn was finally killed, it was Zaynab who ran to hold him and give the *shahadat,* offering his life to God as a sacrifice in the struggle for righteousness.

Part of the narrative of Zaynab is that she led when her brother could not. In the absence of the divinely chosen male leader, the divinely named Zaynab stepped forward, moving beyond her role as companion, confidant, and caretaker. The timing of female leadership and the nature of women's role when males are present are important considerations in the gendering of Shia religion and society.

In the stories about Zaynab related thus far it is not the tales themselves that are so unusual, for all can be found in various oral and written accounts. What is noteworthy is the popular preacher's interpretation of those stories. In telling how Zaynab received her name, for example, Jamila saw the miraculous experience as proving her equality with her brothers the imams. Fatima's and Ali's dying requests that Zaynab look after them is met with Jamila's observation that, after all, an imam should be able to look after himself. For Jamila, Zaynab's added responsibilities to care, nurture, protect, and support her brothers are not seen as lesser tasks dictated by societal expectations of what a woman can and cannot do. Rather Zaynab's role is a testament to the respect and honor in which she is held and to the elevated position she shares along with her brothers the imams. Zaynab emerges as her brother's true partner (*sharik*) when she serves as his confidant, advisor, and helper. She is alongside him as he makes critical decisions about resisting an unjust ruler. Indeed when all the male warriors are dead, it is Zaynab who assumes her brother's leadership role, sanctifying the imam's martyrdom by offering the *shahadat*. This powerful vision of feminine strength, piety, and leadership is sometimes celebrated in poetry that women perform at remembrance gatherings in Hyderabad. In her mourning poem (*nauha*) "Zaynab is the Voice," for example, the Hyderabadi poet Sayyid Rabap Sultana Akbar Patel (1992, 72–73) draws a sketch of the exemplary Zaynab:

> The voice of Ali [Murtaza]* is you, Zaynab.
> The prayer [*dua*] of Fatima is you, Zaynab.
>
> O, who can understand this subtlety?
> The aim of Muhammad is you, Zaynab.
>
> If anyone asks, "Who will follow Husayn?"
> Undoubtedly the Imam's guidance [*huda*] is you, Zaynab.
>
> Through the effect of Fatima's [*Zahra*] milk
> You endured Karbala, O Zaynab.

*Literally, "one who is satisfied." In this poem the writer has used several well-known titles or nicknames for Ali and Fatima. Since non-Shias will not recognize these nicknames, and for the sake of the rhythm of the poem, I have chosen to translate these various epithets in English as "Ali" or "Fatima," keeping the actual Urdu name in square brackets.

In the beginning is Husayn, son of Ali.
The ending is you, O Zaynab.

You possess the reflection of sanctification [*tathir*]
Welcome! Welcome! O Zaynab!

Yours is the voice which rose in the full courts
The daughter of Ali [*Murtaza*] is you Zaynab.

You were the first to make them hear
The calamity of Karbala, O, Zaynab!

Even if worship is the remembrance [*zikr*] of Ali
The remembrance of Ali [*Mushkil Kusha*] is you Zaynab.

The remembrance of Ali embellishes the assemblies [*majalis*]
The embellishment of Ali [*Murtaza*] is you, Zaynab.

On you was the shadow of purification
The cloak of Fatima is you, Zaynab.

Lift your arms and say this, Rabap,
The anguished heart's cry is you, Zaynab.

The poet underscores the elevated place given to Zaynab: she is "the aim of Muhammad," "the remembrance [*zikr*] of Ali." Touched by the "shadow of purification," she is "the reflection of sanctification." Even more powerfully, she is the "ending" of which Husayn is the beginning. The poet sees Husayn's resistance to tyranny as climaxing in the martyrdom of the seventy-two at Karbala. But Zaynab's brave commitment to making the truth known, her "voice which rose in the full courts," is a second important climax, where worship is equated with remembrance. Thus when people ask, "Who will lead us after Husayn?" the poet answers clearly: Zaynab is the guidance of the imam. This is an essential aspect of Zaynab and her leadership, a quality that is shared by Fatima and Hind: testifying to the truth.

Zaynab: Proclaimer of Truth, Defender of Life

In the opinion of Jamila and in agreement with most Shias, of the many qualities and characteristics for which Zaynab is known, the most important is her courage in testifying to what took place at Karbala. As the editors of the Indian monthly magazine *Ja'fari Observer* stated in an article about the shrine of Zaynab in Damascus, the key component of Zaynab's "great and diverse" role was "explaining the reasons of the revolution and conveying and promoting its principles, and especially . . . exposing the oppressive anti-Islamic practices of the Umayyad regime" (Anonymous 1994, 21). Zaynab bore witness in many places: on the fields of Karbala, on the roads and in the towns and villages as she and the other captives traveled to Kufa and Damascus, in Madina upon their return. But she is most remembered for her outspoken and courageous testimony before the rulers in the courts of Kufa and Damascus.

After the slaughter of the seventy-two martyrs, Zaynab, Zayn al-Abidin, and the surviving women and children were taken to Kufa where, two decades before, Ali had sat as caliph. Now, in an ironic twist of fate, they stand before the court in chains. This is a moment well remembered within the Shia community, where tales of Zaynab's speeches are a common reference among preachers and the devout. Of the Shia sources that record this history, the most respected are the writings of the Arab historian Abu Mikhnaf Lut ibn Yahya (d. 774 C.E. / 157 A.H.), whose *Kitab Maqtal al- Husayn* ("Account of the Martyrdom of Husayn") is considered the earliest compilation of Karbala events. Abu Mikhnaf's original work has been lost and survives mainly through its incorporation into the works of others; the Sunni historian Abu Jafar Muhammad ibn Jarir al-Tabari (d. 921 C.E. / 310 A.H.), for example, used it extensively in his comprehensive "History of Prophets and Kings" (*Tarikh al-rusul wa'l-muluk,* translated into English as the thirty-nine volume, *The History of al-Tabari*), which captures some of the details of the well-known exchanges between Zaynab and the powerful rulers.

When the heads of the martyrs and the captives were brought to the Kufan governor Ubaydallah ibn Ziyad, Zaynab entered the court in dirty clothes along with the others and sat surrounded by her maids. Ibn Ziyad noticed her and demanded to know who she was. Despite asking repeatedly, he received no response. Finally, succumbing to the mounting pressure, one of her maidservants volunteered her lady's name: "Zaynab, daughter of Fatima." This set off a dialogue between the local ruler and the granddaughter of the Prophet.

> Ubaydallah said to her, "Praise be to God, Who has disgraced you, killed you and revealed the false nature of your claims." Zaynab replied, "Praise be to God, Who has favored us with Muhammad and has purified us completely from sin. It is not as you say, for He only disgraces the great sinner and reveals the false nature of the profligate." He asked, "How do you consider God has treated your family?" She replied, "God decreed death for them, and they went forward to their resting places. God will gather you and us together. You will plead your excuses to Him and we will be your adversaries before Him." Ibn Ziyad became enraged and burnt with anger. Amr b. Hurayth intervened, "May God make the governor prosperous, she is only a woman. Are women responsible for anything that they say? Do not hold her responsible for her words, or blame her for foolish talk." Ibn Ziyad

> said to her, "God has healed my soul from your tyrant and the rebellious, disobedient members of your family." Zaynab wept and then said: "By my life! You have killed the mature of my family; you have ruined my family; you have cut down my young branches; you have pulled out my root. If this satisfies you, then you have your fill."
>
> Ubaydallah declared, "By my life! This is real bravery. Your father was a brave poet." She answered, "What has a woman to do with bravery? Indeed I have things to distract me from bravery, but what I say is just a spontaneous expression." (Tabari 1990, 19:165–66)

Zaynab came before the governor, the person whose orders brought about the deaths of her sons, her brother, and many of her family members. Traumatized, weary, despondent, and full of grief, she nonetheless managed to meet Ibn Ziyad's claims of triumph with bold defiance. She was not afraid to speak plainly and to rouse his anger. In fact, it is only the intervention of Amr bin Hurayth, the commander of Ibn Ziyad's security forces, that reminds the ruler not to lose control of his temper completely for, "she is only a woman" and cannot be held accountable for her "foolish talk." When Ibn Ziyad finally regains his temper and responds by expressing his satisfaction that God has removed from him the rebellious and disobedient members of her family, Zaynab is overcome by the grief of all she has lost. Yet she is defiant still, accusing the governor of tearing out the very roots of her family. Zaynab's spunk in continuing to defy Ibn Ziyad surprises and impresses him—"This is real bravery"—and he recalls that her father, too, was brave. But Zaynab shrugs off the governor's observation with one of her own: "What has a woman to do with bravery? Indeed I have things to distract me from bravery." Zaynab's words contain a wealth of meaning. Perhaps she is echoing with some irony Amr ibn Hurayth's earlier comment that women cannot be held responsible for their words since they are, after all, "only women." It is also possible that she sees bravery as the preserve of men on the battlefield and is referring to the fact that women have no place there. Or perhaps she is testifying to the physical challenges and losses that men face in battle and sees women's challenges as less taxing. But her final comment and disclaimer that she has things to distract her from bravery is telling. What distracts Zaynab is not only the pain of trauma and loss, but also the very real challenge of protecting and keeping alive those who still remain in her care. If acts of bravery lead men to the battlefield and to death for a cause, women are left to pick up the pieces and carry on in life, continuing to protect those who are dependent and to solve the day-to-day problems they and those they love face.

Indeed there *is* much to distract Zaynab. When Ibn Ziyad notices Zayn al-Abidin and asks who he is, the local ruler discovers that he is the son of Husayn.

In a brief exchange the governor asserts that God killed Zayn al-Abidin's family, and the young man replies that it was people who killed them and that God received their souls at death. Ibn Ziyad is enraged at this bold defiance. He demands that his guards determine whether or not the boy is mature, and when they pull away his waistcloth and find the signs of manhood the governor orders that he be killed. At that moment Zaynab clings to her nephew and pleads with Ibn Ziyad: "Haven't you had enough of us? Have you not sated yourself with our blood? Will you let any of us survive?" Holding Zayn al-Abidin tightly she commits herself with passion to his defense, "I plead to you by God if you are a believer, that if you kill him, you kill me with him." Ibn Ziyad takes a long look at Zaynab after these outbursts, seeing the embattled woman clinging defiantly to her nephew, and then says to his court, "How wonderful is kinship! By God! I think that she really wants me to kill her with him, if I kill him." The governor then gives the order that Zayn al-Abidin be spared and tells him to go off with the women (Tabari 1990, 19:166–67)—an insult, since males remain in the company of women only as children.

After Ibn Ziyad sends the prisoners and the heads of the martyrs on to Yazid in Damascus, Zaynab once again intercedes to save one of her small band of charges. When the captives are presented in the court of Yazid, a Syrian man stands up and requests that the caliph present him with one of the young women in the bedraggled group. He indicates Fatima, the daughter of Husayn, as the one he wishes to have. Fatima shudders and moves away, trying to become inconspicuous in the crowd and clinging to the skirt of Zaynab. But Zaynab has already risen in her defense:

> She said to the Syrian, "By God! You are a liar! By God! You are too lowly born! Such a thing is not for you, nor for him!" Yazid cried out angrily, "By God! You are a liar. That is for me. If I wish to do it, I can do it." She retorted, "No, by God! God would only let you do that if you left our faith and professed belief in another religion." Yazid screamed, distraught with anger, "Dare you face me in this way! It is your father who has left the religion and your brother." Zaynab replied, "You, your father and your grandfather have been guided by the religion of God, the religion of my father, the religion of my brother and my grandfather." He shouted, "Enemy of God, you lie!" She answered, "You, a commander who has authority, are vilifying unjustly and oppress with your authority." By God! It was as if he were ashamed; he became silent. The Syrian repeated, "Commander of the Faithful, give me that girl." Yazid said to him, "Go away! May God strike you dead!" (Tabari 1990, 19:171–72)

Fearless, Zaynab once again takes on a powerful ruler to defend those she loves and the beliefs she upholds. She addresses the Syrian directly, passionately denying that he or even the caliph is a fit match for a woman from the family of the Prophet. Yazid interjects, sharply reminding Zaynab that it is he not she who has the power to decide the fate of any of the captives. Zaynab points out that if he were to give a Muslim prisoner away as slaves or concubines to another Muslim, he would be abandoning the religion which forbids such an act. This swift reply, which displays Zaynab's easy knowledge of religious law, enrages Yazid and he asserts that it is not he but her family who has fallen from the path of God. Zaynab flies in the face of the caliph's anger and steps up her verbal assault. She counters the caliph's arguments quickly and confidently and finally shames Yazid into silence by accusing him of using his power to advance injustice and oppression. When the Syrian breaks the silence in the court by repeating his request to be given Fatima, the caliph vents his frustration and anger on him, conceding the round—and the daughter of Husayn—to Zaynab. In reviewing the oral and written narratives of selected modern South Asian religionists, Syed Akbar Hyder (2006, 100) has argued that the portrayal of Zaynab's brave actions constitutes an interface between womanhood and warrior. She is memorialized and cherished for continuing to "wage her brother's battle" and thus offers a warrior's feminine face.

Yet Zaynab's ferocious and successful defense of her family in situations where the odds (and power) are stacked against her is only part of the story of what her presence meant in the courts, prisons, and roadways of Kufa and Damascus. Shias know that Zaynab's speeches were key in awakening Muslims to the atrocities that had been carried out against the Prophet's family. People who heard her were powerfully moved and compared her oration to that of her father. Before she and other survivors narrated the tragic stories of martyrdom, the Muslim populace seemed only to have understood that the army had successfully quashed a revolt. After listening to their witness, however, more and more people came to know that it was the family of the Prophet that had been slain. As this story spread, unrest grew, forcing first the governor and then Yazid to take action to send them away.

When Yazid finally informed Zaynab that she and the others were free to return to Madina, she refused to leave. First, she said, two conditions must be met: that she be given the heads of the martyrs and that she be allowed to go back to Karbala to perform a proper burial for them. Setting aside an urge to escape a city associated with tragic memories, Zaynab puts forward her clear demands. Thus, according to most Shia understandings, Zaynab took the heads back to Karbala, saw the remains properly buried, and then only traveled on to Madina where she became a testimony to her family's great sacrifice.

As was the case with Fatima and Hind, Zaynab's bold confrontations of those in power aptly demonstrates "witnessing to the truth." To witness to the truth is wholly different from being a witness to events: the first is active, the second is passive. Although many accounts of Shia history frame women as passive witnesses rather than as actors, we see in these women a fearless challenge of the decisions of leaders. They did not simply witness the mantle of leadership pass outside the family of the Prophet or the slaughter or imprisonment of those who refused to bow down before an unjust leader. They spoke courageously against injustice and wrongdoing, passionately testifying to the right path—a course of action that is descriptive of prophets as well as being a defining attribute of God. In fact, according to some religious leaders, witnessing to the truth is equal—or even superior—to being a martyr. This then becomes an alternative role to that of the battlefield warrior, a sanctioned path of courageous action that is open to women.

It is worth noting that the high status of all three women helped make their actions possible: for Fatima and Zaynab being part of the family of the Prophet, for Hind being the wife of the caliph. Without this protective identity the consequences of speaking out boldly could have been very different. Still, as long as one lives in a society with a strong gender hierarchy, every woman has areas of limited power as well as some protection in her lesser female status. As a courtier reminded the Kufan governor enraged by Zaynab's testimony, "she is only a woman" and cannot be held accountable for her "foolish talk."

Summary

What do we learn from stories of Fatima, Hind, and Zaynab? For one, they challenge and expand the gendered way in which human characteristics are constructed. Conservative Muslim societies tend to define women's god-given natures as having the feminine qualities of being supportive, sensitive, emotional, caring, and compassionate, while men are associated with a nature that is decisive, strong, and adept at using the power of reason to think and act (Stowasser 1994, 37). Stories associated with Fatima, Zaynab, and Hind, however, portray women embodying qualities that Arab society defines as masculine as well as feminine. Thus we find not only compassion, generosity, and nurturing love but also decisive and reasoned action in confronting injustice.

In her introduction to Abu Abd ar-Rahman as-Sulami's survey of early women mystics, Rkia E. Cornell (1999, 45) has noted that Muslim thinkers have sometimes dubbed women honorary men because of their inability to reconcile actual women with the qualities associated with females as a group. We do not see this happening here. Rather many of the stories surrounding Fatima, Zaynab, and Hind offer a feminine slant to qualities generally associated with men. For example, in the traditional Shia context bravery tends to be portrayed as courage on the battlefield, death for a cause, or martyrdom before one's enemies. Yet these central women demonstrate bravery in confronting those who seek to harm or perpetrate injustice, protecting those who are dependent and solving day-to-day challenges. Similarly, when women courageously testify to the ideals of society and the path of God, they shift male-centered associations and offer a feminine face to the prophetic godlike quality of witnessing to the truth.

Such strong positive visions are not the understanding of all within the Shia community; rather they are an important part of the religious knowledge accessible to the devout. These feminine portrayals thus provide faithful women with powerful possibilities. When the story of Karbala is one of believers becoming martyrs for their faith, women remain on the periphery for, as Imam Husayn pointed out, "it is not for women to fight." A woman can draw strength from Husayn's example of courage and brave witness, but at some point the story is simply not her own. However, the tradition also offers familiar stories with which she can closely identify. Indeed when we shift from the male perspective and begin to accommodate female stories and views, Karbala becomes the story of tragedy and bravery in which women and men stand together as actors at the heart of the tale. In a similar vein if we frame the founding story of the struggle for succession as one of winning or losing the leadership of the Muslim community, it remains a narrow account of men and power. But when we include the actions and perspectives of Fatima, the story enlarges to one of loyalty and faithfulness: she is present with the Prophet through sickness, death, and burial; she mourns his passing and speaks courageously to uphold the revelation for which he stood. Through Fatima, the tale of succession becomes the story of what it means to be a stalwart believer with an uncompromising loyalty to God's word and God's messenger.

Scholars ignore or marginalize these feminine stories despite their prominence within living faith communities. It is shocking, for example, to find no entry for Zaynab in the *Encyclopaedia of Islam,* a standard reference work in the field of Islamic studies. Almost as startling is her near absence from prominent historical studies. For instance, the respected Shia scholar S. H. M. Jafri mentions Zaynab only once, when he describes how she shielded Zayn al-Abidin from the enemy soldiers during the looting and pillaging of the tents at Karbala (1979, 192). Jafri's silence is particularly surprising given that his subject is an area to which Zaynab made a significant contribution (the early spread of Shia Islam) and that he uses sources (such as Abu Mikhnaf) that give a fair amount of detail about Zaynab's role. John Norman Hollister's often quoted work on Shia history and the Indian subcontinent does not simply fail to mention Zaynab; the author actively renders her invisible. In his analysis of stories about the final resting place of Husayn's head ([1943] 1953, 63–64), for example, Hollister has pointed to three differing beliefs. The first is that Yazid ordered the head carried throughout the kingdom, after which it was buried at Ascalon (and later dug up and moved to Cairo during the time of the Fatimids). The second story is that it was buried in Madina near the grave of Hasan, and the third is that "forty days after Al-Husain's martyrdom at Kerbala the head was buried with the body." Hollister's use of the passive tense in the latter two descriptions effectively erases the actors—arguably Zaynab and her companions—from the story. The marginalization of the granddaughter of the Prophet seems to be the unfortunate rule rather than the exception in standard books on Shia faith and history.

In a similar way we find the cosmic intercessory role of Fatima underreported when compared with that of Husayn, particularly in the writings of Western scholars, including such respected ones as Gustav von Grunebaum (1981, 91–94), Gustav Thaiss (1972, 357), and Mahmud Ayoub (1978, passim).

How can we explain the fact that women are relatively well represented in Shia oral tradition, devotional literature, prayers, and popular beliefs yet somehow overlooked, ignored, or minimized among religious historians and theologians—both Shia and non-Shia? At best, perhaps, the situation reflects a tendency of such authors to see women as marginal to religious thought and its formation; at worst, it indicates misogynist stereotypes of women as emotionally weak, sexually manipulative, and generally inferior to men (Dakake 2007, 213–36). When male historians and theologians hold such views, it is no wonder that they fail to see feminine lives and achievements. When women are not perceived as independent actors, they become simply the passive backdrop to a male-centered cycle of events.

Yet even when women do figure in Shia devotional literature, it is not uncommon to find them portrayed as helpless victims overtaken by a cruel and terrible fate. For example, many male poets and orators portray Fatima as powerless and suffering: miscarrying a child when Umar forces an entry into her house; grieving herself to death in loneliness and despair following her father's demise. Men commonly portray Zaynab and other female characters as mouthpieces through which the Karbala tale is told or as helpless souls overtaken by a cruel and terrible fate. The following Urdu dirge (*nauha*) from a Hyderabad collection of mourning poems (Tabai 1990, 182) is a typical example. The first verse is repeated after each couplet:

Zaynab is a sister taking the place of a mother [*manjai*]
Rocked by sorrow, is Zaynab
Zaynab has brought your head, O headless corpse.

Before the wife of the Governor my head was bare
How ashamed you were, Zaynab, in the jail before Hind.

I did not protest when I was made a prisoner and wandered, head uncovered
Zaynab has obeyed all your orders [*farman*].

The one whom you entrusted to me while you were dying
Tell this dear one [*ladli*] Zaynab has come to Syria.

The wicked one hit your lips with a stick
Zaynab stood silent, shaking with rage.

Brother, take me with you now into the grave
Zaynab is distraught by the terrible suffering [*ranj*] of the world.

In this poem each independent couplet is phrased in two voices: the first-person voice of Zaynab and a nameless third-person voice. The common oratorical device of having the poet or reader assume the voice of a character in the Karbala drama has tremendous impact on the audience at mourning gatherings. The poem's content makes reference to several well-known incidents: Zaynab's promise to Fatima to be a mother to Husayn, Zaynab's bringing Husayn's head back to Karbala for burial, Zaynab's capture and march to Kufa and later Damascus without the outer cloak to which she and the other women were accustomed, Zaynab's meeting with the wife of the ruler, the mockery shown to the head of Husayn in the courts of Kufa and Damascus. The poet paints Zaynab as a passive victim: ashamed before the ruler's wife, impotent with fury in the courts of Kufa and Damascus. The final scene cements this image: having endured so much, Zaynab stands before Husayn's grave overwhelmed by the trials of the world and begs him, "Take me with you."

Although ideas about male superiority are part of the reason for depicting women as passive victims, there are other dynamics that help explain the tenacity of this stereotype. To grasp more fully how women are portrayed, it is important to understand the general function of the extensive prose and poetry dedicated to mourning. The *nauha* cited above, for example, was written for a young men's performance group (*matam-e-guruh*) that recites melodic poetry accompanied by chest beating (*matam*) at remembrance gatherings. The poem is thus meant to arouse emotion and inspire male performers and the wider audience as they commemorate the suffering of the martyrs. In fact, to heighten emotions and increase empathy is an essential aim of remembrance poetry. For poets and religious leaders who have the task of rousing their audiences, depicting women as defenseless victims is useful, for it catalyzes greater participation from the male audience. Men who see themselves as protecting a helpless sister or mother or child are more likely to become sacrificial warriors—whether in political actions such as war or in ritual activities in which they remember the beloved martyrs. In addition, portraying women as helpless in the absence of men feeds a male sense of place and importance in a world where men function as protectors and providers as part of the patriarchal ideal. Clearly, then, the resilience of images of women as powerless victims can be credited at least in part to male investment in such portrayals. To what extent do contemporary Shia women draw upon female stories and characters as a resource in shaping their religious lives?

· CHAPTER 2 ·

A Sacred Community Space

Performing rituals collectively requires space for people to come together. An important religious gathering place for Hyderabad's Shia women is the assembly building cum shrine (*ashurkhana*) known as Yadgar Husayni. This is the only *ashurkhana* of the approximately two dozen major ones in the city that is dedicated solely to women's use. In most other public spaces women participate from the secluded sidelines as witnesses to the central performance of men, although some *ashurkhanas* provide specified times or spaces for women to hold all-female gatherings. Moreover, all the city's other main shrines are administered by male leadership that holds the power to decide how and when the site is used as well as other matters of policy. This is the norm both inside and outside of India. For example, the al-Mehdi Centre in Toronto has a designated "ladies' section" set off from the main complex by a moveable partition. Anjuman Kanezani Zahra (the Association of Maidservants of Fatima) oversees the use of the area, coordinating female ritual performances and managing the circulation of devotional books and other religious materials. Although the women's area is designed to be private, it is not dedicated exclusively to female use. A special door allows men access to the space for religious gatherings or to visit its revered icons, with the admission of males being governed by the needs of the larger community.

Another characteristic that sets Yadgar Husayni apart from the handful of other women-only *ashurkhanas* around the world is that it was designed and is owned and operated by a women's association, the Markazi Anjuman Niswan Barkat-e-Aza (Central Women's Association for Blessed Mourning). Thus the shrine does not belong to a single family or individual but was built by donations from the whole community. This contrasts, for example, with Mehfil-e-Shah-e-Khurasan (Forum of the Eighth Imam), a female *ashurkhana* in the Doongri neighborhood of the South Indian city of Mumbai. Although the Mumbai shrine is used only by women, and a women's association collects an annual membership fee, the small *ashurkhana* remains part of a private home and is the personal property of a single family.

The women's association that founded and runs Yadgar Husayni has clearly shaped a unique institution that reflects a feminine worldview. To understand how this site has meaning for women, it is important to look at how and why women established Yadgar Husayni and how it has become the popular gathering place it is today.

Community Ritual Spaces

In India and throughout the world it is the *ashurkhana,* not the mosque, that is the primary architectural icon of Shia identity. The *ashurkhana* embodies the central stories of Shia faith in ways a mosque seldom can, and it provides a meaningful gathering place for the entire community—women as well as men. Before looking at the unique *ashurkhana* that women established in Hyderabad, it is useful to understand these shrine-cum-gathering places in greater depty. *Ashurkhanas* are popular among urban Shias throughout South Asia, as well as in many Shia communities worldwide. The word literally means "the house of Ashura"—Ashura being the tenth of Muharram and the day on which Imam Husayn and many of his male followers and family were martyred and the survivors of Karbala were captured. Some Shias give its literal meaning as "house of ten days" (a translation also used by Garcin de Tassy [1831] 1995, 149), because many of the shrines come to life with great activity during the first ten days of Muharram. Other names by which local people refer to these structures are *bargah, yadgar, alavah,* or *dargah,* while in North India they are popularly known as *imambaras.* Elsewhere in the world Shias use the term *Husayniyah* (Iran, Iraq, Lebanon), *takiyah* (Iran), or *matam* (Bahrain, Oman). *Ashurkhanas* appear to have emerged in Iran in the ninth century C.E. (third century A.H.), and by the end of that century they were common in Cairo, Aleppo, and many Iranian cities (Ayoub 2000, 875). They spread to India along with many other aspects of Shia culture during the time of the Safavids (1501–1732 C.E./907–1145 A.H.) and proliferated under Qutb Shah patronage.

There are two main purposes that most contemporary *ashurkhanas* serve: to house meaningful icons and to provide a place for the faithful to gather. Among the popular icons one encounters in India are the emblematic crest or *alam,* the tomb replica (*zari*), the coffin (*tabut*), and the cradle (*jula*). Each is a multilayered symbol that links the believer to well-known stories of Shia faith. Many *ashurkhanas* also house evocative artwork, including calligraphy, paintings, photographs of sacred places, architectural embellishments, and more. Locally the word *ashurkhana* encompasses not only independent structures but also private spaces in homes, whether a room that a family temporarily transforms into a shrine during the month of Muharram or a special shelf in a cupboard where family members shelter and display revered objects. Common to all such spaces is a sense of sacredness and an iconic focus on the family of the Prophet.

Although private home-based *ashurkhanas* far outnumber Hyderabad's large shrines, the latter—usually maintained by a trust (*waqf*) and looked after by a family or board of trustees—hold a special and enduring place in the religious lives of Shias. Each community *ashurkhana* has its own unique characteristics based on the history of the shrine, the important dates and rituals celebrated there, and the sacred personalities most closely associated with it. Most Shias are quite familiar with the individual qualities of Hyderabad's two dozen major shrines, and many also are acquainted with the smaller *ashurkhanas* that dot the various neighborhoods in the city and its surrounding districts. Some shrines function throughout the year; others come to life chiefly during the mourning months of Muharram and Safar (see the appendix). Some *ashurkhanas,* such as the one dedicated to Sakina in the Dar al-Shifa complex in the Old City, are primarily sites that house a few sacred objects and that people visit to honor the revered person or persons associated with it, offering prayers and sometimes making vows. Other *ashurkhanas* are designed with spaces that can hold large groups, whether for weekly remembrance gatherings, to practice or perform recitations and acts of self-flagellation (*matam*), to offer daily or weekly religion classes, or to meet other needs of the community. Sometimes an *ashurkhana* is part of a larger complex that may include housing for caretakers or guests, places for preparing and offering ritual meals or performing daily prayers, pits in which ritual fires can be lit, places for processions, and areas where privately owned *alams* and other sacred objects can be temporarily displayed. New *ashurkhanas* continue to be built in the city and to evolve into public shrines from sacred spaces in private homes.

Up until the mid-twentieth century Hyderabad women who wanted to take part in remembrance gatherings would most often make use of home-based *ashurkhanas.* Elite women would organize ritual assemblies on a regular basis, inviting relatives and friends. Working class women, who did not have space or resources to host their own *majlis,* would sometimes participate in rituals organized by their more wealthy relatives or employers. Women from all economic groups, usually accompanied by males in the family, would visit the larger male-run shrines, particularly during the first ten days of Muharram. As still happens today men tend to organize and lead these mixed-gender events while women participated from a segregated area which allowed them to watch the main ritual performance through gaps in a curtain or screen. In 1946 women created an alternative option for themselves by founding Yadgar Husayni. The history of this *ashurkhana* is closely tied to the women's religious association Markazi Anjuman Niswan Barkat-e-Aza and offers a window into gender, agency, and religious practice in Hyderabad Shia society.

Establishing a Women-Only Shrine

Markazi Anjuman Niswan Barkat-e-Aza was founded in 1939 as a sister organization to Markazi Anjuman Barkat-e-Aza (Central Association for Blessed Mourning), a male religious association started in 1934 by four Hyderabad men including Sayyid Chiragh Ali, a respected leader associated with the modern reformer Sir Sayyid Ahmad Khan. When the women of Chiragh Ali's family took the initiative to form Markazi Anjuman Niswan Barkat-e-Aza, it was the first formal religious association for Shia women in the whole of India. From an original ten to twelve founding members, a five-member executive was formed as the Anjuman's managing committee. The leaders encouraged other women to join the fledgling association for a fixed membership fee. Within a few years, the Anjuman's rules and regulations were officially constituted; the association formally registered with the government on 2 January 1946 (Anjuman Niswan Barkat-e-Aza 1981, 4).

Those first associated with the Anjuman were mainly devout women from elite families. Most worked at home and had female relatives and servants to help with the labor of caring for the needs of their extended joint families. They were, thus, a privileged class and had time to commit to this new venture. A prominent and well-remembered figure during these early years was Latif al-Nisa, who served as the Anjuman's first president. A mother of four children and a teacher at the prestigious Mahbubiyah School, she was a woman of exceptional talent and skill and was one of the few women in the Shia community to hold an advanced degree—a master of arts in Urdu language. In addition she was a religious orator (*zakira*), of which there were reportedly less than half a dozen among the community of women. Anjuman leaders also appreciated the respect in which she was held in wider Muslim circles. Her work at the Mahbubiyah School had led to her being invited to speak at different Sunni religious gatherings, including the Prophet's birth anniversary (*Milad-ul-Nabi*). She thus had the potential, they felt, to be an articulate leader and spokesperson for the Shia community (interview, Riyaz Fatima, Hyderabad, 29 January 1997).

In the Shia religious context, a religious association or *anjuman* is an organization that primarily focuses on supporting the performance of rituals associated with mourning gatherings (*majalis,* sing. *majlis*). Thus if a family wants to sponsor a *majlis* individuals often will approach an *anjuman* to request its members to perform at the event. Most Hyderabad *anjumans* are most active during the main mourning months of Muharram and Safar and tend to specialize in organizing and performing recitations of lamentation poetry (*nauhas*) accompanied by *matam* at memorial gatherings and processions. Anjuman Niswan Barkat-e-Aza similarly gave its first priority to assisting women with ritual performance. The members organized a group of voluntary workers to assist those holding a *majlis* or *jeshn* (joyful commemoration) at home. The volunteers contributed by preparing the space, including laying down thin cushioned carpets on which the women could sit, and by looking after practical needs during the *majlis.* Volunteers received donations for these services and gave them to the Anjuman.

The founders of Anjuman Niswan Barkat-e-Aza identified another critical religious need within the community: religious education for girls. The core group decided to hold three-hour religion classes every Sunday and mobilized volunteers: Mrs. Ijaz Husayn offered her home as the first venue and a few women from Chiragh Ali's family agreed to be the first teachers. This informal beginning flowered into a popular weekly religious school (*dini madrasa*) to which Shia girls continue to come every Sunday outside the main mourning season.

It was in the second year of their formal association that Anjuman leaders began to discuss the possibility of having a women-only *ashurkhana*. A female space, they reasoned, would make it possible for women to lead and shape community events more fully and to organize ritual gatherings in a sacred space outside the usual home environment. Creating such a space would make it possible for women having smaller homes to sponsor their own *majalis*. In addition the *ashurkhana* could provide a permanent home for the formal religious instruction of girls. Excited by these possibilities, the women realized that the approaching thirteen hundredth anniversary of the Karbala tragedy would be a perfect occasion to dedicate an *ashurkhana* to Husayn, their beloved third imam. But such a project would be expensive, so they began approaching known philanthropists—all men. They first visited Mehdi Nawaz Jung who, after patiently hearing the women's request, reportedly replied, "This is not ladies' work," and refused to encourage them in the project. They tried with Sayyid Jafar, another well-respected leader in society, but the proposal was once again turned down. The women were discouraged but ultimately decided to go ahead with their dream and raise the money themselves (interview, Riyaz Fatima, Hyderabad, 19 March 1997).

The Anjuman's executive brought energy and creativity to their fund-raising project. They encouraged women to approach their husbands individually, having each household contribute what it could. They also invited women to keep a box in their homes in which they could put a few coins daily, donating the full amount to the Anjuman at the end of each month. Women responded with enthusiasm to these suggestions, for they were already familiar with the practice of regularly setting aside and then donating money or goods for a particular intention (*sarka*, lit. "that which is set aside"). The Anjuman also organized fund-raising events such as "seconds sales," for which they invited women to make handicrafts or donate old furniture, crockery, and other household goods. Sayyidah Jafari recalled one such event: "My mother made sofa sets from small match boxes. Some people made dolls. I made a spicy chickpea dish (*channas*) with my own pocket money. I had six rupees. I made those chickpeas and set them down on a small cart next to my gramophone. At that time there was a popular folk song which everyone knew. The first line went, "Brother, I have brought very hot, tasty chickpeas" (*Channa zor garam babu main laya mazadar*). I played that record while I sold the chickpeas. [She laughs]. When they had been all sold, I had made twenty-three rupees. We donated all that we earned to [the fund for] Yadgar" (interview, Hyderabad, 4 April 1997).

The women worked hard and "Husayn's money" (*Husayn ka paisa*) began to accumulate from every quarter. Anjuman president Latif al-Nisa was particularly talented in mobilizing resources. She spoke regularly about the need to raise money to honor Husayn and was particularly successful in mobilizing women from middle and working classes. Latif al-Nisa's appeals, which she called "begging for my Master" (*Mawla,* that is, Imam Ali), were so moving that everyone who heard her wanted to contribute something. More than one person with whom I spoke told the story of a woman who, though old and poor, came up to Latif al-Nisa on one such occasion and pulled from her wrists her only valuable possession—two silver bangles—which she carefully placed in the president's hands.

Latif al-Nisa believed deeply in this cause and along with other members of the executive were models of scrupulous honesty and selfless giving. Her daughter Miriam Banu, the current long-time president of Anjuman Niswan Barkat-e-Aza, recalls how her mother regularly donated all the money she received for her preaching to the fund for Yadgar Husayni: "My mother would give all the earnings from her preaching as a *zakira* to [the fund to] make Yadgar. She was a good orator, even the men would assemble to hear her. So she was very popular. She would unzip her bag [on a regular basis], turn it upside down and shake it. All the envelopes [containing money given by people who invited her to preach] would come out, or the folded cash. . . . She always kept her personal money in a separate inner zipped pocket so it was not mixed up. She would shake it all out and have her secretary count it and give her a receipt. It all went to Yadgar. She didn't care for her children, didn't care for her parents, but everything was for this" (interview, Hyderabad, 28 June 2004). Latif al-Nisa provides a vivid example of the passion of those committed to making a women's *ashurkhana* a reality. Personal needs, including attention to and financial support for the family, came second to raising money for her imam.

Within a year of beginning the fund-raising, the Anjuman had collected a small but respectable sum. Part of the women's success was a matter of timing: in these years approaching India's independence, before the demise of the Muslim state, many Shia families were reasonably sound economically; some were both wealthy and influential. This undoubtedly contributed to the success of the women's fund drive; their task would have been much harder if they had tried to mobilize for the building project even five years later. With funding secured, the women approached Zayn Yar Jung who, as an engineer, could advise them on the purchase of land and eventual construction. They boldly told him and others with whom they negotiated that since their project was for a religious purpose, they should be given concessions from the ordinary rates and fees. Months before the thirteen hundredth anniversary celebration, they purchased for a nominal price three plots of land in what is today the geographical heart of Hyderabad's Shia community, the Old City locality of Dar al-Shifa.

The women of Anjuman Niswan Barkat-e-Aza chose a deeply significant day in 1946 to commemorate their first step in realizing the dream of a women's *ashurkhana*. For many Shias the second of Muharram is remembered as the day that Husayn purchased the Karbala land where he and his family were to face Yazid's army. Shia tradition relates that Husayn then gave the land back to its owners with their pledge that they would look after the graves of the soon-to-be-martyred and attend to the needs of future pilgrims. Thirteen hundred years after Husayn's death, the women swept their own barren ground and set up carpets and tents to hold a profoundly moving *majlis*. By performing a remembrance gathering on this special day, the women united the building project with sacred time and sacred purpose, adding a personal layer of meaning to the story of Husayn's gift and the holy ground that it eventually became. The Anjuman continues to honor the second of Muharram with a special anniversary *majlis* each year.

Seeing that the Anjuman had spent nearly all its collected funds on the purchase of the property, the leadership once again began to "beg for their imam" in order to raise money for constructing an *ashurkhana*. By then, however, women had enthusiasm, confidence, and experience, and the funds were quickly collected. An inner shrine and large hall were constructed along with a number of exterior shops, the rents of which gave the Anjuman regular revenue and a degree of financial independence. When the construction was complete, the women reverently installed an *alam* dedicated to Husayn and other meaningful items donated by various women and their families, including *alams*, tomb replicas, photographs, carpets, chandeliers, and more. Donations were particularly rich since, following the partition of India, many Shia families had decided to move to Pakistan and were willing to give away treasured objects from their private family *ashurkhanas*.

Yadgar Husayni's popularity grew as more and more women came to see it as a sacred space to gather and perform ritual. In addition to participating in remembrance gatherings sponsored by the association or by individuals, including a weekly *majlis* which the Anjuman organized every Thursday night, women began to use the space to perform daily prayers (*namaz*) and to meet for prayers or other rituals on special days throughout the year. Women members led religious observances such as special recitations of the Quran during the fasting month of Ramzan or the performance of litanies (*amal*) or supplication rituals (*niyaz, dastarkhan*). This growth in religious activity was fed by wider shifts in the society. Middle- and upper-class families were beginning to move away from sprawling joint-family dwellings to smaller single-family houses or apartments,

Main entrance to Yadgar Husayni, a women's ashurkhana *in Hyderabad's Old City*

making space an issue for many who aspired to host their own ritual gatherings. Yadgar Husayni, with its ritually pure environment and ability to accommodate large numbers of people, became an attractive and affordable alternative.

The increased use of the *ashurkhana* stretched existing facilities. By the mid-1980s private donations had funded several additions, including a room for ritual prayers (*namazkhana*) and one for supplication rituals (*niyazkhana*). Still the crowds at a popular *majlis* could not be accommodated within the existing space. The Anjuman thus set a new fund-raising challenge: to construct a new hall that could hold at least three hundred women. The managing committee appealed to the female community, reminding them of the blessing received by donating to a worthy cause. One invitation published in the Anjuman's 1984 (24) commemorative volume in honor of Imam Husayn's fourteen hundredth birth anniversary read, "Appeal for assistance in the construction of Husayni Hall: Give a gift today for the construction of a religious school [*madrasa-e-diniyat*] and receive a reward from the mistress of the worlds" (*Sayyidah Alamiyan;* that is, Fatima). As with its earlier fund-raising efforts, the Anjuman leadership made explicit associations between the shrine project and blessings from the *Ahl-e-Bayt.* They also adopted clever fund-raising strategies such as framing the total construction costs in terms of the cost per woman in the completed hall. They then encouraged each Anjuman member to approach her family for a contribution that would cover the amount of space required by the number of women in the household. Once again the appeal received a tremendous response, and the women collected two hundred thousand rupees within a matter of months. Successful, the Anjuman's leaders laid the foundation stone for Husayni Hall in 1984, and a year later it was ready for use.

Today Yadgar Husayni continues to meet the demands of space and remains one of the most popular sites for women in the community to perform religious rituals. One gets a sense of its popularity by looking at the financial records kept by the managing committee of Markazi Anjuman Niswan Barkat-e-Aza. In 1996 the annual report records that nearly 126,000 rupees were collected from women who paid to use Yadgar for various religious functions, including remembrance gatherings (80,000), and various supplication rites (46,000). Judging from the audited figures and the rates that the Anjuman charges (150 to 250 rupees for rental of its hall), it appears that between 300 to 500 remembrance gatherings (both *majalis* and *jeshns*) were held at the *ashurkhana* in 1996, a figure that Siraj Bahdur Ali, the Anjuman secretary, confirmed as an accurate annual estimate (interview, Hyderabad, 26 June 1997). This remarkable figure conceals seasonal fluctuations; during the main seventy-two-day mourning period, Yadgar sometimes hosts from five to seven *majalis* per day, while at other times of the year there may be a single *majlis* or *jeshn* held in a week. When it comes to supplication rituals, a conservative estimate for the annual number of ceremonies is more than 150—that is, an average of three per week (Anjuman Niswan Barkat-i Aza 1996, 2–4). These figures do not begin to capture the frequency of visits by women who come to Yadgar simply to pray or visit the *alams.* During the period of my research, from ten to forty women and girls dropped in on ordinary days, while on special days, especially during the mourning period, the number easily rose to several hundred.

What has contributed to Yadgar Husayni's tremendous popularity and, indeed, its successful founding and expansion? One critical early factor was certainly the composition of the leadership that catalyzed the project. The women who were initially involved with Yadgar Husayni came from an economic class and position that gave them sufficient time to dedicate to the association and its goals. Many had valuable management and interpersonal skills gained from handling large households and navigating the dynamics of joint families. The leadership also brought useful connections to people and resources since many individuals came from families with ties to the established power holders in pre-independence

The busy interior courtyard of Yadgar Husayni

Hyderabad. Their confidence, energy, creativity, and devotion were further complimented by the woman they chose to be the Anjuman's first president—Latif al-Nisa. Her charisma and personal dedication to the project catalyzed the participation of an ever-widening circle of women.

A second factor that contributed to Yadgar Husayni's success was the project's rootedness in people's faith. Beginning with the germination of the idea, the goal was to honor the third imam. This eased the job of fund-raising, since collecting money for a central beloved imam is very different from raising money for a building project—no matter how worthy. The women made use of this connection, inspiring themselves and others through emotional ties to the family of the Prophet. Thus, for example, the donations that women collected were "Husayn's money," the time frame for establishing the new *ashurkhana* was made to coincide with a significant Karbala anniversary, and the ground-breaking ceremony was organized on an important annual remembrance day that linked the founding of this *ashurkhana* with religious history. It would not be correct, however, to conclude that the project was successful simply because it was a religious one. I once asked one of the community's leaders if women might ever consider establishing a women-only mosque. My friend laughed with amusement at the idea. "What do women have to do with a mosque?" she asked. Part of the reason Yadgar Husayni succeeded, then, is because it addressed a *meaningful* religious goal for local Shia women: providing a place where they could gather to participate in religious activities that they themselves had defined as central and valuable to their faith.

Finally, women's success also lay in having powerful images of strong, active women as models of courage, determination, and purpose. As we have seen, the Shia collective memory includes key stories of Zaynab and Fatima: their fights against injustice, their bold confrontations of power, and their faithfulness to the path of God and the family of the Prophet. These stories are part of what devout women know and serve as a source of inspiration that can catalyze bold public action. Lara Deeb (2006, 149) emphasizes just this point in her study of pious women's community service in Lebanon, noting that interpretations of Zaynab as an active leader "have had major ramifications for the participation of pious women in the public arena."

Religious Meaning and the Feminine Gaze

In constructing a public religious space Yadgar Husayni's leaders have made a range of choices from design and embellishment of the shrine to guidelines for the use of space and donated resources. What do these choices reveal about female religious understanding and Shia faith overall? A closer look at the visual culture of the shrine helps to answer these questions.

Yadgar Husayni is one of several major shrines in the Dar al-Shifa neighborhood of the Old City. It is situated on a quiet lane just around the corner from the Dar al-Shifa complex, the main gathering place for Hyderabad's Shia community. The open outer courtyard and the exterior of the building are unremarkable for, like many public or private buildings within Muslim society, the orientation is toward inner rather than outer display. Once through the building's main arched doorway and curtained entrance hall, however, one descends into an open interior courtyard where sparrows chatter in half a dozen trees and water trills in a stone fountain. The *ashurkhana* consists of various distinct spaces. Most prominent is the expansive Husayni Hall, an open-sided roofed structure that juts into the courtyard at a slightly higher elevation than that of the surrounding space. One must climb a few broad stairs to enter the hall, first removing one's shoes before beginning the ascent into sanctified ritual space. Distinct from this area for religious performance are more mundanely functional interior spaces. Along the eastern wall, and separated from the main hall by the courtyard with the fountain, are a kitchen and eating area, a set of toilets, and a few rooms for women who live at the shrine. Along the northern wall are small office and meeting rooms with a separate exterior entrance to the building. These function as the venue for the monthly meetings of the managing committee and house the records and supplies of the association.

Husayni Hall is bright and airy. The columns that support its high ceiling and separate it from the surrounding courtyard are matched by a set of wide interior columns that divide the nearly four-thousand-square-foot space into two equal parts. The eastern portion of the hall through which one first enters is relatively Spartan, with a few chairs, a somewhat battered couch, and several water coolers. Women mostly use it as an anteroom: a casual place to have a chat without disturbing the events taking place in the western part of the hall. During a major ritual gathering of hundreds of people, however, the crowd overflows to this portion of the hall, even though the large interior columns partially obstruct people's view of events in the main performance area. The polished stone floors throughout the hall are covered by simple carpets. These are replaced by white sheets over cushioned mats during the mourning months of Muharram and Safar, allowing women to sit comfortably while participating in lengthy and frequent ritual gatherings.

The main hall contains three interior rooms, their preeminence being signaled by the fine Persian-style carpets spread outside each entrance. The most prominent of these is known as the *sher nishin,* which literally means "the place where the lion [or tiger] sits." *Lion* is a euphemism for an outstandingly brave man and is one of the popular names of Imam Ali. The *sher nishin* contains the *ashurkhana*'s most precious icons. Flanking it on either side are the prayer room (*namazkhana*) and the supplication room (*niyazkhana*). The position of these rooms within the shrine is intentional and important, with their location along the western wall putting them on an axis aligned with the direction of prayer. Faithful Muslims everywhere face Mecca when performing daily ritual prayers; more precisely, their orientation is toward the Kaba, the large cubic stone structure situated in the center of Mecca's Grand Mosque (*al-Masjid al-Haram*). For most believers this is the closest place to God outside the heavens, and the direction toward it (usually indicated by a small niche known as the *qiblah*) is a central orienting point of ritual and daily life. For example, in many households in Hyderabad one never sits with the soles of one's feet facing the direction of the Kaba, even while asleep. To do so is considered akin to putting one's feet in the face of God—a gesture considered profoundly disrespectful in Indian society. In the same way, when one dies, one's body is placed in the grave with the face positioned toward Mecca and thus toward God. This sense of being in tune with a physical sacred universe is fundamental to Muslim architecture and is built into the very design of Yadgar Husayni.

The spatial orientation of the *ashurkhana* also communicates specific female priorities. The original construction established a devotional space with an inner room to house sacred icons (*sher nishin*) and a hall in which to gather for remembrance rituals. Thus women's first emphasis was on symbols of the family of the Prophet and opportunities to recall, celebrate, and mourn their lives. As women expanded the *ashurkhana* to accommodate its growing popularity, they not only extended the hall to accommodate even larger crowds, but they also constructed rooms with the important religious purposes of prayer and intercession. Although there are several *ashurkhanas* in Hyderabad that have a *niyazkhana* on the premises, in Yadgar Husayni women placed this room for petitioning or celebrating the intervention of the family of the Prophet in a spot that conveys that supplication is the compliment to the daily prayer rite. By making this spatial choice, women communicate that both religious acts are strong and powerful ways to nurture one's connection with the divine.

But it is not just the *ashurkhana*'s layout that communicates female religious understandings and priorities. A careful look at the site's many visual embellishments gives further insights into women's theology. Icons, photographs, and texts fill the *sher nishin* and the *namazkhana* and adorn portions of the *niyazkhana* and the hall. The most visibly powerful of these are the *alams*. When the green doors to the *sher nishin* are open, as they are during most weekdays and during all remembrance gatherings, the *alams* are the central orienting point for all who enter Husayni Hall. Three metallic crests are displayed on poles affixed to an ornate stand, with the central majestic *Husayni alam* dominating the trio. Its brass face, about the size of a large upright tray, is circular and flows into petal-like protrusions along an arched crown. Affixed to its display pole, it stands regally at more than five feet in height. The two silver crests that flank it are each in the shape of an upright hand. This symbol, known locally as *panjah* or *panjatan,* carries deep meaning for most Shias since it—and indeed, the word *panjatan* itself—represents the five central members of the Prophet's family: Muhammad, Fatima, Ali, Hasan, and Husayn. The *panjah* to the left of the Husayni alam is dedicated to Abbas, while the one on the right is dedicated to Ali Akbar. All three are usually decked with garlands of jasmine and rose, with visitors regularly adding new garlands.

There are other icons of religious importance in the *sher nishin.* Prominent among them are two metal-work replicas of tombs (*taziyas*), which are displayed in four-foot-high cases made of wood and glass. One represents the tomb of Husayn, the other that of Zaynab. Around them the walls are adorned with photographs of the tombs of various members of the Prophet's family, as well as two veiled portraits of Ali and Husayn. All these symbols connect viewers with stories from religious memory, helping to deepen a sense of Shia identity. For many of the devout there is a close link between these revered objects and the beloved personalities they bring to mind, creating an intimate tie between the believer and the transcendent. In other words, for many Shia women, stepping into the *sher nishin* is the spiritual equivalent of coming into the presence of Husayn, Abbas, Ali Asghar, Zaynab, and other members of the Prophet's family. A believer sometimes conveys this connection by the way in which she reverently approaches the room: halting before entering or departing to touch the threshold and then her forehead in a gesture of humility and appropriation of blessing.

In the prayer room (*namazkhana*) the visual images help connect the viewer to a broad Muslim identity, stressing the power of communication with God and the beloved family of the Prophet. Well-known prayers of petition (*dua*) and those that ask blessings on Prophet Muhammad and his family (*durood*) adorn the walls alongside many other images including a calligraphic representation of the word *Allah,* an essay on the benefits of daily prayer, a photo of the Kaba encircled by a crowd of faithful pilgrims, and a copy of *Hadith-e-Kisa* (the popular tradition that affirms the blessedness and power of the *Ahl-e-Bayt*). These textual and photographic displays affirm a theology that stresses the primacy of Allah, the sacredness of the Kaba, and the centrality of ritual prayer.

Other objects in the shrine communicate Shia beliefs more subtly. A good example is the wall clock placed next to the doors of the *sher nishin.* On the clock's face are the words "Ya Allah" (O, God), "Ya Muhammad" (O, Muhammad), "Ya Fatima" (O, Fatima), while the names of the twelve imams are displayed next to

The central alam, *flanked by two attendant* alams, *conveys theology by positioning the word* Allah *on the top of the crest, above the calligraphed names of Muhammad, Ali, Fatima, Hasan and Husayn.*

each of the numbers. The overall effect of this timepiece is to have the twelve imams encircle the name of Allah, the Prophet, and Fatima. Another simple yet profoundly theological statement is contained in a glass case fixed to one of the pillars in the hall. The somewhat garish display is the size of a large book and contains a series of small flickering green lights that connect the names of Allah and the five members of the *panjatan.* The positioning of the names is crucial to the message: *Allah* is at the top, and the names of Prophet Muhammad, his daughter and son-in-law, and their two sons are arrayed at the bottom. The string of lights blinks in such a way that light appears to be traveling from Allah down to each of the five. Even the otherwise unremarkable water coolers tell a story, serving as a reminder of the community's promise that no person will ever thirst as the Prophet's family and followers did at Karbala. Thus with eyes of faith simple wall decorations and functional objects become a meaningful testament to Shia faith and community.

Yadgar Husayni's range of symbols and icons, both explicit and subtle, articulates theological basics as clearly as any written treatise. The first precept echoed throughout the *ashurkhana* is the preeminence of God. This is conveyed by the spatial relationship between the word *Allah* and other revered names—Muhammad, Fatima, and the twelve imams—on various decorative objects. A second important testimony of faith is the principle that one is part of a believing community of Muslims (*ummah*). Sunni polemics against Shias tend to emphasize the "otherness" of non-Sunnis. Yet in the *ashurkhana* women's self-definition is intimately tied to beliefs affirmed by the entire Muslim community, whether reverence for the Prophet and sites associated with early Muslim history, a belief in the fundamental acts of worship, veneration for the divinely revealed words of scripture, or an orientation to the Kaba. These affirmations are as much a part of Shia identity as the more divisive symbols that Sunnis commonly associate with Shia belief. Finally, the visual culture of the shrine communicates women's great reverence for the family of the Prophet, expressed in dozens of small ways as well as through major icons such as *alams* dedicated in the family members' names and replicas or photographs of their faraway tombs. While the *ashurkhana* we affirms God as the preeminent source of power and life, it also depicts the Prophet and his family as unique representatives of God's grace who are therefore powerful and worthy of reverence.

Yadgar Husayni's very design and iconography, combined with the stories about its founding and growth, combine to give it a sense of sacredness. For the believer the *ashurkhana* is not simply a gathering place for religious ritual but is also a holy venue where one is especially close to God. One Anjuman leader, Batul, conveyed this most eloquently when she was speaking about a practice that she taught her students at the weekly Sunday school. Before each student goes home, she must come up to Batul and, with a little bow of the head, deliver the brief prayer, "Increase my knowledge" (*Rabe zidni ilman*). Batul smiles as she confesses, "It is my favorite prayer (*dua*), and a prayer made here in Yadgar." She lifts her eyebrows, then raises her eyes expressively, but before she can conclude the sentence a child interrupts her. Even without her final words, however, Batul's meaning is powerfully conveyed in her brief glance heavenward: a prayer offered in Yadgar is even stronger than one offered elsewhere (interview, Hyderabad, 13 February 2000). Like the majority of the women who frequent Yadgar Husayni, Batul is confident that one's prayers are specially heard when they are offered in this holy space.

There is a final observation to be made in analyzing how women use images to shape meaning in a ritual space they themselves have created. Even though the *ashurkhana* was created by and dedicated to female expressions of faith, it is Husayn and other male figures who are at its heart. If men had built this popular local *ashurkhana,* it would be worth pointing out the impossibility of separating women from the central stories and icons, for there are symbols throughout the shrine that connect women to Fatima and Zaynab. But Yadgar Husayni is a female institution and given its female starting point, it is interesting to observe that the feminine presence is indivisible from but not spectacularly central to the space women have created. In fact, one might say that the position of such exemplary souls as Fatima and Zaynab is "taken-for-granted-normal," a position not very different from how women perceive their own presence in society. In contrast, male religious heroes form the center, as is conveyed by the three prominent *alams* in the *sher nishin* dedicated not to women but to prominent men and by the very name of the room, which links it to courageous male warriors. In the *niyazkhana* where women offer prayers for intercession and express their gratitude for blessings received, the only visual image is a veiled painting of Imam Ali. Most tellingly, Yadgar Husayni is dedicated to the third imam, a connection women have honored by linking significant days in the development of the shrine with commemoration points in Husayn's life, giving their initiatives special meaning and blessing.

In some ways, then, the shrine's symbolism mirrors an aspect of the feminine gaze that is very much a part of the dominant Shia worldview: it remains focused on the males at the center and encourages women to faith-filled action. As Saba Mahmood (2005, 175–88) argues in her study of Cairo's vibrant female piety movement, women's agency—the capacity for self-direction exercised on one's own behalf—is not automatically linked to resisting domination, whether it be patriarchy or other forms of oppression. Rather women find and create meaning within the larger structures and power equations of which they are part. In shaping ritual space at Yadgar Husayni women have not sought to "enshrine" women but have affirmed their ties with members of the *Ahl-e-Bayt* in a world where the centrality of males is part of one's identity. That women are an intrinsic part of that world is simply the unemphasized flip side of the coin.

Defining a "Women-Only" Space

Women are strict about preserving Yadgar Husayni as a women-only *ashurkhana,* yet on rare occasions one sees boys or men at the shrine. How do women understand the gendered space they have created? When I once asked one of Yadgar's leaders for permission to videotape a *majlis,* she asked me pointedly whether a man would accompany me to do the filming. She was very clear about the matter: "Men are simply not allowed." Preserving the shrine as a female space allows women the freedom to gather and to engage in religious activity without the encumbrance of veiling—as most do in the presence of men with whom they have no close blood tie. Keeping men from the space also means avoiding issues of power and the distracting sexual undercurrents that are sometimes a part of mixed gender environments. Perhaps most important, insisting on Yadgar's women-only status means that women feel that their presence there is respectable and above reproach: families can be confident that if girls or other family members are at Yadgar Husayni, they are in a safe, protected environment. What, then, are the conditions under which women make exceptions to this strong guiding principle?

The first is the most basic: when women bring a young male relative for ritual or prayer. For example, I once observed a well-dressed woman enter the *ashurkhana* with her seven- or eight-year-old son. When she arrived in the hall a group of women was already performing a ritual of silent litanies. The mother and son took a place behind these women and began their *namaz.* When they finished two cycles of prayer they sat down with some distance between them and began additional silent prayers, using the string of prayer beads (*tasbih*) to count the repeated phrases. The boy and his mother stayed at Yadgar for nearly an hour, the woman deeply occupied in prayer while the boy played quietly with his prayer beads. This kind of accompaniment, which often takes place because a woman is not in a position to leave her child at home, is infrequent but not uncommon.

When I asked a former Anjuman leader about Yadgar's women-only principle and the presence of young boys, she hastened to assure me that there are no hard and fast rules about it. According to her, when a boy attains manhood about the age of thirteen, he should no longer come into the shrine. Most women who frequent Yadgar Husayni would agree. She went on to clarify, however, that the understanding that boys were prohibited had arisen in a particular context: when people of limited means had been taking advantage of gatherings at Yadgar. She explained that some women from low-income families come to religious events simply to collect the blessed food distributed at the end of a ritual gathering (*tabarruk*). At one point women started coming with five or six children whom they had gathered from their neighborhoods so that they could receive a larger share of *tabarruk*. After leaving the event they would collect from each child all but a small portion of the *tabarruk* and take it home to their own families. The Anjuman's leaders felt this was abusing the intent of the gathering but did not think it fair to stop people from attending on the basis of income or social status for such would set up a process of class segregation. Nor could they forbid children's attendance, for while women with a strong degree of economic security might be able to leave their children elsewhere—at home or with their servants or at school—poor women did not always have the same options. Women did not want to abandon principles of justice and fairness, which they identified as quintessentially Shia. "So since you can't stop people from coming, and since you can't stop people from taking advantage of the system," this *Anjuman* leader told me, "you can at least say, 'No boys allowed.' Let them bring a dozen girls if they like" (interview, Hyderabad, 15 February 2000).

There are other circumstances in which Yadgar's leaders have made allowances for male presence at the shrine. The Anjuman's managing committee made the decision to set aside one day a year for the community of men to hold a *majlis* at Yadgar Husayni. Men visit Yadgar on the sixth of Rabi-ul-Awwal, a date that has no strong religious associations and is thus a time when the *ashurkhana* will not have other commitments for holding its own or one of its member's religious gatherings. Women know that the shrine is a powerful place for prayer and remembrance and feel that men should have the opportunity to benefit from it. By welcoming men to visit the shrine for religious performance once a year, the women strengthen the connection between Yadgar and the wider circle of *ashurkhanas* in the city. They also increase male trust and support by allowing men on an annual basis to see and appreciate the space used intensely by the community's women.

Women also have been quite pragmatic in inviting cooperation from men who can assist the Anjuman in advisory or service capacities. The association's leaders reportedly first decided to invite male help when Anjuman Niswan Barkat-e-Aza began to be involved in contractual relationships with legal implications—the employment of teachers and servants, the rental of shops and houses, the provision of charity to the poor, and the receipt of legacies and donations. The women saw the need for specialized help from men for, as one former leader explained, "ladies have their own restrictions" in handling problems involving the government, police, or courts. Thus to increase their effectiveness as an organization, the Anjuman's managing committee formed a board of trustees, seeking the participation of influential Shia women and men whose legal and financial skills, personal connections, or knowledge of various local bureaucracies made them valuable advisors. Today, in addition to having several male members on its board of trustees, the association pays a male financial consultant (at one time, the general manager of the Nizamabad branch of the Charminar Bank) to review its accounts on a weekly basis and to work closely with the secretary and treasurer of the Anjuman.

The Anjuman's leaders also occasionally invite men to Yadgar Husayni to provide special services. For example, I once saw the Anjuman president and secretary walk into the inner courtyard of the shrine in the company of a tree specialist. The leaders had asked him to come in order to investigate two fruit trees afflicted by blight. Interestingly Miriam and Siraj, both elderly grandmothers, made no special allowances for modest covering (*purdah*) for themselves or for the handful of women in the *ashurkhana* during the visit. They had a friendly conversation with the young man, discussed the treatment that would be most effective, then saw him out. This encounter brings to mind Eleanor Abdella Doumato's (2000, 5) observations of pre-1980s Saudi Arabian society in which she notes that women's contact with certain male workers such as business managers, drivers, house cleaners, and tea servers was conceptually treated as if the men were sexually neuter.

Thus although gender separation is an important guiding principle at Yadgar Husayni, it is clear that women leaders operate with discretion and some pragmatism to create what is in fact a permeable boundary. Yadgar Husayni is not completely unique in this regard, for there are many places where Muslim women and men creatively navigate what may appear to be a strict gender divide from the perspective of an outsider. Hyderabad's public wedding halls are a good example. These are the facilities that most families rent to accommodate the vast numbers of guests invited to weddings, engagements, and other major events. Even among conservative families it is not unusual during a wedding to see people breaching segregated space in order to pass messages, catch someone's attention, distribute food, record an event on video, introduce a guest, or pass a child to another member of the family. Another place where segregation strictures are commonly bypassed is in the home when, to skirt restrictions on women mixing with men from outside the household, families sometimes dub a close family friend (such as the best friend of a son of the household) a "cousin brother." When a man has the status of a quasi-relative, women need not veil nor avoid his presence in the home, making ordinary family interactions more relaxed when he is present. Women sometimes use a similar practice to circumvent the requirement that they be accompanied by a male relative during the pilgrimage to Mecca (*hajj*). A woman having no related male to accompany her on this once-in-a-lifetime trip will sometimes travel in a group where, for the purpose of the pilgrimage, she informally adopts as a relative the male kin of another traveler.

Thus although society as a whole may unequivocally uphold the value of a gendered division of space, in practice people make regular compromises and adjustments in navigating boundaries that are dynamic and changeable. Women's choices about gender and space have ensured that, while Yadgar Husayni remains an *ashurkhana* dedicated to female use, it has profited from and enjoyed the support of men. This support is important, for the shrine operates within social and religious systems where men hold significant power. By enlisting male participation in their female venture and by framing the shrine within familiar malecentric visions of Shia faith, the leaders of Yadgar Husayni have avoided the risk of isolating and thus devaluing their initiative in the eyes of the larger community. One can better understand this dynamic and its consequences by comparing women's choices at Yadgar Husayni with a recent venture to build the first all-women mosque in India. The following is summarized from newspaper accounts and the conference paper "Justice in the Name of God: Organising Muslim Women in Tamil Nadu," by V. Geetha (2005).

In 2003 in the South Indian state of Tamil Nadu, Sunni community activist Daud Sharifa Khanam and her six-year-old social welfare organization STEPS (dedicated to steps promoting the empowerment of women) set up the Tamil Nadu Muslim Women's Jamaat Committee. This thirty-five-member all-women body meets monthly and was founded to challenge the authority of a traditional Muslim conflict-resolution system known as the *jamaat* (lit. "congregation"). In India local village *jamaats* are all-male bodies that generally function out of mosques and are engaged in resolving family disputes and other community conflicts, including divorce, custody, and maintenance matters. The *jamaats* have the backing of religious leaders and tend to be funded by endowments and mandatory donations from community members. Women decided to start their own *jamaat* after years of seeing unjust judgments in cases involving women. Since women have been forbidden to enter mosques by religious ruling, they usually cannot plead their own cases directly to the committee but must send a husband or brother as a representative. Many of the women who came to STEPS for assistance were seeking redress from unfair judgments made through this traditional system. Initially STEPS members approached the all-male *jamaats* and urged them to be reasonable and fair while settling disputes. When this had no impact the women decided to take matters into their own hands and founded the Women's Jamaat Committee. Today the all-women group receives more than fifteen petitions a day (most involving marital disputes) and has spread to at least ten districts in Tamil Nadu.

As an advocate for women, STEPS is often in direct confrontation with the male *jamaats* and religious elders. If the men or their relatives involved in a case refuse to heed the committee's decisions, the group threatens to take the case before the police, with whom they have good contacts. The women's committee has faced abuse, intimidation, and slander, including verbal attacks during weekly sermons at village mosques. They even have met resistance from progressive Muslim groups who feel that women should not be represented in decision-making bodies such as the *jamaats.* Still the women have persisted. The Women's Jamaat Committee states its aims as ensuring human rights and promoting social empowerment and improved standards of living for Muslim women.

In 2004 the women expressed their intention to construct an all-women mosque. They envisioned a female-run institution that would be a place for prayer as well as community service; it would have a meeting hall, a shelter for destitute women, and a training and education center for girls. While men could enter and pray, control of the institution would remain firmly with the female leadership. When women first expressed their desire to build a mosque, a local family offered to donate the land. However, following a wave of publicity and an angry countercampaign from male religious leaders, the donors withdrew their offer. Sharifa Khanam then decided to build the mosque on her own land, which already housed the STEPS main office and the meeting hall for the *jamaat* committee. When an edict was publicized stating that Islam does not permit an unmarried woman to build a mosque, the forty-year-old Sharifa accepted a marriage proposal from a progressive businessman. The effort continues to construct the first all-women mosque in India. After nearly five years of fund-raising, the Women's Jamaat Committee has succeeded in breaking ground for the mosque but construction halted after laying the foundation and constructing the basement. Inflation and the resulting escalation of costs has meant that funds have been depleted faster than the women anticipated. Still fund-raising efforts continue and Sharifa pledges that the mosque will be built.

Both the women who founded Yadgar Husayni and those who are trying to establish a women-only mosque in Tamil Nadu sought to build an institution that would meet their devotional needs and be under their control. They differ not only in that one organization is Shia and one Sunni, but also in the focus of their work. Anjuman Niswan Barkat-e-Aza continues to be dedicated to supporting women's religious rituals; STEPS and the Women's Jamaat Committee primarily have addressed social ills—including religious and mosque committee rulings—that directly affect women's lives. The leadership at Yadgar Husayni chose to involve men in realizing their venture. Today the local community views the shrine as one among a number of important *ashurkhanas* in Hyderabad. Sharifa Khanam and her colleagues designed their project within a framework of confrontation and alienated male power structures in the process. Their mosque will be built but the process remains slow. Moreover, as a symbol of female resistance it long will run the risk of physical attack by conservative forces.

The story of the mosque is not meant to suggest that confrontation, including the efforts of the Women's Jamaat Committee, is an inappropriate strategy for change. And it goes without saying that this brief comparison of efforts skims over important differences in class, socioeconomic group, urban/rural settings, and other variables that exert a profound influence on the success of projects. The point is that the efforts of Hyderabad women to involve men reflect an acknowledgment of male-female interdependence in a world where men dominate centers of religious and societal power. Thus, for example, when I once expressed my appreciation of women's success in raising funds to build their own shrine, an elderly leader sharply reminded me that many women contributed money that came from households where men were the sole breadwinners. For a significant number of women, then, mobilizing funds meant convincing male as well as female family members of the importance of the project. As this elder emphasized, donations for Yadgar Husayni reflected support coming through women but not independent of the efforts of men. Although the shrine's leaders have sometimes seen men as obstacles, they also have seen them as community members with whom they need to participate in order fully to realize their goals. This vision of an interdependent community of men and women is an important side to how many Shia women perceive themselves and the world.

Summary

One could argue that the story of Yadgar Husayni is the story of women creatively and passionately overcoming patriarchal pressures to establish an independent women-led public space for expressing female religiosity. Yet, while partly true, such a description neglects several other aspects, including the powerful role of the Shia religious imagination in helping make this shrine a reality. Shia religious history and collective experience include not only the example of Zaynab and her leadership in public spaces, but also women's active mourning presence in the absence of the community of men. These formative stories profoundly shape male and female religious identities and the community as a whole.

As we have seen, most shrines in Hyderabad encourage visits from both sexes, dividing interior spaces into male (central) and female (marginalized) sections during mixed-gender performance times. Many also allow prearranged all-women gatherings to which male access is limited. In contrast, men gain entry to Yadgar Husayni as a religious community only once a year, on a day women see as liturgically unimportant. The net result is that women have greater access to public religious venues run by men, than men have at Yadgar Husayni, where decision making is in female hands. Why is that? One of the keys is that women's presence is essential for male religious identity, while female identity finds resonance in the absence of men.

As witnesses to men's public self-flagellation, women play a crucial role in helping men define their religious identity.

At nearly every remembrance gathering conducted by men, women are present, while men are absent from almost all women-led events. During a male mourning procession (*julus*), women throng the streets through which the procession passes. The traditional dramatized reenactment of the events of Karbala (known as the *taziya*), popular in some communities outside of Hyderabad, generally features only male actors—with even female roles being played by men. Yet women are almost always present as part of the audience. As performance theorists have attested, one cannot say that women have no role in these events, for they are the visible witnessing audience. In contrast, at female rituals there is no witness—except the women participants themselves. The implications of this situation can be seen in Mohammed K. Fazel's (1988, 46) reflection on his childhood participation in a Bombay *taziya:*

> The drums and cymbals, Zuljenah's [Husyan's horse's] neighing, an occasional glimpse of Shimr [the enemy who ultimately kills Husayn] and

> the women screaming and squirming in upstairs classroom windows like nestling crows at feeding time, would transport me to what can best be described as an altered state of consciousness. As the *taziya* grip tightened on my being, so did the toll of the *zanjir* [flail] on my back. One could easily latch onto a particular wail from the storm of sorrow pelting us from the upstairs classrooms. The heavier my flagellation, the louder the wail. I was both grieving and the object of grief. . . . The *taziya* was a crucible where Hussain's monumental sorrow and my existential trappings coalesced.

The presence of women and the sound of their weeping is part of the experience of Karbala—both in the imagined past and the reexperienced present. As Fazel notes, he is both grieving and the object of grief: as he increases the flail's wounding blows to his body, he hears the female cries escalate. Their witness of his suffering is inseparable from his experience of it. In fact, women's grieving witness is essential, for it helps men locate themselves as martyrs. In popular Karbala stories each of the martyrs takes his leave from his senior female relative (most often Zaynab) before going into battle. The leave taking, the women's blessing of their brothers, husbands, and sons, the overwhelming grief upon seeing their menfolk slain—all help to define the event. In contemporary religious practice, as captured so powerfully in the reflections of Mohammed Fazel, how would the male performer know he was lost without the wailing of women as a measure of it? Could men march in procession without women watching and weeping? In front of whom would they process? If there were no women, would there be a remembering Shia community? Without the witness to tell the tale and grieve the loss, the martyr simply fades away. This is why the female voice surfaces repeatedly even during male recountings of the martyrdom stories. At the climax of the *majlis* sermon it is the cries of Sakina, Fatima, or Zaynab that most commonly testify to the sufferings of the Prophet's family, even when it is through the voice of a male *zakir* that the tale is told.

In his comparative study of female spirituality Jordan Paper (1997, 240) has observed that "the religious activities of the female, in a culture with extreme gender occupational specialization, are essential to the success of the primary male occupation." To buttress his argument, he cites an Inuit man's explanation of the role of women in hunting, a seemingly all-male activity: "It is a mistake to think that women are weaker than men in hunting pursuits. Home incantations are essential for success in hunting. . . . It makes the animal well-minded." The female role of witness is just as essential to male practices within the Shia religious tradition. In contrast, no male witness is needed for female ritual performances, since part of women's imagined experience is that of male absence. In fact, one could argue that the absence of men is part of what assists women in their imagined experiencing of the pain of the Prophet's family. Transported back to the plains of Karbala where the corpses of the martyrs are all that is left of most of the Prophet's male line, the women align themselves with the experience of Zaynab and other grieving women to embrace an experience of all-consuming loss. It is the absence of beloved men that shapes the most profound religious experiences of many women. These essential presences and absences are central to how the Shia community defines male and female and undoubtedly help a community envision and support a female-only gathering place such as Yadgar Husayni.

· CHAPTER 3 ·

Remembrance Gatherings

Throughout the calendar year Shia women organize and participate in mourning assemblies (*majalis;* sing. *majlis*) and celebratory gatherings (*jeshns*) to remember the family of the Prophet. Remembrance gatherings are the most widespread and influential communal events across the Shia world (Nasr [1975] 1981b, 232) and are mournful or joyous depending on the occasion being commemorated. The distinction between the two events largely revolves around the story being told and how one chooses to tell it. In the *jeshn* we hear litanies of praise, with the poets and orator recounting the qualities, accomplishments, and miracles of the family of the Prophet. The *majlis* is filled with the tales of their terrible sufferings, with passionate recitations moving participants to an experience of grief and self-inflicted pain. Participants convey the character and difference between these two events through oral narration and embodied experience.

Women are a primary force behind a great many of these popular community gatherings, including the hundreds of household-sponsored assemblies held in Hyderabad each year and attended by both men and women. Women are also the chief organizers for the ritual gatherings linked with weddings or funerals. They mobilize extended family networks to participate in the event, help coordinate transportation of guests, oversee the cleaning and preparation of the ritual site and its objects, see to the preparation of food and blessed presents (*tabarruk*), and, in female gatherings, arrange for people to give the oration and recite poetry. Women are able to dedicate the time needed for these tasks (and for their participation and leadership in the rituals themselves) because most work at home and thus have a degree of flexibility in arranging their schedules and priorities. However, opportunity alone does not explain women's active engagement. What is it about commemoration gatherings that make them so prominent in devout women's lives? And what factors help women construct meaningful ritual?

There is considerable overlap in how Shias observe two rituals: the *majlis* and the *jeshn*. The *majlis* is the older and more widely practiced. Each of these two rituals has three main purposes: communicating the story of what happened to the family of the Prophet (*Ahl-e-Bayt*), bringing sacred connection, and conferring blessing on the faithful.

The Female Roots of the *Majlis*

The Urdu word *majlis* can mean "assembly," "meeting," "congregation," or "party," being a noun form of the Arabic root *jls* ("to sit") and thus a "sitting." Among Hyderabad Shias it has the more specific meaning of an assembly to remember and mourn the sufferings of members of the family of the Prophet. In other parts of the world, including Iran, such a commemorative gathering is known as *taziyah majlis* ("consolation" gathering), *majlis-i rawzah-khani,* or simply *rawzah-khani* after the first and most famous compilation of Karbala martyrology, *Rawzat al-Shuhada,* written in Persian in 1502 C.E. (908 A.H.) by Kamal al-Din Husayn Sabzawari.

Shias popularly believe that the first lamentation gathering was held by Zaynab and the surviving members of the family of the Prophet in 61 A.H. while they were still in the court of Yazid in Damascus or when they returned to Karbala upon their release from captivity. The most popular accounts describe Hind the wife of Yazid and her companions from the court as present at the *majlis* which, according to some stories, lasted for seven days (Ayoub 1978, 152). The women narrated the tragic events that took place at Karbala, focused on the gallant lives lost, and voiced their pain and grief. According to the Lebanese scholar Muhammad Mehdi Shams al-Din, who chronicles in detail the development of Shia commemoration practices, women engaged in highly emotional accounts of the battle, the eulogizing of martyrs, a wailing kind of poetry, and self-inflicted pain—the beating of face and breast (1985, 144). Once Zaynab, her nephew Ali, and the rest of the party reached Madina, the city became "a house of mourning" for those loyal to the Prophet's family. After initial public outbursts of emotion, men and women began gathering in homes to mourn the slain martyrs. These home-based assemblies were crucial, for public gatherings carried tremendous risk. In the eyes of the Umayyad rulers mourning assemblies were subversive acts, stirring up sympathy and support for the followers of the rebel Husayn. In fact, according to tradition, it was just this perception of threat that ultimately caused the rulers to exile Zaynab, as Shams al-Din (145) has described: "These rites [of remembrance under the leadership of Zaynab] and the anti-Umayyad reaction they generated in Medina prompted the governor of Medina Amr ibn Sa'id ibn al-As to write to Yazid ibn Mu'awiya: "The presence of Zaynab among the people of Medina is inflammatory. She is eloquent, clever, intelligent. She and those with her are determined to take vengeance for the death of al-Husayn." Shams al-Din goes on to note that Zaynab was forced to leave Madina a mere eight months after the tragic events at Karbala and that she died the following year while still in exile. Despite her absence, however, gatherings to remember the family of the Prophet continued to grow in popularity. Over the ensuing generations they developed a rich ritualistic style that powerfully demonstrates group piety and is a key expression of Shia religious identity.

In the development of the *majlis* there is a clear tie to female mourning traditions that have existed in Arab society down through the ages. In fact, women were so known for their passionate and emotional responses to death that the grieving female became a powerful icon of bereavement in Arab culture. For example, in reporting on the return of Zaynab and her party to Madina, the historian Ibn Tawus noted that "they [men loyal to the family of the Prophet] grieve for them with the grief of bereaved women" (Shams al-Din 1985, 184). Part of this tradition included composing poignant verses of mourning and praise for their dead; indeed it was widely accepted that a hero's mother and sisters played a special role in offering poetic eulogies (Nicholson 1907, 126). This tradition puts into a larger context the poetic response of Umm Luqman Zaynab bint Aqil ibn Abi Talib when she learned of the death of her brothers and others of her clan on the plains of Karbala. Historians record that she came out into the street with the women of her family, weeping, untying her hair, twisting her clothes, and reciting: "What will you say if the Prophet asks you: 'What have you, the last *umma* [the community of believers], done / With my offspring and my family after I left them? Some of them are prisoners and some of them lie killed, stained with blood. / What sort of reward to me is this after I had advised you, that you should oppose me by doing evil to my family?'" (Tabari 1990, 19:178).

Thus in the mourning traditions during the time of the battle of Karbala, women capitalized on the poetic mourning tradition powerfully to express their love and bereavement, eulogizing the departed. This type of poetry was often recited in a wailing style and was accompanied by physical demonstrations of grief, including loosening one's hair, rending one's clothes, and striking one's head, face, or breast. These elements—lamentation and wailing, recited verse, and the physical demonstration of pain and suffering at one's loss—are today essential parts of the Shia *majlis* tradition. So, too, are the goals of communicating the events of Karbala and mourning the lost martyrs, which were the central aims of the gatherings Zaynab and others organized. Seeing these clear female roots of the *majlis,* we can ask whether it would still exist if women had not witnessed and responded to the events of Karbala. In other words, if women were not part of the original party that traveled with Husayn, would the tragedy have been immortalized through other rituals or, perhaps, would it have faded from memory altogether?

Shams al-Din (1985, 144) notes that flagellation, inconsolable weeping, and lamentation were not originally part of men's mourning repertoire. Yet today these powerful acts of bereavement are as popular in male assemblies as in female. It seems clear that men adopted women's mourning styles to appropriate the tremendous power inherent in the Arab symbol of the grieving female. This would not be the first time that men have borrowed from the female religious imagination to create rituals. Juan R. I. Cole (2002, 145–46) chronicles how the nineteenth-century ruler of Awadh Nasir al-Din Haydar Shah (r. 1827–1837) not only continued innovative religious rituals initiated by his mother Badshah Begum, but also created new ones in which he assumed a female role. On the birth anniversaries of the imams, the ruler would mimic a woman suffering through the pains of childbirth; later, with a jewel-studded doll in his lap, he would receive the traditional dishes fed to women who have gone through labor. Just as Haydar Shah used ritual to appropriate the power of women's life-giving role in birthing the imams, men have borrowed the power inherent in the grieving female as they constructed the rituals of the *majlis.* It is thus ironic that Shia patriarchal society dictates women to be the sidelined audience during male-led performance at mixed-gender gatherings. Their marginalization is normalized through a Shia historical memory in which the strongest models of community leadership are the examples of the Prophet and the imams. Yet Shia collective memory also includes tales of Zaynab's courageous and inspired leadership in the absence of men, presenting a powerful feminine role model.

A Contemporary *Majlis* in Hyderabad

Each year in Hyderabad, during the first ten days of Muharram alone, Shias organize hundreds, even thousands, of *majalis.* They are held in homes, on open grounds, in meeting halls, and in shrines. After the climax on the tenth, the day known as Ashura, the number declines. Still, individuals, families, and groups continue to organize and attend *majalis* in homes and public *ashurkhanas* on a regular basis throughout a longer mourning period. While these type of commemorative gatherings are common all over the world, the length of this main mourning period varies from place to place. In some regions it is composed solely of the first ten days of Muharram; in others it concludes with Arbain, the fortieth day after the martyrdom. The longest period seems to be in the Indian subcontinent where, in some areas such as Hyderabad, many Shias observe a mourning period of two and one-quarter lunar months; that is, the whole of the Muslim months of Muharram and Safar, and up to the ninth day of Rabi-ul-Awwal. There are other times when Shias gather for *majalis* outside the main mourning period. These include the death anniversaries of key members of the *Ahl-e-Bayt* (see the appendix), as well as events having personal meaning to the organizers, such as funerals, weddings, and death anniversaries of certain family members. Some *ashurkhanas* in Hyderabad, including Yadgar Husayni, hold mourning gatherings on a regular weekly basis (often on Thursdays). *Majalis,* then, are not confined to a given season but occur throughout the year—the numbers being greatest, however, during the Muharram season.

Mourning gatherings are more numerous and more popular today than they were a century ago (Pinault 1997, 86). At the beginning of the twentieth century most Indian *majalis* were organized by members of the upper classes, people who had not only the time and financial freedom to host such events but also sufficient domestic space to dedicate to a personal *ashurkhana*. Wealthy women would invite relatives, friends, and even servants to participate in their home-based gatherings, as Mrs. Meer Hasan Ali, the English wife of a learned Shia from Lucknow, aptly chronicled in her early-twentieth-century accounts ([1832] 1917, 18–30). Today, however, working-class and lower-income families also access the perceived blessing of hosting these gatherings—if not in their own homes, then in community shrines such as Yadgar Husayni where there is sufficient space.

Every *majlis* has its own form, whether simple or complex. The style and ritual components vary from gathering to gathering and from place to place. These variations generally reflect differences in local practices, ritual histories of a given family or shrine, personal preferences of the organizers, the holy personalities being honored at the gathering, and other factors. For example, in the *majlis* described below, a ritual procession of the icons known as *alams* (reminiscent of battle standards) is a regular part of the event. The women parade these popular symbols to help in remembering the suffering and death of the honored martyrs. Not every *majlis* contains this element of performance, but whenever women commemorate this particular anniversary day at this particular shrine, the *alam* procession forms an integral part of the ritual.

Rituals, however, are not static manifestos but actively performed beliefs, changing over time as performers choose to retain, emphasize, or introduce meaningful elements. Thus we find significant shifts when comparing today's mourning practices with those popular a hundred years ago or those sponsored during the Qutb Shah period (1512–1687 C.E.). For example, we no longer find once-essential props such as large brass lamp stands, tall camphor candles, and imposing wooden cut-outs (Rizvi 1986, 2:334–47); nor do we observe public spectacles including men acting like lions or mendicants (Shureef 1832, 98–148). Muharram fire pits are relatively rare, and mourning colors have shifted from green or blue to black or white (Hollister [1943] 1953, 167–68). Some elements, however, remain constant. Almost all contemporary *majalis* include an oration and the melodic recitation of remembrance poetry, helping participants to focus on some aspect of the trials and sufferings of the *Ahl-e-Bayt* and their followers. Also central is the shedding of tears by participants, reflecting the crucial purpose of sorrowfully remembering the terrible losses suffered by the Prophet's family. The mourning usually reaches its climax with the performance of *matam*, the rhythmic—often impassioned—beating of one's chest in time to a melodious dirge (*nauha*). Other common *majlis* elements in Hyderabad today include the display and honoring of revered icons, the formal offering of prayers, the calling down of blessings, and the closing distribution of an item that is specially blessed (*tabarruk*)—usually food.

The *majlis* described below is one held every year on Arbain, the fortieth day after the martyrdom of Husayn and his followers (the twentieth of the month of Safar). This anniversary day is second in importance only to the tenth of Muharram, the day on which Husayn and other Karbala martyrs died. To begin to grasp its meaning, one must realize that for most Muslims in the Indian subcontinent the fortieth day after a person's death is the end of the main mourning period. It is an important commemoration day (along with the third, seventh, and tenth days following death): an occasion of sharp grief and a time when family and friends commonly offer special prayers and conduct rituals in memory of or on behalf of the person who has died. One woman explained to me that the fortieth day is also a time of inescapable sadness, for in putting an end to the formal mourning period one experiences the first sharp loneliness of life without the beloved. Most believers thus experience Arbain (and the third day after the tenth of Muharram) as a reprise of intense sorrow, a day to touch again and grieve a collective loss.

Like time, place contributes powerfully to the meaning of a ritual. This particular *majlis* was held on the grounds of a hilltop *dargah* (shrine) dedicated to the Twelfth Imam—the spiritual figure whom Shias see as ever present but hidden from the world. The place had deep meaning for the organizers, who were the female descendents of the shrine's founder. Mrs. Walida Nasir, the elderly granddaughter of the founder, had invited me to join sisters, daughters, nieces, in-laws, and others for this special commemoration gathering. She took care to see that I understood the story behind the shrine's origins before the ritual began. As a young man, she explained, her grandfather had been drawn to the area, wandering and exploring while the land was still quite wild. One day he met an Arab goatherd who told him to take off his shoes (a common sign of reverence for holy ground) and climb the hill. Only later did the young man pause to reflect that it was odd to find an Arab in the area. He climbed the hill with great difficulty, struggling through the undergrowth until he finally emerged at the top. Below him the immense rocks of the Deccan Plateau stretched to the horizon, embracing a distant glittering reservoir and winding swaths of verdant landscape. The young man found the scene tremendously moving. When he later tried to find the Arab to thank him, he discovered that the man had disappeared. He was never seen again. Concluding that the mysterious figure had been the Twelfth Imam, Mrs. Nasir's grandfather decided to build on the rocky hill a *dargah* dedicated to this revered soul. He mobilized support from many "high and noble people" and had an Italian architect design the structure. One day, while digging the foundation and moving great piles of earth and rock, the construction workers discovered a very old ring. People eventually determined that the ring was from Iraq, establishing a clear tie with the land of Karbala and the Twelfth Imam. Everyone involved with the project desired the ring and tensions mounted. Someone finally suggested that all should try it on; it fit perfectly the finger of Mrs. Nasir's grandfather. He kept the ring with him always, and after his death it eventually came to Mrs. Nasir.

Stories like these are more than family history. In the believer's eyes they connect the space with the beloved presence of the family of the Prophet, transforming the ritual site into one that is holy and specially blessed.

The venue for Mrs. Nasir's *majlis* is a low-roofed dwelling on the grounds of the shrine. One room is empty except for a simple carpet and a large clay pot of drinking water. The other room contains eighteen *alams* in wooden stands on a raised bench, a silver cradle (*jula*), and a stylized replica of a corpse on a bier (*tabut*). As women arrive for the event they bow and touch the *alams,* greeting them in the traditional respectful way in which one greets one's elders. When nearly twenty girls and women have arrived, Mrs. Nasir signals the start of the *majlis* by reciting a *nauha* written by her father. She stands on the open threshold facing a rain-washed expanse of rock, angling the yellowed notebook with its neat faded handwriting toward the waning light. A young girl stands beside her holding a green flag embroidered with the names of the *panjatan:* Muhammad, Fatima, Ali, Hasan, and Husayn. Mrs. Nasir's voice is frail but tuneful as she paints the pitiful scene of brutality and loss. Halfway through the recital her lips quiver and her cheeks shake as tears roll down her face. Her voice wavers for a moment, then gathers strength. There are now nearly thirty women in the room, and most are marking the rhythm of the poetry by beating their chests (*matam*). Many are weeping. One woman with her head thrown back and her eyes raised heavenward is particularly intense, accompanying the words with terrible double-handed blows to her chest. Intermittently she cries out in a powerful and compelling voice, "Husayn! Husayn!" or "Zaynab! Zaynab!," timing her calls to the break of a verse.

Later Mrs. Nasir explains that these initial few *nauha* are done in the name of Husayn and other martyrs but are usually performed as part of a procession to the shrine. A crowd gathers at the base of the hill then processes up it, led by the *panjatan* flag; the group sings *nauhas* and pauses to do the powerful *matam* along the way. On this occasion many people have not come because of the incessant monsoon rains, and the women have chosen to modify the procession and perform it in the building itself.

When the initial round of *nauhas* is complete, a woman recites a prayer of blessing (*ziyarat*); then the group sits down cross-legged in front of the *alams.* A middle-aged woman has situated herself before the microphone and begins to recite an elegy (*marsiya*) about Husayn. When she finishes there is a disorganized flurry as the group seeks to find a poem to recite next. A dozen women page through different collections—copybooks with hand-written lines, thick bound volumes, paperback books, pamphlets and booklets like those one can buy in the bazaar—searching for their favorite poems. In the end they recite four, all written especially for this day of Arbain. During the final *marsiya* Mrs. Nasir's sister leads the chorus. Her voice is hoarse and loud as she cries out the refrain, "*Chalo*!" ("Let's go!"). The women join her, shouting, wailing their pledge that they, too, are coming to Karbala. Mrs. Nasir and her sister are beside themselves in grief, sobbing, sighing, and beating ferociously on their chests in response to the poignant words.

As the room finally settles down to quiet sighing and weeping, the orator (*zakira*) stands up and moves to the doorway. She is a slight woman with dark winglike brows above shadowed eyes. This is her first major sermon and she stands, hands somewhat stiffly at her sides, facing the others. Someone moves the microphone before her and adjusts it. The *zakira* begins her oration in gentle, measured tones, speaking of duty and commitment, of doing what is difficult but necessary. Her words are precisely modulated, and sometimes she pauses a few seconds too long, as if trying to recall the next sentence. Soon, however, she is describing the scene at Karbala. As she narrates the deeds of the martyrs her voice increases in strength and pitch and her eyes darken. Her voice becomes animated as she describes the heartbreaking scene of death and cruel parting. The audience is now beginning to wail. The twenty-minute oration reaches its climax, and the weeping women start chanting "Husayn! Husayn!" and get to their feet. A few accompany the words with *matam,* but there is no strong sustained beat as women busy themselves taking the *alams* off the stands and handing them out. A woman who cradles an infant in one arm picks up the *jula,* while four others lift the large *tabut,* each holding one of the bier's wooden handles.

The women file outside into the steady rain, Mrs. Nasir's tuneful voice leading the *nauhas.* The group parades across a large rock toward a smoking incense burner, then begins to process around the burner, the *alams* held upright, the responsive dirge continuing. Beneath their bare feet, the rock bears the faint impression of a circular path, perhaps worn away by years of people tracing these same steps. When the group has circled three times, Mrs. Nasir's sister spreads a thick velvet cloth on an empty tray. The women, still singing, remove the metal crests from the poles on which they are borne and place them on the tray, each facing the direction of Mecca. When all eighteen *alams* are piled up, a woman covers the tray with a white cloth. The *tabut* and *jula* are similarly covered, and the women bring the icons back indoors. Once inside, they join in the poetry recitation with greater strength and force. Most arrange themselves in two lines facing each other. The woman leading the recitation stands apart at the head of the line, a microphone before her. As she sings out the melodic *nauha,* most of the group performs pounding double-handed *matam* to the beat. Tears stream from the eyes of some of the women, and the neck and chest of others turn red from the beating. The reciter's voice breaks with emotion, then strengthens and goes on. The group performs three *nauhas,* their powerful grief reaching a crescendo. Finally a woman calls out for the prayer of blessing and visitation (*ziyarat*). The group faces west as their sobbing slowly fades, and the prayer is recited in Arabic. A long prayer of supplication (*dua*) follows, the women raising their arms before them, palms open. As the *majlis* finishes, some of the women return to the covered icons. One buries her head in her arms and weeps, her body covering the tray. Another kisses the cloth. Others sit down to talk, as Mrs. Nasir and her sister slowly circulate in the small crowd, inviting their guests to stay for dinner.

This *majlis* displays all the common elements of mourning gatherings: melodic remembrance poetry, an oration, the beat of *matam* to tuneful dirges, the offering of prayers, the calling down of blessing, and the closing distribution of a blessed gift—in this case, a shared meal. We also find features that are not a regular part of all *majalis,* most notably, a procession of sacred symbols. Each of the elements contributes to at least one of three main purposes: it communicates the story, brings sacred connection, or confers blessing. Each ritual component—the oration, the poetry, and the procession—is central in nurturing a collective memory of events that lie at the core of Shia identity.

Communicating the Story

The oration (*zikr*) is often the main inspiring focus of the *majlis,* and in an average gathering of an hour and a half in length can take up forty-five minutes or more. Women sometimes arrange to have a well-known *zakira* (female orator) lead this portion of the event, for a good orator has tremendous power to move an audience and create a mood. On many occasions, however, a family chooses to have one of its own members deliver the oration, as did Mrs. Nasir and her relatives. In this particular case the oration was relatively short—only twenty minutes—a circumstance that reflected the choice and skill of the *zakira* and the fact that the organizers wished to reserve significant time for the poetry and procession. This balance of oration, poetry, and ritual performance is a matter of preference and circumstance and varies from *majlis* to *majlis.*

A *majlis* oration commonly consists of three parts: a general discourse in which the speaker elaborates on a topic she sees as important for the community's knowledge and growth, the *fazail* or exposition of the virtues of one or more members of the family of the Prophet, and the *masaib* which presents a passionate recounting of some aspect of the tragedy. A skilled orator makes the transitions between all three parts seamless: the lessons of the general discourse give rise to praise of certain qualities of the *Ahl-e-Bayt* and lead to a climax in the heartrending account of their sufferings. The general discourse almost always starts with a preliminary recitation either from the Quran or of a saying (*hadith*) of the Prophet or one of the imams. This is then linked to the larger topic. For example, when a *zakira* chooses to focus on the subject of intercessory prayer, she may begin with the Quranic verse "Call ye unto Me, and I will answer you" (40:60). Or if her focus is on the person of Husayn, she may begin with the words of the Prophet "I am from Husayn, and Husayn is from me" before delving into the accounts of the courage and fortitude of the Prophet's grandson. Most *zakiras* see this discursive portion of the *zikr* as an opportunity to enlighten or remind participants about an aspect of history or certain moral principles or the rightness of particular actions. It is a largely intellectual exercise providing insights into broader theological truths that often go beyond the simple events of Karbala (Howarth 2001, 278). In contrast, the *fazail* and *masaib* are designed to appeal to one's emotions. These emotional elements—particularly the *masaib*—can be considered the heart of the oration, for a crucial aim of the *majlis* is to inspire in the audience an overwhelming response. The *zakira* wants to move her audience to tears and, if time is short, she will narrow her talk to focus simply and poignantly on the sufferings of the family of the Prophet.

The recitation of powerful melodic poems of mourning almost always brackets the oration, with at least one or two poems preceding and two or three following the *zikr*. The amount of time given to this activity depends on the organizers, the poetry reciters, and the response of the crowd. In Mrs. Nasir's *majlis,* poetic recitations took as much time as did the oration. The poetry consisted of two of the most popular forms of remembrance poetry in Hyderabad: the *marsiya,* a mournful requiem that usually focuses on a particular event or on the character of one or more members of the family of the Prophet, and the *nauha,* a tuneful dirge that is usually accompanied by the rhythmic slapping of one's chest (*matam*). In most *majalis* in Hyderabad, *marsiya* recitation precedes the *zikr,* while the more powerful and participatory *nauha* recitation follows it. Those who lead these portions of the gathering usually decide in advance which poems they will recite. However since the *majlis* described above was largely an extended-family event, the women chose many of the poems by collective demand in the midst of the ritual. They performed the heartrending poems in the most common style: one or more leaders reciting the verses while the whole of the assembly joined in repeating the chorus. The following example, translated from a contemporary Urdu *nauha* (A. D'Souza 1997, 89), gives a flavor of this type of poetry:

Husayn arrived at the helpless corpse of Qasim
He saw [his] state and could not look again.
Sitting by his side, he cried with tear-filled eyes,
"We have come for you, bridegroom—rise, rise!
Rise from the burning earth, [my] son—rise, rise!

"Qasim, your mother is anxiously waiting.
Young Sakina is restless at the door of the tent.
Take the name of your grandfather [and] rise, my darling!
A bridegroom does not sleep on the ground—rise, rise!
Rise from the burning earth, [my] son—rise, rise!"

Successful mourning poetry always paints a powerful emotional picture for the faithful audience. In this *nauha* we find Imam Husayn coming to the battlefield to find his slain nephew. The young man's death is so brutal that the imam has to turn his eyes away. We hear Husayn crying out for Qasim to rise up from the scorched Karbala plain. In desperation he evokes the young man's mother and niece (Sakina) who anxiously await him and, in a subsequent verse, the wife whose life will soon be filled with pain. Husayn urges the lifeless Qasim to call on God's help, using the name of his grandfather the Prophet. Surely God would not will the massacre of such a "flower like" innocent. This picture of crazed grief is intensely moving, especially when it is phrased in its original melodious rhythms and being expressed—as is often the case—in the first-person voice of one of the *Ahl-e-Bayt*. The poem is steeped in pathos: a young man lying on the dusty baked earth on what should be the happiest day of his life, a day when he would normally be honored and celebrated as the beloved, respected groom. It is also rich in meaning, for the audience is familiar with the details of the story and needs only hear a person's name or an allusion to a series of events in order to make larger connections. For example, the faithful believer already knows that Husayn raised Qasim like a son, that Qasim was considered the fairest of his generation, and that he was pledged in marriage to Fatima Kubra, Husayn's daughter. They know the grandfather on whom Qasim should call is the Prophet, that Qasim's niece Sakina will be confused and devastated by the cumulative losses and sufferings, and that her father Husayn will soon die as well. Listeners form a powerful yet plaintive chorus as they join the imagined voice of Husayn, repeating the last pitiful line with those who lead the poetry: "Rise from the burning earth, [my] son—rise, rise!"

The recitation of a *nauha* is always punctuated by rhythmic chest beating (*matam*). Sometimes the *matam* is led by a trained group that specializes in its performance. At other times, as in the family *majlis* described above, everyone who has gathered participates passionately. Although women do not practice the forms of *matam* involving blades, knives, or swords (an exclusively male practice), their chest beating is not soft or gentle. In the *majlis* described above, most women performed the punishing two-handed *matam* with stunning force and for long periods of time. For them this self-flagellation is integral to the commemoration of Arbain. Abida Sultana, a successful middle-aged business woman now settled in Canada, has explained what is being communicated through this practice:

> If someone dies in my own family, even someone very close to me, we will not do *matam*. It is something we reserve only for the *masumeen* [the "pure ones": the twelve imams, Fatima, and Muhammad]. We will not even wear three black items if our own family members die. We reserve that, too, for the *masumeen*. As far as men and women, what goes on in people's heads is very individual. It is part of our collective memory to not forget. We know the family of the Prophet were not allowed to grieve, therefore we are joining them in their grief. We are saying, okay Lady [*Bibi*] Zaynab, we remember and we will grieve. Especially to do the *matam*, keeping the beat, the resonance of the words, . . . it is very powerful. It is also a way to keep the message alive. That people had the strength and the courage to stand up and act against injustice. In this way we say, yes, I am with you. I totally appreciate what you did. (Interview, Toronto, 6 April 2001)

To inflict physical pain upon oneself, then, is part of the practice of grieving for special souls whose death one honors even above the loss of one's own family members. This practice is especially poignant given that the devout believe that Zaynab and other members of her family were denied the right to mourn their loved ones properly and to receive the comfort and consolation of family and friends who could join in the grief of their terrible loss. *Matam* provides a uniquely embodied way to express one's loyalty, solidarity, and grief.

But *matam* is a gendered practice. Male performance includes not only self-inflicted blows to the chest but also the exclusively male practice of shedding one's blood through the rhythmic use of swords, knives, or blades. Through these actions Shia males convey a message to the family of the Prophet that can be summarized as "If I were with Husayn on the plains of Karbala, I, too, would have shed my blood for you" (Pinault 1992, 106). Women's message is different. Their commitment is not to sacrificing their lives—for even the women who were present at Karbala could not do that. The women survivors of Karbala bore their pain courageously in the presence of their enemies, testified to the truth and the injustice of what they had seen, and kept alive the memory of those beloved souls who had the strength and courage to resist injustice at enormous personal cost. Most simply put, the message inherent to female *matam* is "I am with you, and by enduring this pain I give a tangible sign of my love, appreciation, and willingness to suffer alongside you." Through self-flagellation, then, both men and women express their personal solidarity with the family of the Prophet. However, for men solidarity means to fight and give one's life, for women it is to suffer, testify, and endure.

In any one gathering there are variations in the way people practice *matam:* some perform it with great passion, some keep the beat with moderate force, and others tap their chests lightly in time with the tune. As Abida Sultana points out, "what goes on in people's heads is very individual." Factors that influence women's choices regarding the performance of *matam* include health, age, the occasion being marked, and personal preferences. There is also some difference of opinion among believers about the "excessive" practice of *matam.* In Abida Sultana's view, "I happen to believe that we sometimes overdo it. What is reasonable, perhaps three or at most four *nauhas.* But sometimes people will go on for an hour. Someone like me will be way in the back of the crowd, tapping lightly on my chest. I will be doing the *matam,* but restrained. I will not be disrespectful and say people should not do this, but I am not right up front" (interview, Toronto, 31 March 2001).

Women thus differ in what they define as acceptable expressions of ritual remembrance: what some view as legitimate, others may see as "overdoing it." In the *majlis* described above the women were largely like-minded: almost all participated enthusiastically in extended periods of forceful *matam.* In a larger and more heterogeneous group, or on a less emotionally intense occasion than Arbain, one can witness a wider range of participation. Interestingly, even though Abida Sultana may not wholly support the intense prolonged *matam* that some women embrace, she does not challenge those whom she feels may be going too far. To do so would be "disrespectful." Instead she chooses to distance herself physically, standing at the back of the crowd and tapping lightly on her chest. Although women vary in their acceptance of extended forceful *matam,* few choose openly to oppose a practice that so powerfully expresses personal solidarity with the family of the Prophet.

The third major element in Mrs. Nasir's *majlis* that helped with the retelling of the core stories of faith was the procession of treasured icons. The paraded symbols differ in *majlis* in which a procession takes place, but they are always filled with meaning and connected to the story being communicated. For the women who gathered with Mrs. Nasir at the shrine of the Twelfth Imam, the *alams, tabut,* and *jula* collectively became the men and boys who died at Karbala. The cradle, for example, evoked the infant Ali Asghar, killed by an arrow through the throat as he was held in Husayn's arms. The young mother who carried it bore it along with her own child, creating a poignant symbol of the stark contrast between life and death. The *alams* represent a host of beloved souls who were cruelly slaughtered. When the women removed the icons from the poles on which they had been raised, they created powerful symbolism in the changed posture of the ornate standards. From their upright proud display they assumed a passive horizontal position on a bier (a tray), a graphic depiction of the martyrs passing into death. Along with the cradle and the bier, they were draped in funeral white, again evoking death. Such performative acts offer a powerful entry into the experience of Karbala, providing the believer with an avenue that goes beyond the oral recounting of what took place. As is the case with *matam,* the body and senses are fully involved, providing those familiar with the symbolism a way to experience physically the pain and grief of the story and to pass from the present to the keenly imagined past.

Thus the storytelling portions of the *majlis* serve two main functions, echoing the goals of Zaynab and her companions in the wake of the Karbala massacre. The first is to provide an occasion to hear and speak the truth of what happened to the family of the Prophet, providing crucial lessons for one's life and faith. The second is to mourn for the family of the Prophet. According to popular belief, every tear shed in active remembrance of the family of the Prophet counts toward a mourner's ultimate salvation (Shams al-Din 1985, 80–82; Ayoub 1978, 142–44). Many Shias understand that Fatima, the mother of the martyred Husayn, plays a crucial role in this. She draws comfort from the love, loyalty, and devotion she witnesses at the *majlis* and in turn intercedes with God on the Day of Judgment, rewarding those who are faithful to her family. But it is not simply a quest for reward that motivates women's participation. As one woman explained to me, Fatima knew that she would die young and her sons would be martyred after her. Since she would not be there when they died, "she wanted to know who would do *matam* for them. She wanted to be reassured that there would be a people who would mourn for her sons and keep their memory alive." That, she stressed, is how the Shia community came to be (interview, Hyderabad, 17 June 1997).

Believers thus find a powerful motivation in their loyalty to the family of the Prophet and their commitment to stand beside family members in their grief. In the transformation of time and space inherent in this ritual of remembrance, they weep alongside Fatima, Zaynab, and other blessed souls. In fact, the *Ahl-e-Bayt* are the invisible presence among the gathering, as the *majlis* audience knows. Ritual leaders sometimes remind their listeners of just who is among them when they gather to mourn: "When I held a *majlis* in my home in remembrance of Husayn, he came and his mother was also present. When I called out for Husayn, the Prophet came too, as he had said, 'I am from Husayn and Husayn is from me.' Because the Prophet Muhammad is the 'Master of the Prophets', Adam, Abraham, and all 124,000 prophets came following afterwards. . . . All of them came to the *majlis.* They became the guests and I was the [host]" (Howarth 2001, 118). As this Hyderabad *zakir* emphasizes, the members of the family of the Prophet are not just distant spectators. They are present among the crowd, witnessing the grief and being consoled by it. Believers thus stand amid a transcendental community of those who are beloved to God and follow the right path. This connection to sacred souls is a powerful purpose of the remembrance gatherings.

Prayer and Connection

Prayer is the recitation of powerful sacred words or words audibly or silently addressed to sacred beings and is a thread woven throughout the *majlis.* Most Hyderabad gatherings start with a prayer of benediction, are punctuated with supplications, and close with a prayer of greeting and blessing.

The prayer known as *Fatiha* is a popular choice to open a *majlis. Fatiha* in Arabic means opening and is also the name of the first chapter (*sura*) of the Quran. When a Muslim says she will recite *Fatiha,* however, she is generally referring to a formulaic recitation in Arabic consisting of several parts: a thrice-repeated blessing on the Prophet and his family (also known as *salawat* or *durood*), the first chapter of the Quran, and another repetition of the triple *salawat.* The full *Fatiha* prayer is thus translated:

O God! Bless Muhammad and the family of Muhammad!
O God! Bless Muhammad and the family of Muhammad!
O God! Bless Muhammad and the family of Muhammad!

In the name of God, the Beneficent, the Merciful.
All praise is [only] for God, the Lord of the worlds.
The Beneficent, the Merciful, Master of the Day of Judgment.
Thee [alone] we worship and from Thee [alone] we seek help.
Guide us [O, Lord] on the Right Path.
The path of those upon whom Thou has bestowed Thy bounties,
Not [the path] of those inflicted with Thy wrath, nor [of those] gone astray.

O God! Bless Muhammad and the family of Muhammad!
O God! Bless Muhammad and the family of Muhammad!
O God! Bless Muhammad and the family of Muhammad!

This popular formulation praises God, asks for God's guidance, and petitions God mightily to bless the Prophet and the *Ahl-e-Bayt.* With the inclusion of the best-known chapter from scripture—which places God at the center of all things—it is a clear testimony to one's Muslim identity. Yet it also affirms Shia identity by surrounding the Quranic verse with petitions for blessing on those who are most beloved by God. Sunnis as well as Shias consider the *Fatiha* to be a powerful sanctifying prayer. It is the one most often used to bless food (including *tabarruk*), transforming the ordinary into something imbued with the sacred. It is thus a fitting way to sanctify and bless a *majlis* that is about to begin.

The call for blessings (*salawat*) is not simply a part of the opening prayer but is a commonly repeated refrain that punctuates the *majlis.* It is well known to Muslims for, like *sura Fatiha,* it is a regular part of the daily prayers (*namaz*), having arisen early in Muslim history in response to the Quranic injunction to greet and bless the Prophet: "Verily God and His angels bless the Prophet! O' ye who believe! Send ye blessings on him and greet him with a salutation worthy of the respect [due to him]" (33:56). During commemoration gatherings the call for this prayer is often delivered by a *zakira* or a member of the audience who seizes a moment in the middle of the oration to cry "*Salawat*!," to which the crowd loudly responds, "O God! Bless Muhammad and the family of Muhammad!" ("*Allahumma salla ala Muhammad wa-Ala Muhammad*"). This call for benediction is particularly popular in large gatherings where it functions to unify the audience, to whip up enthusiasm, and to punctuate a point in an oration, or simply to allow the *zakira* to catch her breath before continuing her delivery.

There are shorter prayers delivered in a similar responsive style; most are a form of supplication to Ali or one of the imams. Thus a leader in the gathering may cry, "Call on Ali!" ("*Nadi-Ali!*"), to which the audience replies, "O, Ali!" ("*Ya Ali!*") or "O, Hyder!" ("*Ya Haydari!*"), the latter being one of the popular names of Ali. This abbreviated prayer carries a host of meaning for most Shias, for the story of its genesis is well known among believers. According to the collection of the words and deeds of Prophet Muhammad and the imams (*hadith qudsi*), the Prophet and his forces were locked in the battle of Khayber, unable to gain entry to the impregnable fort of their enemies. The Prophet had informed his followers that they would overcome their foes within forty days, but at the thirty-ninth day they still had not breached the imposing gates of the fort. The situation looked grim. Praying to God for direction and enlightenment, the Prophet received the response, "Call on Ali!" He followed God's command and Ali, who had been sick, miraculously joined the battle and successfully transformed the Muslim army's fortunes. The prayer, then, attests to believers' faith in the God-given power of Ali, the possibility of miracles when one calls for help with a sincere heart, and one's identity as loyal followers of Muhammad and the Imams.

Finally, almost every *majlis* (as well as *jeshn* and *namaz*) closes with a genre of prayer known as *ziyarat* (lit. "visitation"), a term that is also used to describe a gravesite visit for the purpose of praying for the dead. Believers stand to face the direction of the graves of those whose presence is evoked as a single person recites the Arabic formulation on behalf of the whole gathering. *Ziyarat* prayers arose in the second century A.H. to meet the needs of faithful Shias who were unable to visit the burial site of Husayn on the anniversary of his martyrdom. The fifth imam had proclaimed that a pilgrimage to Karbala on the day of Ashura was equal to a thousand hajj pilgrimages (the obligatory journey to Mecca required of all Muslims who have the means). The imam also noted that if one lived too far away to reach the sacred site on that day, one could turn one's face toward Karbala and pronounce "many salutations of peace on the martyred Imam and curses on his murders," followed by ritual prayer and a *majlis* attended by all one's friends and relatives (Ayoub 1978, 189). The point of this "pilgrimage from afar" was to be totally immersed in the tragedy, to offer condolences, and to express one's loyalty to the *Ahl-e-Bayt.* Over the centuries the *ziyarat* prayer has widened to address a whole host of sacred revered souls. The following is a translation of a contemporary prayer offered in the name of the martyrs of Karbala:

> Peace be upon you all, devotees of God and His Lovers! Peace be upon you all, O selected ones of God and His dear ones! Peace be upon you all, O supporters of the religion of God! Peace be upon you all, O supporters of the Prophet of God! Peace be upon you all, O supporters of the Commander of the Faithful (Hazrat Ali A.S.) Peace be upon you all, O supporters of Fatima the most exalted amongst the women of the worlds! Peace be upon you all, O supporters of Abi-Muhammed Al-Hasan (A.S.) son of Ali (A.S.) the pure, the guide and the trusted one! Peace be upon you all, O supporters of Aba-Abdillah Al-Husain! May my father lay his life for you all and may my mother too sacrifice her life for you all! You have become blessed and blessed is the land in which you are buried. You all have attained greatest success and how I wish I was along with you all to achieve the same glory that you all attained. (Ali 1996, 80–81)

Most *ziyarats* begin, as does the one above, by greeting the holy soul who is being honored. If the gathering is being held in the name of a particular imam, organizers often choose a *ziyarat* that is specifically addressed to that soul. In the *ziyarat* quoted above, the prayer addresses all the martyrs of Karbala (as might happen at a *majlis* commemorating the anniversary of their deaths) and gives special mention to Ali, Fatima, Hasan, and Husayn. It begins with a common respectful salutation among Muslims, "Peace be upon you" ("*al-salamu alayka ya*"), and addresses the souls with well-known descriptive epithets. For example, Fatima is the "most exalted amongst the women of the worlds," and Ali is "Commander of the Faithful." Generally characteristic of this genre of poetic prayer are its rhythm and repetitive style. Sometimes it takes the form of greeting the figure being addressed with many different names, fleshing out his or her character and standing. For example, a *ziyarat* to Fatima greets her in peace as the "daughter of the prophet of God," "daughter of the Friend of God," "daughter of the Respected of God," "daughter of the Trustee of God," "leader of all the women of all the worlds," "[one] who was tormented, who was not given her dues."* There is a soothing force to this recited litany, with each name, title, and descriptor being prefaced by a wish for God's peace. A *ziyarat,* then, is a prayer of affirmation of the glorious and elevated status of the soul being addressed. Although it can vary in form, length, and content, its purpose remains constant: to provide the believer with an opportunity to come respectfully before the *Ahl-e-Bayt.* Standing in the exalted presence of those who are named, one calls for God's blessing upon them and may even make a petition for them to intercede in the lives of their faithful devout followers.

Blessing and Power

Blessing surrounds and inhabits the *majlis,* most tangibly in the gift known as *tabarruk* which every person receives who attends a remembrance gathering. *Tabarruk* literally refers to "a portion of presents [or what is left of food presented to great men] given to their dependents." It is thus a present to the soul or souls in whose honor the *majlis* is held but one which is passed along to those who attend the gathering. In Hyderabad *tabarruk* usually consists of a piece of bread or a bit of cooked food or sweets or sometimes a full meal. When the host gathers or prepares this gift, she or other organizers first see that it is blessed (usually with the *Fatiha* prayer) in the name of those honored by the *majlis.* Then unless it is a meal to be consumed at the gathering, the *tabarruk* will often be prepacked in individual bags and kept ready near the door to speed the process of distribution when people leave. Although food is the most popular choice, the host occasionally offers a more enduring item such as a handkerchief (for wiping tears shed for the family of the Prophet), a cup (to symbolize the quenching of the thirst of those who suffered at Karbala), a sticker carrying words of blessing on the family of the Prophet, or other item that she considers meaningful. The form of *tabarruk* is contested, with some Shias feeling that the custom has become too elaborate. One woman in her seventies complained to me that when she was growing up it was not a very important part of the ritual; today, in her view, it is a status symbol. Others with whom I spoke disagreed. Since those who attend a *majlis* are viewed as a special blessing, it is important that one offer them a "good" *tabarruk.*

As a sanctified gift *tabarruk* cannot be casually discarded because of the risk of desecrating it. It is meant to be wholly consumed or carefully kept, and many women take it home to share the blessing with family members or others who

*Taken from the anonymously published collection *Hadiyah al-zairin* [A Pilgrim's Guide to Righteousness] (n.d.), 4.

could not attend the event. Any uneaten portions of food—for example, bones or seeds—are usually disposed of with care and respect, often by burying them or placing them in a safe place. Devout Shias will even be careful with the water used to wash their hands after touching such food, seeing that it is poured on a plant, for example, rather than down a drain. In short, *tabarruk* is an embodiment of blessing. It is the source of good fortune for the sincere giver as well as the receiver. A woman related to me the story of a man who had a single water buffalo and always distributed "pure milk" tea after the *majlis.* Over time he profited in his dairy business and eventually owned a herd of ten buffaloes. This faithful Shia reportedly attributed his prosperity to the blessing that came from performing this act of generosity and service to those who mourn the family of the Prophet (interview, Hyderabad, 14 October 1998). This story underlines the fact that a *majlis* is a source of blessedness or grace (*sawab*) to all those who attend and participate, including the host. In fact, the popular belief is that the greater the number of people who gather for a *majlis,* the greater the blessing for the organizer. Most hosts thus welcome and encourage the widespread announcement of their gathering—by word of mouth, formal invitation card, or announcement at preceding gatherings. They are buoyed in this belief by the sayings of the imams, such as that of Jafar ibn Muhammad al-Sadiq who told a companion, "Al-Fudayl, I love these [remembrance] gatherings. . . . God will have mercy on a man who keeps the memory of our situation alive" (Shams al-Din 1985, 152).

The blessing of a remembrance gathering is not just about what is given or received. Place and time contribute their own blessedness to the event. In one sense, as is true for ritual prayer (*namaz*), place is unimportant. Just as Prophet Muhammad taught his community that "all the world is a mosque" (and hence available for prayer), so too most Shias know that a *majlis* can take place anywhere. However, although Mrs. Nasir and her companions could have held their *majlis* at any one of their homes, they chose to mark this special day of mourning in a place they saw as particularly holy. The sacredness of the site, like that of Yadgar Husayni, had been built up through the accumulation of stories, signs, and objects, including the tale of the discovery of the location and the mysterious encounter with the Arab goatherd and the ring "from Iraq" that conveyed a blessing to the devout man inspired to build a shrine to honor the hidden imam. These stories helped make the site deeply meaningful not only for Mrs. Nasir and other family members but also for the wider community that sees the shrine as a testament to their ongoing association with the beloved Twelfth Imam. In the same way that a martyrdom anniversary carries a special temporal holiness, a shrine or other sacred site carries the blessedness of place. It is a near and present reminder—a shorthand symbol—of the power of God and those whom God loves.

Like the remembrance gathering itself, it becomes a doorway through which one finds transcendent connection.

A Joyful Occasion: The *Jeshn*

The word *jeshn* comes from the Pahlavi word *yajashn,* and means a banquet, feast, festival, jubilee; rejoicing, joy. In Hyderabad it signifies an assembly which commemorates joyful episodes in the lives of the *Ahl-e-Bayt.* Shias in Iran use the more complete expression *majlis-i jeshn* to refer to a "gathering of rejoicing," or, more specifically, *mawludi* (from the Arabic *milad,* birth) when the occasion is a birth anniversary. The term used in the Lebanese and many Arab contexts is *mawlid,* a term also applied to birth celebrations of the Prophet and Muslim saints. Like the *majlis,* the *jeshn* has the purpose of remembering and honoring the family of the Prophet, whether the focus is on a particular member, the group as a whole, or an important occasion in their lives. The fundamental difference between the two types of assemblies is that the purpose of the *majlis* is to remember the death and suffering of one or more of the *Ahl-e-Bayt,* whereas the *jeshn* serves to recall and celebrate happy occasions in the lives of these personalities. The anniversaries that are marked are primarily birthdays of the *Ahl-e-Bayt,* the wedding of Fatima and Ali, and the occasion on which the Prophet named Ali as his successor (known as Ghadir-e-Khumm).

It is difficult to pinpoint the emergence in history of Shia celebratory gatherings, largely because historians have given far greater attention to mourning practices. It does seem clear, however, that the institution of the *jeshn* arose much later than that of the *majlis.* As we have seen, it was immediately after the tragedy at Karbala that gatherings emerged to communicate what took place and to mourn the martyrs. The Shia found in these events a vehicle to express their shock, grief, and anger and to keep alive the memory of the ill treatment of the family of the Prophet. Mourning gatherings were also popular because they helped to spread the news of the tragedy, elicit sympathy and support, and hasten the revolt against the Umayyad rulers, ultimately leading to the downfall of the dynasty (in 750 C.E. / 132 A.H.). As the Shia community moved through this early period, traumatized and struggling for its survival, there seemed to be little space for or interest in commemorating "happy" occasions. Eulogizing the family of the Prophet did take place but not at gatherings dedicated to this purpose. Rather it seems to have been incorporated into the process of mourning at *majalis* or delivered as odes (*qasidas*) by popular poets who recited before the public, particularly in bazaars. According to Mohammad-Djafar Mahdjoub (1988, 54–57), the first extant documentation of poetry recited for marketplace audiences dates from the twelfth century C.E./sixth century A.H., although the practice of eulogizing Shia heroes existed long before.

Mahdjoub notes that some poets had their tongues cut out in reprisal, highlighting the risks of celebrating the family of the Prophet during this period of Sunni dominance.

As Shia dynasties—or rulers favorable to the Shia cause—emerged, however, the scene began to change. It appears that the Buyid rulers of Iran and Iraq (945–1055 C.E. / 339–447 A.H.) sponsored commemorations of Ghadir-e-Khumm, the day on which Shias celebrate Prophet Muhammad's naming of Ali as his rightful successor. The Fatimid dynasty in Egypt (969–1171 C.E. / 358–567 A.H.) seems to have introduced the large scale celebration of the Prophet's birthday, with rulers inviting scholars to address the gathering and distributing sweets and money to the crowd (Schimmel 1987, 455). In India, by the sixteenth century C.E./tenth century A.H., the Qutb Shah rulers of Golconda (Hyderabad) were lending royal patronage to the celebration of the birthdays of the Prophet, Ali, and Ghadir-e-Khumm, among other festivals (Naqvi 1993, 202). It was during the same period that Safavid rulers in Iran institutionalized the celebratory feast to commemorate the death of the third caliph Omar—whom Shias generally revile for his opposition to Ali and his aggression toward Fatima. Azam Torab has noted that conducting a "burlesque" event that showed disrespect to the historically Sunni-recognized caliph was a means of eliciting consent to the change of religious direction from Sunni to Shia (1998, 131). In fact, with the exception of the Prophet's birthday, all of these early-observed anniversaries are primary markers of Shia identity, for they underline the fundamental belief on which the two groups disagree: that Ali, the first imam, was the rightful heir to the Prophet. It is thus not surprising that Shias (or a ruler favorable to them) would highlight such occasions to assert their divergence from former Sunni leadership. However it is probable that, as with the *majlis,* Shias privately observed certain celebratory anniversaries from a time much earlier than their first state-approved appearances. Greater political safety for Shias simply meant that commemorative rituals could have more public visibility and prominence.

Although we currently do not have much detailed information on what earlier *jeshns* looked like, we know that some of the common elements in Hyderabad under the patronage of Muhammad Quli Qutb Shah (1580–1611 C.E.) and Abdullah Qutb Shah (1626–1672 C.E.) included poetry of praise (*qasidas*), decorative light displays, fireworks, special food (particularly sweets) and drink, new clothing among the guests, the sharing of perfume by the host, and the dispersal of alms. Many of these elements continue in today's local gatherings. Gone are some other components such as the dancing girls and royal procession (with a specially decorated elephant) that marked the celebration of the Prophet's birthday and the practice of playfully sprinkling colored powder over one another (as is practiced in some Hindu festivals) during the anniversary of Ali's birthday (Naqvi 1993).

Two major additions to the contemporary style of *jeshn* practice are the *zakira* (or *zakir*), who gives an oration, and the overall proliferation of commemoration days themselves with, for example, the birthdays of all twelve imams being honored as well as those of the Prophet, Zaynab, Fatima, and Abbas. Most Shia weddings also include a *jeshn* as part of the celebration rituals.

The contemporary *jeshn* contains many elements of the traditional *majlis.* Most often it starts with a blessing or benediction: in Hyderabad this is sometimes the *Fatiha;* at other times it is *Hadith-e-Kisa,* the tradition that affirms the primacy and divine blessedness of the *Ahl-e-Bayt.* There is usually an oration (*zikr* or *khutba*), though its aim is somewhat different from that of the *majlis.* Its main focus is to communicate stories of strength, power, and blessing or to highlight the superior qualities for which the person being honored is known. This is not the occasion to narrate hardships and suffering, so the *zakira* avoids heightening emotions or escalating a process of grieving, although she may make a veiled reference to the shadows of grief yet to come. Without the shift from reasoned explanation to highly emotional recounting, so typical of *majlis* sermons, the *jeshn* oration tends to be more unified. Melodic poetry generally precedes and follows the *zikr,* but it is usually in the form of praise poems known as *qasidas* or the salutation poetry called *salam. Matam* is not part of the *jeshn* practice. Most gatherings, however, do conclude with a *ziyarat* prayer and a parting blessed gift (*tabarruk*)—usually food.

Within this array of *jeshn* elements people's creativity results in considerable variation, as it does in the *majlis.* Icons such as the *alam* may be an important part of the ritual or there may be no *alam* present at all; a recitation of the full Quran may precede the *jeshn* or children may read praise poetry in honor of the Prophet's family; there may be a procession as part of the celebration or a lavish meal to conclude the event. In other words there is not one set style but a broad range of performative elements that help accomplish the common goal of remembrance and celebration.

The following description of a portion of a typical *jeshn* to conveys the flavor of such an event and a sense of how it differs from a *majlis.* This particular gathering was organized by the managing committee of Yadgar Husayni on the occasion of the birth anniversary of the eighth imam. As on most celebratory occasions, Yadgar Husayni is decorated to reflect a joyous mood: colorful lights adorn the outer walls and the usual faded curtain in the entryway is replaced by a rich red cloth. Gilded green brocade hangs behind the *alams* in the shrine's central inner room (*sher nishin*) and decorates in the hall the pulpit and the *takat,* a low bedlike structure on which people sit. The hall floor is spread with fresh white sheets, and garlands of jasmine and rose are heaped on the pulpit. An ornate incense holder (*udan*) and gold fan stand ready to perfume the air. Over the course of an hour a hundred or so women slowly assemble, wearing saris and long tunics with pants in a rainbow of colors. As they arrive, most take a moment to greet the *alams,* then sit on the floor chatting in small and large groups as children run about the hall excitedly.

Tahira Mohamed, an engaging elderly orator, arrives wearing a gray and orange silk sari and accompanied by a young woman who supports her by the arm. The two join a half dozen women standing near the *sher nishin* and proceed to garland all three *alams.* A woman then takes the remaining garlands from the pulpit to a spot near the entrance of the hall and begins to drape them over a crossbar fixed to a long brass-topped rod. When the rod is held aloft, the strings of flowers hang down from the crossbar at the top, obscuring the pole and swaying gently over the hands of those who hold the rod upright. This simple device aids in processing garlands in full view through a crowd.

By now about thirty women have gathered near the end of the hall. Tahira Mohamed and a gray-haired companion hold the garland procession pole, while a middle-aged woman settles a tray covered with a brocade cloth on her head. Then the small line of women begins to make its way toward the *sher nishin,* reciting a melodious ode (*qasida*) that speaks (among other things) about bringing to one's beloved the gift known as *sandal*: sandalwood paste prepared from the extract of the Asian evergreen tree (*chandana*) that is popularly associated in India with wedding rituals and other happy events. As the group slowly processes, women press forward from the crowd to kiss the garlands reverently. When the small parade reaches the *sher nishin,* one of the women lifts a fragrant string of flowers from the pole and carefully secures it over the main Husayni *alam.* She similarly adorns the other two *alams,* leaving fragrant ropes of flowers covering each crest. She then takes a small clay pot from the tray and, holding it in her hand before the *alams,* gracefully traces a large circle with her arm fully outstretched: first extending the *sandal* pot above her head and then moving it clockwise in a fluid circular motion. This is a common gesture in the broad Indian ritual context, and is known as *arati* in Hindu rituals. After tracing a circle three times, the woman turns to those who have accompanied her and, first dipping her fingers into the clear *sandal* oil, makes a brief mark (*tilaka*) on the brows of those who come forward. Other women push forward to be similarly marked by oil they understand to be blessed by Husayn and his revered companions.

Meanwhile a small group of women has sat down at the *takat.* One woman rises to place a thin garland of jasmine around the neck of a woman sitting cross-legged in front of the microphone. Others pass around a small pile of books. The woman at the microphone begins a tuneful ode (*qasida*) and the others join in, mainly repeating the refrain. Occasionally someone calls out "*salawat,*" and the women in the hall respond with the traditional words of blessing on the Prophet and his family ('*Allahumma salla ala Muhammad wa-Ala Muhammad*'). After three *qasidas* are recited, the main leader moves aside and another takes her place. There is relatively little audience participation in reciting the poetic refrains, a marked difference from how most *nauhas* are recited during Muharram remembrance gatherings. Also different is the absence of younger reciters; many are gray-haired, and all are at least in their thirties. As the tuneful odes continue, a few women are invited to the *takat* by the others already sitting there. Most smile and protest mildly before eventually joining the small group.

The melodic odes continue for nearly half an hour, before the microphone is moved to the pulpit. Tahira Mohamed rises with difficulty from her informal seat on the portal of the *sher nishin* and hobbles over to the stairlike structure. She bends to kiss it, then begins a shaky climb to the traditional third step. A woman extends a steadying hand and then places a garland around her neck. Setting the garland aside, Tahira Mohamed begins her oration with a melodious recitation from the Quran. A host of anecdotes follows, sketching out the life of Imam Reza and highlighting his kindness to the poor and weak. Many of the stories are miraculous tales: of a small bird that is restored to life, cloth that is mysteriously used to make clothes for a poor man's daughter, a lion's attack that is forestalled. She reminds people of the imam's popular name *Imam-e-zamin* (the one who stands in guarantee for another) and narrates how he received it for halting a hunter's killing of a deer when the imam learned—from the deer—that she must feed her hungry offspring. The imam promised the skeptical hunter that the deer would come back and waited in her stead with the hunter. When the deer did return, fawns in tow, the hunter released her out of respect for the imam and the miracle he had witnessed.

After relating these stories Tahira Mohamed emphasizes how people of good faith seek the intervention of the Prophet's family. Those who don't believe in supplicating Imam Reza are misguided and will later repent. She calls out for the audience to give the *salawat* blessing. But forty minutes into her oration, the responsive cry lacks certain vigor. Tahira Mohamed chastises the crowd for not responding with greater force, asking "Where is your respect?" When she again invites the *salawat,* her listeners enthusiastically call out their blessing on the Prophet's family. As they finish, a woman sitting close to Tahira Mohamed cues another popular refrain: "*Ya Ali! Ya Haydari! Ya Safdari!*" (all variations of the exclamation "Oh, Ali!"). The crowd's response gives Tahira Mohamed a moment to sip a glass of water and catch her breath before continuing to elucidate the special qualities of the beloved eighth imam.

As the description above illustrates, a *jeshn* shares several elements with a *majlis,* including the broad purposes of communicating a story, bringing sacred connection, and conferring blessing. The ritual elements that contribute to the latter two aims are the various prayers and the rituals around the *tabarruk* (including how it is blessed, given, and understood); these are much the same for both kinds of gathering. There is even a similar understanding of the blessing inherent in participating in remembrance rituals. For example, Imam Reza is reported to have said, "Whoever narrates our virtues through his poems, Allah will grant him a house in paradise, the size of which will be seven times the size of this earth."* Perhaps the only minor difference between the two types of ceremony is that the *tabarruk* in a Hyderabad *jeshn* is more likely to be sweet, reflecting the cultural equation of sweets with joy and celebration.

And yet the *jeshn* and the *majlis* are not the same. The *jeshn* is characterized by a mood of celebration that vividly shapes how and what women choose to communicate.

Communicating the Joyful Story

Recited verse occupies a central part of most *jeshns,* with odes known as *qasidas* being the most popular verse employed in Hyderabad. This genre of monorhyme praise poetry has its roots in pre-Islamic Arabia, where it usually was a means of giving acclaim to a ruler or patron. As it continued its development through the Muslim period, it became a popular form of praising God, the Prophet, and Muslim saints and heroes (Sperl and Shackle 1996, 4–24). A well-known Arabic *qasida* composed in praise of the fourth imam gives a sense of how this poetry began to be shaped in the Shia context. The author, the renowned poet Farazdaq, was a contemporary of Imam Ali Zayn al-Abidin and composed the poem to mark an occasion when the Prophet's great-grandson and the Sunni caliph were both trying to reach the Kaba during the hajj. The throng of pilgrims parted to give way to the imam, while the caliph had to struggle to make his way through the crowd. This offended the caliph, and he sarcastically asked to whom it was that the people showed such favor. The following verses are just a few from the poet's long reply:

> It is he whose footsteps are well known to every spot
> And it is he who is known to the Bayt [the Kaba] in Mecca,
> the most frequented sanctuary.
> It is he who is the son of the best of all men of God [that is,
> Prophet Muhammad]
> And it is he who is the most pious and devout, pure and unstained,
> Chaste and righteous and a symbol [of Islam].
> This is Ali [ibn al-Husayn], whose father is the Prophet
> And it was through the light of his [the Prophet's] guidance

*Quoted in the anonymously written and locally circulated booklet *Imam Mahdi and Our Duties Towards Him* (n.d.), 17.

That the darkened road changed into the straight path . . . .
Whosoever recognizes his God knows also
The primacy and superiority of this man [Ali ibn al-Husayn]
Because religion reached the nations through his house. (Jafri 1979, 248)

The purpose of a *qasida,* demonstrated well in Farazdaq's poem, is to proclaim the greatness of the one about whom one writes. The poet underscores the subject's ties with sacred and revered symbols, such as the Kaba, and his link to the Prophet who brought religion to the nations. In fact, using a familiar literary device to stress the fifth imam's close ties to the Prophet, Farazdaq collapses the actual generations between the two figures and transforms their relationship into that of son and father. Superlatives describe Zayn al-Abidin's qualities, and the poet asserts that someone who recognizes God (that is, a faithful Muslim) will also recognize the superiority of this member of the *Ahl-e-Bayt.* It is interesting to note that although Farazdaq was imprisoned for his spontaneous recitation, he was subsequently released when he began to compose poetry satirizing the caliph—a testament to both his skill and his renown as a poet and to the power and respect that poets wielded in Arab society.

We find in contemporary *qasidas* all the same elements utilized in Farazdaq's poem: ties with sacred symbols, links to the Prophet and his bloodline, generous superlatives, and incidents that demonstrate the subject's excellence and virtues. *Jeshn* organizers or *qasida* reciters generally choose poems that extol those members of the Prophet's family being honored at an event. Thus, for example, the following *qasida* is meant to be performed at a *jeshn* commemorating the birth of Hasan, the second imam:

In the house of Fatima [*Zahra*], the bearer of radiance [*Anwar*] has come,
The successor of Ali [*Haydar-e-Karrar*] has come.

In the house of Ali [*Haydar*] the celebration of birth is welcome,
The leader of the youth of Paradise has come.

Those satisfied to remain apart from the remembrance of his wellbeing
Have the look of someone sick.

Today, whoever has a need has come asking
To take alms [*sadqah*] to the door of Ali [*Murtaza*].

There was talk of kindness and there was remembrance [*zikr*] of generosity,
Hasan's name came repeatedly to people's lips.
The unbelievers were astonished when they saw the warrior skills of Hasan [*Shabbar*]:
Who is this likeness of Ali that has come?

Friends have said that today is the celebration [*jeshn*] of Hasan.
Jawaid has arrived with verses of high praise.*

This poem reminds the listeners of Hasan's generosity, kindness, and bravery and also uses popular names to link him with his revered family. Like his mother, the "shining" one (*Zahra*), he is the bearer of radiance; like his father, the "attacking lion" (*Haydar-e-Karrar*), he is a warrior. And believers know that "leader of the youth of Paradise" was an epithet given to Hasan and Husayn by the Prophet himself.

The poem also blurs the distinction between past and present. In the first two verses the listeners are in the house of Ali and Fatima as the couple celebrates the birth of their new child. In another couplet they are on the battlefield as the astonished enemy beholds the likeness of Ali. In still other parts of the *qasida* they are firmly in the present as the poet (Jawaid) arrives with verses of high praise, and Hasan's qualities are extolled in the celebration of the *jeshn*. Past and present unite in the couplet that describes needy people coming to Ali's door on the occasion of Hasan's birth. The verse evokes the common practice in the Indian subcontinent of a family distributing blessed alms (*sadqah*) when a child is born. However, it also reminds the listener that this is the day when "whoever has a need" can ask and receive a blessing from Imam Ali. This comingling of past and present is not just a literary device but reflects as well the believers' experience at remembrance gatherings when linear time dissolves into overarching sacred time.

Following an initial recitation of poetry, most *jeshn* have an oration. As with the *qasidas*, the focus is usually on stories that highlight the qualities and greatness of the persons being honored. The stories range from fairly well documented historical accounts to popular "miracle tales," such as those presented about the eighth imam in the *jeshn* described earlier. During that oration the *zakira* also reminded her listeners to perform supplication rites to bring their needs before Imam Reza and other members of the Prophet's family. As she noted, a true believer trusts in the power of the *Ahl-e-Bayt;* doubters will one day repent. Thus an oration serves as a teaching moment: reminding the audience of the life and qualities of a sacred soul and guiding the actions of the faithful believer.

Oral narratives such as and oration function as the key way to communicate Shia theology in many *jeshn*. However, as we saw with the *majlis*, a third means of sharing a message is through physical performance. In the *jeshn* described earlier the organizers chose to begin their event with a procession. This is familiar in the South Indian cultural milieu where processions are a common part of social and

*Translation of the poem "Zahra ke ghar men paikar-e-anwar agaya," by Jawaid Badauni; http://smma59.wordpress.com/tag/qaseeda-writeups/ (accessed 1 August 2007).

religious observances. Familiar, too, are the offerings that the women processed: garlands of sweetly fragrant flowers and sandalwood oil. Floral garlands have been used from ancient times in India as gifts to honor respected persons or deities. Sandalwood paste is a precious and revered commodity used in sanctifying and celebratory rituals at weddings, temples, and shrines of Muslim saints. In fact, offering *sandal* is equated with honoring the beloved—a theme that the women highlighted in the melodious poetry which they chose to recite as they processed. After the women presented these gifts before the *alams,* they made the sandalwood oil available to believers, rubbing a bit on the forehead of anyone who came forward to receive it.

There are parallels here with localized religious practices; for example, many Hindus make an auspicious mark (*tilaka*) on a devotee's forehead as a sign of blessing from a deity. Juan R. I. Cole (2002, 138–60) has pointed out that in the development of Indian Shia ritual women have tended to be more open than men to wider expressions of faith. Looking at eighteenth- and nineteenth-century Lucknow, Cole finds the "feminine imagination at work" in how women from various social classes melded elements of local female and family life-cycle rites with the celebration of events related to the life of the imams. Cole argues that women appeared to be less communally minded than men of similar class and background and attributes this to wide-ranging feminine networks that brought women into contact with those of other religious traditions. Cole has pointed out that, although some Shia clergy of the period accused women of being unorthodox in their thinking and practices, the reality was that such women were generally quite strict in their Muslim religious observances, whether daily prayers and fasting or Muharram rituals. In other words Shia women did not leave their faith; rather they supplemented it with religious discourse and practices appropriated from other traditions and made meaningful within their own. Cole's observation about women's "wide-ranging networks" is equally true today. In addition to relationships with Hindu neighbors, coworkers, market vendors, and school teachers and fellow parents at school gatherings in the religiously mixed environment of Hyderabad, women encounter Hindu cultural and religious traditions through cinema, popular television programs, and local religious displays. Many women who are deeply rooted in Shia faith and tradition are comfortable with practices that draw from broader Indian cultural practices, whether they involve using incense or sandalwood paste as a mark of celebration or making particular gestures to convey offering and blessing. Further research could help illuminate gender differences in this aspect of religious identity and ritual practice in multifaith settings like that of India.

Yet women's performative use of fragrant oil in the *jeshn* (to give just one example) is about more than just culturally familiar ways to honor sacred personalities.

These powerful props create tangible links between the faithful and the revered souls being celebrated. As the believer receives oil on her brow, strokes a garland, or eats one of its flower petals, she physically embodies her connection with the family of the Prophet. Similarly, when she adorns herself with bright colors, colorful bangles, or glittering jewelry—celebratory signs normally reserved for such events as weddings—she manifests the joyfulness shared with the *Ahl-e-Bayt.* This sensory experience of celebration is further expanded by decorating the ritual space with festive curtains, lights, and vibrant luxuriant cloth. In contrast, during a *majlis* women embody suffering by donning monochromatic dress and adopting a starkly simple décor, putting away all glitter, color, and comfort to walk alongside the grieving *Ahl-e-Bayt.* In other words, such props help women embody their relationship with the family of the Prophet.

Women are creative in their use of common ritual objects to convey meaning. Flowers, for example, are a feature of both *majlis* and *jeshn,* yet the spirit in which they are given and what they convey are totally different. During the months of Muharram and Safar, with their haunting shadows of death and suffering, a woman demonstrates respect and love for the family of the Prophet by adorning the *alams* with garlands of jasmine and rose. These often tearful presentations of the *majlis* are reminiscent of the custom of draping a dead body with fragrant flowers before its burial or the common practice of putting a garland on the photograph of a departed family member. During the *jeshn,* however, one offers flowers in a style that is closer to the way in which someone welcomes a beloved or respected dignitary, presenting a necklace of flowers as a mark of honor and affection. These performative elements, powerfully experienced through the senses, are important tools in communicating the central stories of Shia faith.

Summary

The *majlis* and *jeshn* are the most common religious gatherings in the Shia community, giving shape to a pattern of sorrowful and celebratory days that enlivens the calendar year. Why are they so prominent in female lives, and what assists women in constructing meaningful ritual? One factor is certainly that women are actively involved in carrying them out, creatively fashioning rituals that reflect their religious needs, aspirations, and visions. Women's active engagement is linked to a system of segregation that limits female participation and leadership in mixed-gender environments and constrains male presence in female gatherings. In addition, remembrance gatherings are multilayered rituals that invite participation whether it be in preparing and decorating the space, assembling or preparing the *tabarruk,* giving orations, reciting melodic poetry, performing *matam,* creating and taking part in processions, or simply collectively mourning for, celebrating, and blessing the *Ahl-e-Bayt.* Although the role of ritual leaders is important, the role of audience is equally vital, with women actively participating through weeping, calling out of prayers and blessings, and physically embodying the connection with the family of the Prophet through their behavior and dress.

Women's active participation is also aided by the fact that commemoration gatherings are one major religious practice where women are welcome to partake in the ritual irrespective of whether or not they are in a state of elevated purity according to established religious custom. Muslim rituals such as fasting, daily prayers, and pilgrimage to Mecca are all contingent on a woman's being in a physiologically "clean" period. As a result most adult women must calibrate their ritual participation with their menstrual or postpartum cycles, putting a temporary halt to practices when they begin to bleed. In remembrance gatherings, however, the only restrictions for a menstruating woman regard touching an *alam* or leading the oration. Women explain this greater openness by noting that the *majlis* and *jeshn* involve listening to orations and reciting inspired verse, not voicing God's word through reading the Quran, something most women are hesitant to do during an "unclean" period. Others express the importance of not excluding anyone from participating in remembrance gatherings, since telling faith-inspired stories is crucial to spreading religious education, and expressing grief or joy is meritorious and a source of blessing. One articulate leader went even further, asserting that the freedom in these gatherings offers an important example for all religious rituals. This university-educated teacher argued that exclusion from fasting, prayers, and other religious practices is largely a male-imposed stigma that has no basis in the Quran. Noting the example of a neighborhood Sunni mosque that now admits women, she posited that, although change takes place slowly, it will come eventually because "there are no restrictions [in the Quran] on women for these things" (interview, Hyderabad, 1 February 2000).

The opportunity to connect with one's emotions, especially grief and loss, is undoubtedly another factor that contributes to female participation in remembrance gatherings and one that may help explain differences in the popularity of the two types of event. Mourning gatherings far outnumber celebratory ones in the Shia community and also tend to draw larger crowds. One can observe that a *majlis* is often more vibrant than the celebratory *jeshn,* with greater numbers of people participating and the very air crackling with emotion. While there may be a number of reasons for this, one is certainly the power of the cathartic experience of grief. A well-orchestrated *majlis* creates an intensely moving experience for the believer. In melodic poetry, with its words of sorrow and pain, the narration of the tragedy that engulfed the *Ahl-e-Bayt,* the active grieving of participants, the pounding beat of *matam* as people passionately express their sorrow, the symbolic reenactment of the death of beloved souls—all combine to highlight the tragedies of life and to bring to the surface one's own experiences of sorrows and sufferings. There is solidarity and comfort in the fellowship of grief, and the *majlis* provides an environment where it is not only acceptable to grieve but is also laudable to do so.

Aiding women's active engagement with remembrance gatherings is also a cultivated sense of familiarity. A *majlis* procession of *alams,* for example, is highly evocative because it closely mirrors locally observed funeral practices: the body arranged and laid out at home, the family gathered distraught around it, neighbors and friends coming to mourn and console, the body being covered in a shroud and taken away in procession for burial. Likewise, the procession in the *jeshn* described mirrors a marriage procession, with gifts such as fragrant sandalwood paste ritually brought to the house of the bride or groom. Because these images are so familiar, the believer can draw on her own experiences to enter more easily the emotional scene of an earlier time. Karen G. Ruffle (2011, 85–94) makes exactly this point in her detailed discussion of the Hyderabad mourning assemblies that annually recreate the premartyrdom wedding of Husyan's daughter Fatima with Imam Hassan's son Qasim. The *mehndi,* or henna, ceremony, the name of which refers to the ritualized painting of a bride's hands and feet with henna in preparation for their wedding, is preeminently Indian, with its emphasis on local wedding rituals and Indian conceptions about widowhood.

Important to these performative elements are props such as the *alam* that remind the believer of the presence of the *Ahl-e-Bayt.* Other ritual elements evoke the presence of cosmic souls, elements such as the greeting of the *ziyarat* prayer and the stories associated with such holy sites as the shrine to the Twelfth Imam. Remembrance gatherings are a means that allows the believer to stand alongside these revered souls in love and loyalty. As Ali Mohsin Khan, president of Hyderabad's Elia Theological Association, has remarked: "We strongly believe that Hazrat Fatima, the mother of Husain, comes to every *majlis.* We seek to have as many people present as possible, so that when the *majlis* ends and Fatima returns to Paradise, she'll feel satisfied at seeing so many people honor her son. Our sole purpose in all this . . . is to satisfy Husain's mother" (Pinault 1997, 87). Remembrance gatherings, then, are not so much a recalling of events and persons locked in the past as they are a renewing of relationships in the present.

Although the *jeshn* and *majlis* are important religious gatherings that contain a wealth of teaching and ritual, they are also social occasions that meet the needs of many women. Remembrance gatherings are occasions to catch up with friends, to share problems and joys, to immerse oneself in prayers, to give attention to children or to sleep, to test possible alliances for future arranged marriages, or simply to take a break from household routines and family demands. Men and women may view the social benefit of religious gatherings differently, as Toby M. Howarth (2001, 262) has suggested in quoting a Hyderabad *zakir* that says: "If women have a women's *majlis* in the home, they will spend the whole day; they will go for two hours before to chit chat, and stay afterwards for two hours, wasting the whole day. On the Last Day, we will be questioned as to how we have used our time." This male preacher brands women's socializing as squandering a God-given resource of time in which one could be more productive. Although I did not encounter this critique among the men with whom I interacted, I do not doubt that it exists. Perhaps it reflects in part a difference in how men and women frame religious experience in terms of relationship, for, counter to this *zakir*, female religious leaders clearly acknowledge that ritual gatherings are important times to nurture connections that go beyond one's immediate household.

CHAPTER 4

The Female Face of Religious Leadership

Collective ritual is shaped by active leaders. In gatherings such as the ones just examined, women act as hosts and organizers, poetry reciters, orators, and those who lead the breast-beating (*matam*). Among all these roles, it is the orator (*zakira;* lit. [female] "reciter") whom Shias see as having the most profound influence on ritual assemblies. The *zakira* (or the male *zakir*) is the person who assumes responsibility to keep alive the founding stories of the faith and is thus a primary conduit for religious knowledge. Indeed hers is the most prominent position of religious authority open to Shia women in India. In Shia Islam a woman can become a *mujtahid,* a religious scholar accredited as having the power to exert independent judgment (*ijtihad*), but not a *marja al-taqlid,* a *mujtahid,* one whom others follow and who is considered the most learned religiojuridical authority in the community. In reality very few women have achieved the position of *mujtahid,* and those who have, such as Sayyidah Nusrat Begum Amin (1886–1993), tend to be from Iran or Iraq, the perceived heartland of Shia Islam. Hence for the majority of women, and especially for those in South Asia, the greatest opportunities for religious leadership lie within ritual spaces among the community of women. In seeking to understand how gender impacts ritual leadership, it is useful to begin with a review of the origins of the *zakira*'s role.

The Origin and Development of the *Zakira*'s Role

The word *zakira* comes from the Arabic word *zikr* which means remembrance, recitation, or narration. In the Shia context a *zakira* (or *zakir*) is one who remembers and narrates the incidents connected to early Shia history, particularly the events surrounding the Karbala massacre and its aftermath. In Iran and other parts of the Indian subcontinent, this person is known as a *rawzah khan,* a "reciter of the *Rawzat*" (a seminal sixteenth-century C.E. martyrdom account that achieved such popularity that mourning gatherings as a genre were named for it). Shias know that Zaynab, the granddaughter of Prophet Muhammad, functioned as the first *zakira* when she led a mourning gathering in Damascus with the women of the family and court of Yazid, the caliph. She and those who followed her drew upon an already existing mourning tradition that included poetic tributes, weeping, and the physical demonstration of grief. They also stood within an existing and celebrated narrative tradition. Arabian society placed a high value on the tribal spokesperson (*khatib*) and the poet for their verbal dexterity in extolling the deeds and qualities of the tribe and exposing the weaknesses of enemies and opponents. The role of *zakira*, then, developed from these strong roots in mourning and narrative traditions.

From the beginning the main function of the *zakira* was to relay the story of what took place at Karbala, to testify to the courage and bravery of those who were martyred, to express grief and pain at the loss, and to inspire loyalty, empathy, and sorrow in her listeners. These goals have guided orators throughout the centuries and continue to offer direction and inspiration to today's *zakiras*. Thirteen hundred years have brought about changes in the style of ritual leadership, as women have chosen different ways to realize these and other goals. Although there is a scanty historical record, one can trace the development of the *zakira*'s role through a series of small windows that offer glimpses of her performance. The clearest points of reference are in the immediate aftermath of the Karbala tragedy and in the period from the mid-nineteenth century to the present—with a few additional snapshots in between. Assessing these brief historical mentions delineates three broad stages in the development of the *zakira*'s style: the early spontaneous oration and poetry (performed by relatives of the martyrs); the recitation of established stories, poems, and rhyming narratives; and the inclusion of learned disquisitions along with the traditional stories.

There are no firsthand historical accounts of the initial remembrance gatherings organized by Zaynab and other women in the family of the Prophet, although there is considerable documentation of the sharp waves of grief and lamentation that news of the deaths of Husayn and others caused. One finds many faith-based accounts that try to fill in the details. A typical example is found in the Indian-published biography of Zaynab compiled by Yousuf N. Lalljee (n.d., 88–89). Lalljee describes Zaynab addressing multiple *majalis* where she "apprised the Syrian ladies of the cruelty and atrocity of Yazid and of the merits of Imam Husain":

> O Ladies of Syria! You are unaware of the terrible tragedy of Kerbala. How Husain, grandson of the Holy Prophet along with his kith and kin were massacred hungry and thirsty, how horses trampled their bodies and were left even without a burial. How their heads were mounted on spikes and carried along with us all the way to Syria. After the martyrdom we were made captives by the order of the shameless ibn Ziad. They took us to Kufa bare-headed and were made to sit on camels without saddles and the

> divinely commissioned Imam was in shackles and fetters and with a heavy rope around his neck and made to walk behind the camels. Such a scene of horror is unimaginable and you cannot visualise how terrible it was.

Although women's traditional mourning practices at the time of Husayn's death tended to feature verse rather than prose oration, it is likely that Zaynab took the opportunity offered by these well-attended gatherings to voice at least some of the details of what had taken place, perhaps as described in this faith-based account. She thus continued the announcing role that she and her nephew the fourth imam had assumed following their capture at Karbala. While historical records may never tell us exactly what Zaynab said or how she functioned in the gatherings she catalyzed in Damascus, Karbala, or Madina, we do know that these events were so powerful they began to alarm the ruling authorities, who called Zaynab's presence "inflammatory." It is clear that the granddaughter of the Prophet was a powerful and courageous orator whose skill in delivering a message and thinking on her feet reminded those who heard her of her father, Imam Ali. In the post-Karbala climate, gatherings to mourn the dead were one of the few opportunities for a group to assemble without being accused of insurrection. It seems indisputable that the passionate narrations of Zaynab helped rouse people's sympathies and fuel a desire for revolt, for the Umayyad rulers stated their fears about the power of this "eloquent, clever, [and] intelligent" woman and sent her into exile.

As the Umayyad government clamped down on expressions of solidarity with Husayn, the family members and those who were loyal to them held mourning gatherings in private, mainly in the homes of leaders. It was during this time (and with the encouragement and patronage of the imams) that poetry and prose honoring the dead and recounting the events at Karbala began to accumulate. Skilled reciters emerged and assumed increasing leadership in the mourning gatherings, frequenting the homes of the imams and leading the lamentations (Ayoub 1978, 152). By the fourth and fifth centuries A.H. a class of "professional" storytellers and "wailing reciters"—both male and female—had developed. Historical sources make mention, for example, of the "famous" and "accomplished" Khallab of Baghdad, who in 323 A.H. was reciting poetry in the wailing style in the homes of local leaders. Her recitals apparently were heard and appreciated by men as well as women, although her fame as a powerful and poignant voice of Shia faith ultimately led to her death (Shams al-Din 1985, 169, 172).

These experienced and respected mourners who chanted elegies and recited stories seem to have occupied the main position of leadership in remembrance gatherings. In fact, if the imam was present he would sit on the floor in deference to the poet who stood and recited from the pulpit (Wafa 1978, 6). The "readers for

Husayn" (*qurra al-Husayn*), as they were known, continued in the footsteps of Zaynab and other early leaders who acted as important catalysts for the community's mourning process. Eventually their repertoire included written martyrdom narratives, the recitation of which occupied a central place in remembrance gatherings from the fifteenth to nineteenth centuries C.E. (Ayoub 1978, 20; Howarth 2001, 37–58). This stage also saw an expansion of the topics addressed, reflecting the development of Shia theology. A brief glance at popular martyrdom texts of that time reveals how the tragedy of Karbala began to be set into a wider context. The renowned and highly popular *Rawzat al-Shuhada* ("Garden of the Martyrs"; 1502 C.E.) by Kamal al-Din Husayn Sabzawari, for example, begins with chapters entitled "The trials and tribulations of some of the prophets," "The persecution of Prophet Muhammad by the Quraysh and the martyrdom of the Prophet's uncle Hamza and Jafar bin Abi Talib," "The death of the Prophet Muhammad," "The life of Fatima Zahra," "The life of Imam Ali," and "The life of Imam Hasan." It is only after Sabzawari provides this extensive foundation that he moves on to relate the stories of what happened to Husayn, his family and followers. Although the *zakira's* role during this period was largely one of reciting from a text rather than offering a learned disquisition, this broadening of focus was another step toward the contemporary practice of including a general discourse along with the narration of the sufferings of the family of the Prophet.

There are two historical accounts—from Iran and North India—that help shed light on women's leadership at this stage in the development of the tradition. In her chronicling of the women's movement in Iran, Badr al-Moluk Bamdad (who in 1936 was among the first female students admitted to Tehran University) noted that *zakiras* (called *rawzah khans* in the Iranian context) were a "long-standing tradition" in the society. During the eighteenth and nineteenth centuries female members of the Qajar ruling family, and their upper-class contemporaries used to invite learned women into the harems to recite at mourning gatherings. "The reciters were always literate women with a feeling for poetry." They seem to have been part of a cadre of female religious teachers (*molla-bajis*) who had responsibility for providing religious instruction to the harem inmates, as well as helping to organize and facilitate their performance of ritual duties. Bamdad (1977, 20–22) names several prominent *rawzah khans* and mentions how some won great fame and popularity, rising to "high positions" due to their exceptional talent. Upper-class women made use of female religious leaders throughout the year, not just during the profusion of commemoration ceremonies held during the months of Muharram and Safar. For example, Mah-Taban Khanom, the wife of Prime Minister (1871–1873) Mirza Husayn Khan Sepahsalar, invited *rawzah khans* to her home for weekly remembrance gatherings which she organized for friends, relatives, and acquaintances. These leaders also were invited to feasts of supplication (*sofreh*) where their hosts gave them the "utmost attention and respect" and made use of their "help in phrasing prayers." It seems clear, then, that the Iranian *zakira* of this class and period was literate in Arabic and Persian, with a knowledge of Shia history and poetry, as well as of prayer, scripture, and ritual.

We find a somewhat similar account of women's leadership in Northern India during the same period. Mrs. Mir Hasan Ali, an English woman who had married into a Shia family and resided in Lucknow, described Muharram gatherings in the early part of the nineteenth century. She made the following observations about the women who were enlisted to lead commemorations in the female quarters of private homes:

> The few females, who have been educated, are in great request at this season; they read the Dhie Mudgelluss [*Dah Majlis*], and chant the Musseeah [*marsiya*] with good effect. These women, being hired for the purpose, are detained during the ten days; when the Mahurrum ceases, they are dismissed to their own homes, loaded with the best gifts the good lady their employer can conveniently spare, commensurate with the services performed. These educated females are chiefly daughters of poor Syaads, who have not been married for the lack of a dowry;—they live devoutly in the service of God, according to their faith. They are sometimes required, in the families of the nobility, to teach the Khoraun to the young ladies. ([1832] 1917, 23–29)

Hasan Ali's description offers us some further insights into how female orators functioned during this period. First, as in the Iranian case, the emphasis during the *majlis* seems to have been on reading from established martyrdom texts and reciting mourning poetry. The *Dah Majlis* ("ten assemblies") was the heart of the daily Muharram ceremonies, being an abbreviated version of the *Rawzat al-Shuhada.* Various scholars over the centuries had abridged copies of this famous Persian text and divided it into ten, eleven, or twelve installments in order to facilitate the recitation during the mourning season (Rizvi 1986, 2:352–55). The invited leader was responsible for reciting the daily portion at women's gatherings. She also was the one to perform moving elegies (*marsiyas*) in the local language of Urdu. In contrast to the modern period where we find separate individuals leading the poetry and the oration, this precursor to the modern *zakira* appears to have specialized in both types of recitation. Hasan Ali also mentioned that families hired such women to give regular Quran instruction to the young females in a household. Clearly, then, these talented leaders were literate in at least three languages:

the court language of Persian, the local language of Urdu, and the scriptural language of Arabic. In addition they were familiar (to varying extents) with Shia history and the Quran and had committed to memory dozens of poems, verses, and prayers. Hasan Ali's description implies that this level of education was rather rare in the society of women. The women who assumed these positions came from families who traced their descent to the Prophet (known as *sayyids*) and attributes in part their high levels of learning to the fact that they remained unmarried, their families being too poor to assemble a suitable dowry.

Elderly women in Hyderabad with whom I spoke also recalled this stage in the development of the *zakira*'s role. They related how women of the upper classes organized *majalis* at which they and their guests heard or recited poetry, practiced *matam* (rhythmic breast beating), and listened to written narratives that retold the stories of Karbala. Professional female performers were commonly invited to recite the mourning poetry while the guests reclined on bolsters, often with a bowl of roasted anise seeds circulating among the crowd. One of the women would then read from a written account of the martyrdom event using "Muharram books" or "*majalis* books" (probably including the *Dah Majlis*) containing separate readings for each day. Among those who recalled these affairs, a few commented that the ladies who gathered were more spectators at an event than participants in it.

We can make several observations about the development of the *zakira*'s role in the *majlis* up to this point. First, we note that at times this religious leader had responsibility for reciting poetry and for narrating or reading martyrdom accounts—a mixture that probably echoes the original mourning practices of Zaynab and other women of the Prophet's family. This stands in apparent contrast to the male tradition in which poetry and prose seem to have been more distinct streams of performance (Howarth 2001, 19–64). We also observe that at least from the eighteenth century (and probably earlier) the *zakira* commonly played a larger religious leadership role in the female community: being invited to help women formulate prayers for supplication, to oversee rituals, and to teach the Quran. During these centuries she was often among a relatively small number of literate educated women having facility in language, including the sacred language of the Quran (Arabic), and the language of poetry and religious commentary (Persian, Urdu). Finally, we see that the goals of the first *zakiras*—to tell the stories; to extol the courage and bravery of the martyrs; to express one's grief and pain; and to inspire empathy, loyalty, and sorrow in one's listeners—have remained fairly consistent throughout the development of the orator's role. As we will see, in the modern period the *zakira* takes on an additional goal of educating her listeners on religious themes wider than the Karbala story. This is in keeping with the growth of Shia theology and the general expansion of the subject of narration from an initial focus on the immediate tragedy to an inclusion of stories about the Prophet, his family, the imams, and other prophets who suffered in the service of God.

The Modern *Zakira*

As we have seen, the biggest difference between the premodern orator and the contemporary *zakira* is that the latter generally supplemented her stories about Karbala with an extempore religious discourse (*bayan* or *taqrir*). There was not a distinct category of female extempore preachers—although Zaynab appears to have combined extempore oration with poetry in the earliest mourning gatherings, and later "professional" female poets and storytellers probably made some personal words of introduction or explanation before or after their recitations. By the nineteenth century women's roles in the female-led *majlis* seem to have been largely ones of performing already written compositions, both poetry and prose penned by men and women. For *zakiras* in the earliest part of the twentieth century, then, the biggest step forward was to free themselves from this tie to established texts to offer thoughtful orations of their own. To deliver an extempore *zikr* was the major innovation of the modern era for women—even though, in fact, it was reclaiming a space Zaynab seems to have occupied fourteen hundred years earlier.

Oral accounts of women in their seventies and eighties suggest that it was at the very beginning of the twentieth century that this extempore style began to emerge, although the exact dates and details are still somewhat unclear. Toby M. Howarth (2001, 50–56) drew upon interviews with women in Hyderabad and Lucknow to argue that it was in the 1930s and 1940s that women first began their extempore preaching. In delineating this change, however, he is precise to separate discourses on the events of Karbala from talks focusing on wider issues—the latter, in his view, were the truly modern innovation. Howarth based his conclusion on the fact that male extempore oration about Karbala already existed in the premodern period. In the Deccan region, for example, formally trained male religious scholars (*ulama,* pl. of *alim*) had been giving sermons in conjunction with mourning commemorations at least as far back as the Qutb Shah period. Thus, in Howarth's estimation, the modern innovation was to broaden the subject beyond the Karbala context, not to deliver extempore oration per se. Yet, this distinction holds little meaning for women. The early preaching that Howarth cites was almost always delivered by trained and accredited religious scholars (the *ulama*), an exclusively male group in which women were not represented. Unlike men, women in the premodern period had almost no established or legitimate religious platform for public address. Those who emerged as leaders in female gatherings were often among a relatively small number of literate educated women having facility in language, including the sacred language of the Quran (Arabic) and the language of poetry and religious commentary (Persian, Urdu). Such women often played a larger religious role in the female community, helping women formulate prayers for supplication, overseeing rituals, and teaching the Quran. The significant change for such female leaders was the opportunity to give a talk relying on their own oratory skills rather than expressively reciting from a prepared text. As was the case with men, and no doubt influenced by them, the scope of their performance gradually widened to include not only the recounting of stories of Karbala but a broad range of other subjects as well.

The switch to extempore performance seems to have been catalyzed by several factors including reform movements to recognize women's rights and abilities, the push for women's education, the rising number of literate women who could make use of written materials, and the increase in discursive sermons at male-led gatherings. Interestingly, this last major watershed in the development of the *zakira* tradition witnessed a brief time during which male orators addressed female gatherings. This trend seems to have been short-lived in Hyderabad and perhaps even hastened the rise of female extempore orators. One reason it did not persist was practical: many women did not feel comfortable removing the outer veil or cloak in the presence of an unrelated male. Thus they remained in *purdah* (seclusion; here created by clothing, in other contexts by the physical division of space) for the whole gathering—something they never did in meetings involving only females. Second, some *zakirs* seemed to assume that women knew very little and therefore gave talks which some in the audience found patronizing. It appears that, as a group, women did not encourage male leadership in female gatherings. Rather, a handful of women used their own skills and abilities, capitalized on existing opportunities, and, within a relatively short period, became strong preachers of the faith.

It is interesting to contrast this point of history with that in other settings and cultures, for the practice of male leadership in female mourning gatherings continues in some religious circles in present day Iran (Good 1978, 486; Fischer 1978, 204). Azam Torab (1998, 151–156, 411–14) has described Tehran women who invite male religious leaders (whom she calls cantors) to offer short prayers, sermons, and martyrdom recitations at female mourning gatherings. Her portrait of *purdah* and the dynamics of power is revealing. The presence of men is particularly curious given women's otherwise strong and creative religious leadership and their vivid ritual life, all of which Torab documents well. A fascinating comparative project would be to analyze the development and dynamics of gendered leadership in female religious gatherings in India and Iran.

Grandmothers in Hyderabad's Shia community vividly recall the passion and delivery of pioneering female orators from the 1930s and 1940s (although they also allude to a prior generation of *zakiras*). These include Latif al-Nisa, the first president of the women's religious association that founded Yadgar Husayni, and other well-known women in the community, such as Sughra Begum, Mehdi Begum, Sughra Sadiq, and Fatima Begum. These leaders had an intensity that many women still remember. "It was fantastic," remarked one woman in her late sixties. "They could make you roll in tears in ten minutes. They were really emotional" (interview, Hyderabad, 20 June 1997). The chief aims of the early-twentieth-century *zakiras* were to remember the tragedies endured by the Prophet's family, to weep for them, and to inspire others to feel the pain and loss they suffered. A successful *zakira* was a gifted storyteller who could help her audience experience the agonizing grief of the original events. Such women knew the Karbala tragedy and could embellish it to quickly bring the crowd to a frantic pitch.

To deliver an emotional address that inspires and transforms one's audience is still an important part of how people judge a successful *zakira*. Yet, oration styles have changed—a process that some women see as ongoing. "Blind faith still exists," said one sixty-year-old, "but education is changing the whole way we think and learn. The way we were taught twenty or thirty years ago is impossible today. We [*zakiras,* teachers] have to be able to give satisfactory answers to the questions young people ask" (interview, Hyderabad, 4 April 1997). In other words the techniques a *zakira* used to capture and hold the attention of an audience in the 1930s or 1940s may not be as successful today. "People are less willing to accept the simple description and emotionalism of earlier days," said one popular *zakira.* She noted that an analytical approach is essential, as well as an organized presentation of the topic. In her mind her career as an educator and her role as a religious orator were closely linked, for they draw on the same skills of organization, analysis, and presentation (interview, Hyderabad, 26 March 1997). Another woman, who emigrated from India and now lives in Canada, noted that the subject matter covered in women's orations has also expanded: the "better ones [*zakiras*] are talking about social issues" (interview, Toronto, 6 April 2001).

Not all *zakiras,* however, felt comfortable delivering a reasoned discourse of the more academic variety. And, despite changes in how people learn and what they value, some still long for the earlier days. As one woman summarized, "Before it was short and sweet. Perhaps now they [the *zakiras*] want to show all their knowledge in two months [the mourning period]. . . . Now, before I go [to a *majlis*], I find out who is the *zakira.* If it's someone I know gives a long-winded talk, I won't go. I get bored and my back hurts" (interview, Hyderabad, 20 June 1997). In other words there is some tension between reasoned exposition and emotional recounting of the tragedies that overtook the beloved family of the Prophet. The modern practice tends to be to combine both styles in one address. A *zakira* will begin her talk with a preliminary recitation from the Quran or some words from

Prophet Muhammad or one of the imams. She then usually links this excerpt to a learned disquisition—theological or other—that illuminates some aspect of her listeners' faith and the world in which they live. In the celebratory *jeshn* she goes on to offer stories of strength, power, and blessing, highlighting superior qualities and remarkable incidents involving one or more members of the Prophet's family. In mourning gatherings she may briefly expound on these virtues, but her main emphasis tends to be on delivering the passionate recounting of some aspect of the sufferings of family of the Prophet (*masaib*), through which she seeks to move her audience to tears. In fact, when time is limited or the occasion demands, the *zakira* may confine herself to simply narrating these tragic accounts.

The Choice and Demands of Leadership

The women who take up the task of being an orator at remembrance gatherings are an extremely varied group. They may be twelve years old or eighty; have a university doctorate or no formal schooling; be well-off or working class; be married, widowed, or unmarried; be grandmothers, mothers, or childless. What they have in common is a devotion to the family of the Prophet, time to prepare and deliver a message, and an ability to communicate in Urdu. How do women make the choice to be *zakiras* and what are the gendered demands they face when they do?

Women in Hyderabad today estimate that there are between twenty-five and one hundred *zakiras* in the local community. Their count, however, refers to orators whom they hear fairly often or whom people invite to lead remembrance gatherings. It does not include women who give talks occasionally but do not have an ongoing commitment to performing this role. As one *zakira* noted, "There are two types of *zakiras:* those who make it a career, and those who do it because they get an opportunity to talk" (interview, Hyderabad, 18 February 2000). In other words the role of orator is owned not just by those who see it as a calling but by a larger more informal network of women as well. This circumstance accounts for the diversity in the age, education, and experience of *zakiras,* as well as a range of motivations for assuming leadership.

Women who choose to function only occasionally as *zakiras* do so for a variety of reasons. Sometimes they are encouraged by female relatives who are sponsoring a gathering within an extended family circle. Family elders often give a young woman an opportunity to lead a *majlis* or *jeshn* as a way to boost her confidence and skills and to encourage her to grow into this leadership role. Others feel that everyone should have at least one opportunity to prepare and deliver a talk, since all believers should be able inform people about what happened to the Prophet's family. One young graduate noted very practically that "each of us should have at least one woman in our own family who can lead [a commemoration gathering] if someone from outside is unable to come" (interview, Hyderabad, 26 June 1997).

Finally, some hosts encourage less well-known women to speak when they are looking to set their gathering apart from the large number of assemblies being held on popular commemoration days. They may seek out and invite a woman whom they feel has a different perspective from what one ordinarily hears. For example, a woman who retired from a prestigious law career was asked by a relative to be the orator at her upcoming *majlis.* The legal scholar smiled wryly as she related their conversation: "I asked her 'Why do you want me? I don't do all that.' But she said 'No, come. I want you to speak about women's rights in Islam.' As part of the *zikr,* she said. I wasn't very sure about going but she was quite insistent. So I will be at her *majlis* next week" (interview, Hyderabad, 20 June 1997).

When it comes to the women who regularly take up the *zakira*'s role, many begin their careers while still in school, with the support and encouragement of their families. Others start later, after marriage or children or beginning a job. There is no set pattern. Once a *zakira* begins, her work is intimately linked to demand. As women see and appreciate the way she leads an event, some will invite her to gatherings they or their friends and relatives organize. The leader's popularity grows as she builds up a loyal following, her circle of invitations expanding as positive reports about her performance spread by word of mouth. Some women have steady careers from the time they begin giving orations. Others may persist for a time, then stop or take a break. A woman may interrupt her career because of demands of school, job, or health, or, most commonly, because of choosing to give more time to family or children.

For those who make a commitment to this leadership role, there are demands. These include pressures for time, balancing home and family commitments, transport, and maintaining religious purity. Time pressures for a popular *zakira* can be intense during "the season." In Hyderabad a *zakira* might speak at four, five, or even six *majalis* a day during the main two-month mourning period, addressing anywhere from a dozen to several hundred people on each occasion. Those who are in particular demand—and can free themselves of work and family commitments—sometimes travel outside of Hyderabad for part or all of the Muharram period, preaching to Shia communities in Europe, Africa, North America, Australia, or other parts of India. Each commitment that a *zakira* makes requires time to prepare an oration, to travel to the venue, to participate in the event and deliver the sermon, and to mingle with hosts and guests afterwards. One of the biggest challenges for a successful *zakira,* then, is having enough time to keep up with the demand. Keeping family members abreast of scheduling details is also a challenge. A popular orator will move from *majlis* to *majlis* during the peak months of Muharram and Safar, and her family may be unable to contact her during the day. Indeed they may not even know exactly where she is. I remember trying to contact Jamila Jafri during the month of Safar in order to clarify a few points in my research. Over the course of a week I phoned three times and dropped by her house an equal number of times. Still I could not catch her. As a woman in her sixties, Jamila has the trust of her extended family and is used to arranging her schedule and traveling independently. Younger women often need to be more explicit with parents or in-laws about their whereabouts in order to be able to travel freely.

Absences from the home can be demanding since most Indian women—on their own or with other women in a joint family—hold a primary responsibility for running their households. Most adult women, even those with careers outside the home, see their primary occupation as caring for a home and family. Unlike their male counterparts who are supported by women who cook for them, care for their needs, and look after their home and children, female orators must creatively address the issue of domestic support. How a *zakira* handles this aspect of her work depends upon two main factors: the support she receives at home from her husband and extended family (or her family of birth if she is not married), and her family circumstances, including her age and stage in the life cycle. For example, when a woman is first married and living with her in-laws (as most do), her new family may be concerned about long unsupervised absences from home and may limit her ability to travel independently without her husband or female relatives accompanying her. When she has young children, her primary energy and time may go toward caring for them and contributing to the household work. If the family has economic needs, or the woman has a career, she may hold a job that occupies portions of her day and takes her outside the home. The women who find it easiest to make time available to perform as a *zakira* are usually those who live in a large or extended family with other females in the home to assist with household tasks and those who have families with sufficient income to employ household servants.

Many *zakiras* struggle to balance home and family commitments, and the busiest tend to be those who are relatively free of the work of child bearing and rearing, and who have a degree of stability, familiarity, and respect within the joint family of which most are part. Older women usually have greater freedom of movement than do younger ones, partly because those women's child-related responsibilities are over and partly because family and society see older women as more stable and less sexually available than younger ones and hence exert less control over their movements. Middle-aged or older women also seem to have greater experience and confidence in navigating patriarchal social systems, whether in the family or in the larger society. Thus, as Nancy Tapper (1978, 377) noted in her study of an Iranian tribal community, female leadership is profoundly influenced by a woman's age and stage of life. Society's vigilance around younger women's movements, and women's primary responsibilities as caregivers for children and other family members, profoundly impact the pool of potential *zakiras*. This situation contrasts sharply with the situation of male aspirants who throughout their life cycle are relatively free to travel and interact socially and are less burdened by home-based responsibilities.

Gender also impacts practical issues such as transportation. Most women in Indian society are not completely independent when it comes to movement, relying on rides from others or on systems of paid or public transport. Transportation can be hard to coordinate with a busy schedule. Some women request their hosts to arrange a vehicle, some get around the city using Hyderabad's network of motorized rickshaw taxis, and others have their own vehicles or make arrangements for a driver to take them from event to event. One *zakira* I knew paid a rickshaw driver a regular salary during the "season" to be her dedicated driver. This issue may become less pressing for a younger generation of middle-class women who are learning to drive motor scooters or mopeds in increasing numbers. Female drivers, including those who are modestly veiled, are becoming a more visible part of the dense traffic on Hyderabad roads, contributing to a social climate in which women are accepted as drivers, not just passengers.

Another gender-influenced demand that shapes a woman's ability to exercise her role as a religious leader is ritual purity. Most Shias recognize that occupying the orator's pulpit (*minbar*) is a serious responsibility that demands preparation, prayer, and purification. As Keith Guy Hjortshoj observed in his study of Shia practice in North India, there is a certain amount of sanctity associated with the *minbar*, and speakers generally perform ritual ablutions before mounting it (1977, 127–28). While both men and women see religious purity as a requirement, most men understand it to refer to one's thoughts and conduct, a *zakir* being well aware that he is an example in the community and must be above reproach. Although this is also true for women, the main focus for most female orators is the presence or absence of "impure" blood, for its association with being unclean renders one unfit to occupy the highly respected pulpit. A menstruating woman or one who has just had a baby cannot, then, perform as a *zakira* until she is again ritually pure. For a popular *zakira*, this regular physiologically imposed break from her role can be very inconvenient, even exasperating, for it sometimes falls in the middle of the main mourning period—the busiest and most demanding time of the year. It is not surprising, then, that many *zakiras* see menopause in a positive light, for there is now no monthly flow of blood to interrupt their important leadership tasks. The availability of birth-control pills also means that it is possible for women to have some control over the timing of their menstrual cycle. Some Hyderabad Shias use contraceptive pills when timing pilgrimage events including the hajj, but I am uncertain of the extent to which they are used to assist *zakiras* in remaining "clean" during the main mourning period.

The most important demand for a successful orator is to retain the support of a community of listeners, for she is dependent on her audience for future invitations—a relationship that influences the talks she chooses to give from the pulpit. As long as a *zakira* remains effective, engaging, and available, meeting the challenges of her chosen work, she will continue to be in demand. When a popular *zakira* decides to limit or curtail her career, she generally does so by accepting fewer and fewer invitations. However, not all orators choose to bring their ritual leadership to an end; some continue to occupy the *minbar* well into old age. Among these, some *zakiras* become less effective: their narration may wander or they may give bits and pieces of stories and traditions that do not fit together coherently. Leaders who "comes to the end of their creativity," as one woman described it, gradually decline in popularity as the ritual organizers seek out others who have greater power to move an audience. Still, a *zakira* who is past her prime generally continues to be supported by loyal friends and family who respect her past leadership and value her presence at gatherings held in smaller family circles.

Qualities and Qualifications of a Good *Zakira*

Becoming a *zakira* is only partly about making a choice and meeting demands. There is also the question of the qualities necessary to fulfill the role. The most basic requirement is knowledge of the stories around the events of Karbala. As Akhtar Zaidi, one of the most prolific male *zakirs* in Hyderabad, remarked in an interview with Toby M. Howarth, "If a person can recite the narrative of the Sufferings of the Karbala martyrs, then he (and one should add, she) is a *zakir*" (2001, 89). At the most basic level it is that simple: a leader must have sufficient knowledge of Karbala so that she can inspire the community in remembering and mourning. Yet, as Howarth has pointed out, at least three other fields of knowledge are also important in helping a *zakira* be successful: the Quran, particularly passages that are important for Shia exegesis; the *hadith* material (the recorded sayings and actions of Prophet, the imams, and Fatima); and narratives of the early stages of Shia history.

A successful *zakira* must also have good rhetorical skills, for her oration (*zikr*) tends to be the main inspiring focus of a remembrance gathering and often occupies more than half the time in an average assembly of an hour and a half. Presence of mind and confidence are essential, given that a *zakira* presents her ideas and relates her stories without the use of notes. She also needs to know how to pace her delivery and assess the needs of the crowd. Finally, and most important, she must be able to rouse the emotional pitch of her listeners. Although she may touch upon a broad range of religious issues in the discursive portion of her *zikr*, her role in the *majlis* is not successful unless she helps lead her audience back to the plains of Karbala, where the pathos and tragedy are so great that faithful believers are overcome by grief. The following description of a *majlis* held at Yadgar Husayni in 1995 on the morning of Arbain (the fortieth day following the tenth of Muharram) offers an example of this process.

> Yadgar Husayni's cavernous hall is filled with women: slim young girls, stooped worn figures, mothers with small children, whole families—but no men. Nearly two thousand women will gather for the *majlis* which is to start at 9:30 A.M. Gone is the fresh white cloth that has covered the floor since the beginning of Muharram; today women stand or sit on the bare stone floor. Two silver tomb replicas (*zaris*) enclosed in glass cases—one the tomb of Husayn, the other the tomb of Zaynab—have been pulled from their usual alcove and stand alone in the very center of the hall. The central icons are a reminder of the partnership of Husayn and Zaynab. Visitors sprinkle flower petals or place garlands on the *zaris*; others lie sobbing across them, and still others kiss the fragrant flowers or press their cheeks against them tenderly. Many of the women are weeping; all are solemn and dressed in black, the color of Muharram. After a while a small group sits down cross-legged before a microphone and begins to recite the *marsiyas.* One mournful elegy after another fills the hall; today many focus on Zaynab, her grief, her courage. The crowd sighs and weeps and moans. More women fill the hall.

Twenty minutes later Jamila, the *zakira* for this *majlis,* steps to a microphone at the head of the hall. The room is quiet except for the sound of shuddering sobs. Beneath the veil of the delicate black sari that covers Jamila's hair, her face is lined with grief. Today she gives no reasoned sermon; the *minbar* has been pushed aside, and Jamila stands alone before the microphone, facing the women and the two tomb replicas standing in their unadorned simplicity at the center of the hall. She begins with a prayer—a short passage from the Quran—and then cries: "It is a day of cruel parting." Weeping, sweating, she laments the death of the martyrs, the loss that leaves Zaynab to carry on alone. There is no intellectualizing, no carefully reasoned sermon, only deep emotion. People avidly attend to the *zakira's* words; only a few are hiding their faces, immersed in their own private grief. Overhead the fans slow to a halt as the electrical supply is cut, a common occurrence in summertime Hyderabad. The microphone, however, is hooked up to a battery-powered generator, so the oration is not interrupted. For twenty minutes Jamila stands, describing the cruelties of a family torn apart by tragic violence. At times she can hardly speak through her tears. Finally she wails, "They are going!" Choking with emotion, she recreates the loss of the captives who are being taken off to Kufa. The women in the hall are with her, responding fervently: wailing, weeping, many slapping their thighs in self-inflicted pain. Jamila continues to call out amid the crescendo, her voice cracking with emotion. Finally she brings her oration to a close with a sobbing call for blessing on Husayn, Abbas, Ali Asghar, Zaynab, and others of the suffering family of the Prophet.

As the *zakira*'s voice dies away, the hall resounds with the wailing of the crowd. Then a gray-haired woman with a pure strong voice begins the *nauha,* the sharp slapping beat of the *matam* keeping the rhythm. A group fanned out around her sings the verses with feeling, and the chorus is picked up by all in a growing crescendo of voices: "Zaynab, I am coming!" The words hang in the air, conveying infinite sadness as the women promise that they too will be at Zaynab's side as she is forced to part with all those she has loved best in this world. The dozen women leading the chorus are pounding their chests with resounding force, many doing the punishing double-handed *matam.* As the *nauha* draws to a close, the hall resounds with the passionate cry: "Husayn! Husayn! Husayn! Husayn!" Then, in a sound more poignant than words, there is the haunting echo of thousands of hands striking sharp blows to the chest, the rhythm pulsing, driving, and intensely moving.

In this vignette we see that a good *zakira,* like a good actor, takes one beyond one's surroundings, transporting the listener back in time. If a skilled thespian plays Hamlet, audience members no longer see the actor before them but feel as if they are in the castle experiencing Hamlet's anguish. In the same way the voice of the *zakira* becomes the voices of Sakina, Abbas, and Zaynab. The barrier between past and present dissolves and one experiences the primacy of a loss that took place fourteen centuries ago. As the *zakira* Jamila takes on the voice of Zaynab, wailing for her brother, her son, her family, she becomes every woman who has suffered the loss of a beloved. She is a mother, a sister, a daughter, a wife—raw with the pain of losing a child, a friend, or a family member. Hearing her anguish, it is almost impossible not to identify; she becomes one's own voice, naked with emotion, as one confronts the immensity of loss and the inescapable tragedies of life. In the hands of a good *zakira* an oration becomes a moment of connection and catharsis. The *zakira* becomes a pathway to connect with and express the community's collective memory.

A successful *zakira* also exercises tremendous skill in gauging a crowd, making wise choices about the style and length of her presentation. In the example above Jamila knows that on this major day of mourning—the important fortieth day following the anniversary of the martyrdom—there are many *majalis* planned as well as a major public procession (*julus*) through the Old City. Most people will be busy at home conducting the rituals of taking down and putting away the *alams* that have adorned their homes and thus bringing to a close the main mourning

Overcome by grief, a religious orator (zakira) *pauses in telling the story of Karbala.*

season. A long speech would be a distraction on Arbain, and Jamila keeps her oration relatively short. She also chooses to stick to the emotional narration of the Karbala story, avoiding an overly intellectual prelude. This heightens the sense of the tragedy: it is no ordinary day when one needs to build up to the story of loss. Rather it is a day that epitomizes quick and cruel partings, touching the very heart of people's faith. The *zakira*'s passionate preaching and display of grief rouses the crowd, successfully paving the way for a seamless transition into the *matam*-punctuated lamentation poetry. The pitch of emotion rises through her oration and climaxes as the crowd joins in a collective expression of grief, guided by the leaders of the rhythmic poetry recitation.

Although it is possible to analyze the components of effective leadership by observing how the most successful *zakiras* operate, I wanted to know how ordinary women judged a *zakira*'s effectiveness and success. I therefore asked women in the community, "What makes a good *zakira*?" I found the answers illuminating.

"Knowledge," replied one young mother who proudly identified her family as orthodox, observing all the commemorative days of the family of the Prophet. "The *zakira* should know the gist of the whole Islam: the history, the Quran, the traditions. And the oration [*zikr*] of Ali should embellish her whole talk." In other words a good *zakira* is one who draws deeply on a wealth of tradition from respected sources, intricately weaving into her talk the words and examples of Imam Ali, revered by Shias for his goodness, his leadership, and his loyalty to the Prophet.

"Confidence," answered a university graduate who recently completed a course in fashion design. "She should be able to speak in front of an audience with ease." She took another bite of the food we were sharing and added, "And knowledge. She should be familiar with the whole of Islam."

"See, anyone can read the traditions," explained one young teacher. "We've grown up with these stories our whole lives. We hear them every year. Even I can relate them." She paused to give me an earnest look. "But a *zakira* has something more. When she relates the *masaib* [the emotional latter part of the oration] . . . she should be crying." She stops for a moment, thinking. "Another thing. She must practice what she preaches. That is very important."

"A *zakira* must be religious," answered a grandmother who is the respected mother-in-law in a traditional joint family home. "She must do her *namaz* [ritual prayers], *rosa* [fasting], all that. She must have knowledge, right from the time of the Prophet onwards. The whole Islamic history. She must be able to explain why a thing is, how a thing is. There should never be any doubt when people ask her. . . . She must teach what Islam means, . . . what it *really* means." She paused, searching, then began to narrate a well-known story from the life of the Prophet. "Each day, as the Prophet passed through a particular street, an old woman would throw garbage on his head from her window. The Prophet never said a word, even when curses were hurled down as well. One day he passed along the street but was not assaulted in the usual way. The second and the third day were also quiet, prompting the Prophet to stop and make concerned enquiries about the woman, who turned out to be ill." The mother-in-law paused to see if I had gotten the point. "Islam teaches us to be kind. A *zakira* must teach us Islam."

"The most important thing is a person's interest. Her enthusiasm. Without strong will power, she will not have the strength to become a *zakira*." The woman who made these comments is a mother in her thirties who works for a Shia social-service organization. "You see none of this is taught in schools or colleges, so she must learn on her own. When she is a child, her parents and elders teach her. But at a certain time the child must decide to learn for herself. It's a question of interest. A child may be good in school but have no opportunity to really express herself. Or she may already be a leader in school and this quality of leadership carries over."*

To summarize: a successful *zakira* according to many women in the community is one who confidently and knowledgeably teaches the intricacies of Shia faith and history. She knows the "whole of Islam," its subtle messages as well as its main precepts, and never hesitates in her replies to people's questions about religion. She is herself a religious woman, known to "practice what she preaches" from the regular duties of faith to the guiding moral principles. A dedicated and successful communicator, she provides an emotional recounting of the tragedies of the family of the Prophet that not only demonstrates her own grief but also moves her audience to tears. Finally, she has a strong interest and enthusiasm, for in pursuing knowledge and gaining the skills characteristic of a good *zakira* she must "learn on her own."

Gaining Religious Knowledge

How do women gain the knowledge and training needed to be effective in their leadership roles? At the time of my research in Hyderabad from 1994 to 2002, *zakira* training was still largely informal, although this situation is starting to change. For generations, as in Muslim societies around the world, girls acquired most of their religious knowledge at home, usually through elders in the family who were knowledgeable about prayers and household rituals. For instance, a woman now in her sixties recalled learning Arabic from her mother who would make her recite from the Quran daily before breakfast. Some elite households drew upon male family members to teach Arabic or Persian; others engaged tutors—usually men, but occasionally women—to assist girls in learning these foundational languages.

In Hyderabad the women-only *ashurkhana* Yadgar Husayni started holding formal religious classes for Shia girls in the 1940s well before the shrine itself came into existence. Women in their sixties recalled their parents sending them in covered carriages to attend the weekly Sunday school held at women's homes. At its peak in the 1970s Yadgar Husayni's morning religious school was regularly attended by 100 to 150 girls ranging in age from five to fifteen. Today enrollment is half that, a drop women explain by pointing to new options for religious instruction at Shia-run schools, increased pressure and commitments for secular study (including tuition classes), and the distraction of pastimes like television.

The syllabus at Yadgar Husayni's religious school focuses on religious concepts that underlie students' faith, including Shia traditions, scriptural verses, and

*All quoted statements taken from interviews conducted in Hyderabad during June 1997.

prayers of supplication, blessing, and praise—many of which the girls commit to memory. Students also master Arabic as well as Urdu (the mother tongue for most students but one that few know how to read or write), with the brightest girls studying in depth Quranic verses and accompanying commentary with the guidance and help of their teachers. All this study is useful for the budding *zakira,* as is the small collection of religious texts and devotional books that Yadgar Husayni maintains. Still, even though the women's association that runs the school has as its expressly stated aim "To try to stimulate, especially among young educated girls, the knowledge of oration (*zakiri*)" (Anjuman Niswan Barkat-e-Aza 1981, 5), it has not been systematic in pursuing this goal. There is, for example, no guidance or mentoring for preparing and delivering religious oratory, a feature that is part of the training for boys at one of Hyderabad's religious schools (Howarth, 2001, 90). This absence of a formalized system of training may be due to a lack of organization in developing a methodology, the time limitations of teachers, or simply the fact that women do not feel any pressing need for formalized instruction since informal education has been working well so far.

New options for women's formal religious instruction continue to emerge, including online resources, short courses, and all-women institutions of religious learning (*madrasas* or *hawzas*). This change reflects a worldwide expansion of religious education opportunities for Muslim women over the last several decades. Among Indian Sunnis, for example, there is a shift from providing basic instruction at home, in neighborhood mosques, or at school to offering specialized education that culminates in a degree in religious studies such as *alima* (masc. *ulama*) or *muftia* (masc. *mufti*). Eight to ten percent (more than three hundred) of India's estimated thirty-five thousand *madrasas* are female institutions; all were established after 1950, and their number continues to grow (Winkelmann 2005b, 36). Among Shias there are relatively fewer options for formal religious education. Although documentation is scanty, it seems that Jamiat al-Zahra, established in Lucknow in 1990, was the first dedicated school to offer women advanced religious training. The Hawza al-Imam al-Qaim (Islamic School of the Twelfth Imam) in Hyderabad's Old City was founded in 2001 and runs a four-year program of part-time evening classes for young women, as well as a full-time study program for young men. In 2005–2006 fifty-two female students were enrolled; six received full five-year scholarships to study at Iran's Jamiat al-Zahra, the highly respected women's seminary founded in Qum in 1984. The links with Iranian-based women's seminaries continue to grow, building on well-established historic ties between Persia and India, although they develop at a slower pace than in other countries such as Pakistan and Lebanon (Abou Zahab 2008, Abisaab 2006). It is still too early to gauge the impact of these educational exchanges on women's ritual gatherings in Hyderabad.

In general, then, it is still true to say that the majority of Hyderabad women do not follow a formal process in learning how to be *zakiras.* Several people with whom I spoke observed that young orators tend to "come up on their own." Their informal paths to religious competency and leadership tend to be as variable as the characteristics of those who have chosen to take up the role: some started their careers as teenagers or in college; others assumed leadership later in life when their children entered school or they became established in a job. Most, however, name their experiences as young women or girls as seminal to their preparation. Common components include exposure to religious gatherings, playing minor performative roles in rituals, the support and encouragement of family, the presence of role models and mentors, and initial opportunities to function as an orator.

The most basic foundation for a *zakira*'s functioning as a religious leader is her personal experience of ritual traditions. This exposure to the everyday practices of Shia faith usually starts quite early, for children are an integral part of social interactions in Indian society. Babies and young children accompany female relatives at home-based rituals, local pilgrimages, and community gatherings. Thus, by the time they enter their teens, many children will have witnessed and participated in hundreds of remembrance gatherings, giving them a feel for the rhythm of these rituals. One has only to sit through a commemoration gathering to witness this foundation being laid, as the following brief description of a *majlis* held on the eighth of Muharram (1997) shows.

The melodic chanting, "Husayn! Husayn!" reverberates through the room. Approximately sixty black-clad women sit cross-legged on the floor behind a slatted bamboo screen that separates the elongated alcove of the women's area from the main hall. Inside, nearly two hundred men are getting to their feet as the *majlis* oration comes to a close and the haunting refrain of a *nauha* rings out over the crowd. The melody is achingly sad and the words paint a picture of isolation, pain, and bravery as the martyrs embrace their tragic fate. Some of the women have now also risen to their feet; others remain sitting, including a woman cradling an infant across her folded legs. Tears glisten on her cheeks as she gently rocks her baby. A few women are talking among themselves, and one summons a child, drawing the little one to her lap. From the men's side of the screen the beat of the *nauha* pulses stronger, the crowd keeping the rhythm with blows to their chests. Between the slats and through the bodies one catches a glimpse of those leading the recitation. A group of teen-aged boys and young men cluster around two men near the microphone. Many are beating their chests with stunning force, chanting the chorus in ringing voices. Now most of the women are on their feet, many raising their voices in the chorus, their hands marking time on their bodies.

Several women adjust their modest shawls (*dupattas*) so that they can slap their chests with little intervening cushion. Others keep the beat with a less vigorous but steady rhythm. Slowly the recitation reaches a crescendo. A girl of about eight years old squeezes by, weaving her way through the crowd with a toddler on her hip. The woman who was cradling the baby is now standing, her child nestled against a shoulder. The young mother's hand gently taps out the rhythm on the baby's back. The child sleeps on. Lips moving silently, the woman mouths the chorus, tears streaming down her face. As the hall echoes with rhythmic grieving, her hand keeps a steady rhythm on the back of her child, pulsing like a heartbeat.

As this brief description demonstrates, it is most often in the laps of mothers, grandmothers, and aunts that a child first feels the pulse of the *matam* and hears the wailing of parents and relations. As the child grows, she becomes accustomed to the routines of the "crying parties" and moves easily in the ritual environment, much like the eight-year-old girl in the description above who made her way through the crowd with her sibling on her hip. This exposure does not systematically impart the details about faith and practice but it provides basic knowledge about how one conducts and leads rituals, as well as an easy familiarity with the basic stories of the faith.

A second powerful root in a young woman's development as a *zakira* is active participation in the rituals. Many *zakiras* describe adults who have encouraged their early involvement in the *majlis* or *jeshn*. A parent or relative may give a girl an opportunity to hold a revered icon during a procession, to read a story about one of the *Ahl-e-Bayt,* or to help recite remembrance poetry. This last activity is a fairly common first step for developing leadership. Commemoration poetry tends to be recited together with others, giving children an opportunity to perform before an audience with the support of a larger group. Parents sometimes proudly invite their children to recite at home during ritual events or when relatives or friends are visiting. It is not unusual for young girls to collect remembrance odes to recite on such occasions. One woman described her experience of this kind of informal training: "My father and mother made me memorize couplets [of poetry]. That's how we [the children] started. At the *majlis,* the children would always recite first. It was a way of building our confidence. . . . So at an early age my mother and father began to teach us these things. By the time I was a preteen I was reciting praise poems (*qasidas*) and elegies (*marsiyas*). I would be the accompanying vocalist (*bazu*) for my mother as she recited" (interview, Toronto, 6 April 2001). For this woman and many others, reciting poetry helped build confidence in addressing a crowd, particularly when one has the example and support of her parents and relatives. In this woman's case her mother and father were themselves active participants in religious gatherings and encouraged their children to do the same. Such positive ritual experiences strengthen the foundation for women's leadership at a later time.

Family support is thus a strong factor in the success of many *zakiras.* Adults generally take great pride in their children's ability to deliver a religious talk, as was stressed by a young *zakira* whom I casually met in a Shia locality in Hyderabad. One evening in the Old City I was stopped just outside a friend's home by a confident young woman of about eighteen. Her long patterned shawl identified her as a Shia. She and the five veiled women whom she smilingly introduced as her mother, her aunt, and her sisters had seen me briefly at a large gathering at the home of a common friend. After asking my name and offering hers, Miryam asked me why I was studying her community and was delighted to discover that a "foreigner" was interested in her faith. She explained that tomorrow she, her sister, and her mother would be traveling to Karbala for a pilgrimage (*ziyarat*). She was visibly excited at the prospect of her first visit to Iraq. For her mother, she explained, it was the second trip, and her aunt had already been there five times. As we talked, and she learned of my interest in women's leadership, she proudly asserted, "I am a *zakira,*" and went on to explain what had made her a good one. "It is the people around you. The elders. My father helped me a lot, he is a *zakir.* Both my parents give a lot of support. They encourage you. They tell you the stories, give you things to read. Others too: when you first give a talk (*zikr*) they say, 'Good for you; that was well done.' Like that they make you feel good. But it is something that has to be in your heart. At first I was not so interested, but then I started to feel to do it" (interview, Hyderabad, 17 June 1997).

Miryam stressed that a good *zakira* needs a personal inclination to take up the role. To be successful one needs to be self-motivated: one must "feel to do it" or have it "in your heart." Yet her parents' support was also significant. Miryam credited their encouragement and their ability to offer her potentially useful resources such as stories and "things to read." Her mother, her aunt, and a wider circle of relatives provided words of encouragement ("Good for you!" "Well done") that were especially helpful in the early stages of her career as a *zakira.* The family had also given opportunities for Miryam to visit sites that are sacred to Shias the world over, broadening her exposure and experiences. In addition, the fact that her father is a *zakir* means that this confident young woman has a close personal role model and mentor as she develops her own style of sermon delivery. Like Miryam, many of today's successful *zakiras* have a parent or relative who is an established orator and has, at times, lent them advice or support.

Perhaps the most essential part of the informal training process for *zakiras* is an opportunity to lead remembrance gatherings. At the early stage of an orator's development, it is usually parents and relatives who provide these opportunities.

A fledgling orator can draw upon much information—written, oral, and experiential—as she prepares for and delivers her talk. She often chooses to keep her *zikr* short, selecting a simple topic for the discursive part of her oration. While some women excel from their first performance, most *zakiras* take time to develop their skill and power. It is mainly experience and dedicated preparation that make the difference between a young woman who gives a narration in the presence of her family and relations and one whom the community recognizes as a knowledgeable *zakira*. Each performance provides an occasion to deepen her knowledge of history, tradition, and the personalities of the *Ahl-e-Bayt*, as well as to advance her skills in developing a theme, presenting her ideas clearly, and touching people's emotions.

A *zakira* draws on several sources for her knowledge and information, oral tradition being one of the most common. As one *zakira* explained, "We hear the stories from other learned orators and then pass them on ourselves. This is how the authority [of the stories] is transmitted" (interview, Hyderabad, 26 September 1996). The advent of audio and video recording and the Internet has given *zakiras* the opportunity to listen to a much wider array of learned scholars than previous generations were able to hear. These orations are a primary source for stories about the *Ahl-e-Bayt* or points of religious belief. Books offer an additional resource and a wide variety is available. *Zakiras* today have access to multilingual editions of the Quran, for example, allowing them to read the revealed text in their mother tongue of Urdu alongside the Arabic, deepening their understanding of the scripture. They can also use religious treatises and study materials that have been translated from the classical languages of Arabic and Persian. Shia publishing companies in India, Iran, and London have produced relatively affordable books and pamphlets, including condensations of Shia history, books of prayers, narrations of stories about the imams and other members of the Prophet's family, and explanations of aspects of theology, law, and religious practice. All these are available in local bookshops and often circulate informally among friends and family or accumulate in small library collections such as the one at Yadgar Husayni.

As one well-educated Shia woman in her fifties commented, these resources mean that today's young *zakiras* are better equipped to offer a reasoned discourse than were their counterparts of a generation or more ago: "What has happened now is that there is a whole class of *zakiras* who have come up. They have studied the Quran much more, they've read the Urdu translation much more than my mother's generation. They have taken time for their studies, some even go to Iran—even for a month—to learn more. They also read books; there are many Urdu translations now of Persian books. . . . My younger sister has done this. She started reciting *majlis* when she was in medical college" (interview, Toronto, 6 April 2001).

Compared to *zakiras* who saw their primary task as offering an emotional recounting of the Karbala story, many of today's orators make use of a wider array of religious resources. A number of highly motivated women seek out opportunities for exposure and study programs abroad. Still the process of gaining religious knowledge continues to be largely informal and self-directed, requiring a high level of personal dedication and commitment and the support of family mentors.

Rewards and the Issue of Payment

The work and responsibility of being a *zakira* come with certain rewards. One is the respect of the community, which may take the form of receiving special attention at weddings or other private gatherings, being invited to speak at secular occasions, or receiving special gifts at times of major feasts. Another tangible reward is the "gift" or "present" known as *hidayat* or *nazrana.* These are words used in religious circumstances when people feel that the word *price* or *fee* is inappropriate. For example, one is never charged a price for a Quran but pays a *hidayat.* When a woman invites a *zakira* from outside the family to lead a remembrance gathering, she usually offers her a monetary gift (a hundred rupees or more) in addition to meeting her traveling expenses. Many early *zakiras* seem not to have received cash; rather their hosts demonstrated their appreciation and respect with a special meal and/or gifts of food and sometimes household goods or clothing.

The issue of *hidayat,* however, can be contentious, for there are people who perceive a tension in performing a religious act and receiving payment for it. The feeling is that accepting money turns the deed into a commercial transaction that lessens or negates its religious value. More than one woman with whom I spoke related the story of an early Hyderabad *zakira* who reportedly decided to stop her career as an orator rather than accept payment. One of the woman's peers had tried to encourage her to accept cash gifts, as that woman did herself, saying that it would look bad if she was taking money while the other woman always refused. "I won't turn it into a trade," the older *zakira* reportedly replied. From that time on she eschewed all outside engagements and confined her orations to events within her family. Some of today's *zakiras* share the feeling that one should not introduce money into what is essentially a religious service. One earnest college-aged student told me, "I don't take any money for it [performing as a *zakira*]. Even the auto fare I pay from my pocket. I also only take one *tabarruk.* Some other *zakiras* take extra from the hosts. I accept only one. I have been encouraged like this. [She gestures at her mother]. She has told me that it's a good thing to do this without taking money. They have guided me like that" (interview, Hyderabad, 11 June 1997).

Yet the role of *zakira* involves a certain financial outlay. A popular orator who daily attends three, four, or five gatherings during the busy Muharram season can incur significant transport costs. She may also need extra domestic help or family support to carry out the many household tasks she is unable to do. Although the choice not to accept payment may be viable for some women, particularly younger ones who speak only occasionally and are supported by parents or relatives, it is difficult to see how a popular *zakira* can afford to subsidize personally her ongoing participation in Hyderabad's exceedingly busy mourning season. In order to find out more, I talked with Jamila, one of Hyderabad's popular *zakiras,* about her experiences with and perceptions of *hidayat.*

> People have been taking *hidayat* all along; right from the beginning everyone has taken it. Some depend on it, and it is "good money"; it is very honest money. It is not gotten through corrupted means but is earned by reciting God's name. Personally, what happened to me was that I came from an upper-middle-class family, so I was not dependent on this money for my livelihood. When I first started speaking, I spoke mainly for the family, so it didn't come up. Then I started becoming more popular, and people started offering. But I would refuse. For a very long time I did not take the money. After a period of time I was asked to speak at Bombay. When this happened there were actual negotiations: they said, we'll pay you so much for your "to and fro" charges, and TA [travel allowance], DA [dearness allowance], and a fee for the *majlis.* I was excited. Not because of the money, but because of the chance to go and talk at Bombay. The money was not important to me. I had a lecturer's post at the university. I was earning well; at least it was good enough for me. Now this may not be true for others.
>
> Once I had taken *hidayat* at Bombay, I decided, why should there be any difference? And I started accepting this money in Hyderabad, too. Up to this date, I have never asked anyone to give—you can ask anyone about this. But I have not refused to take what people have offered. People usually give me an amount inside an envelope. I don't look at the amount. At first I was hesitant to spend it. So I would put it there [she waves toward another room], in one place, kept away. Soon there were so many envelopes. So I told the children, when I die you can perform my last rights with this money. But then I decided to use the money to go on a *ziyarat* [pilgrimage]. I took out all the money and went on a *ziyarat.* But I do so many *majalis, jeshn,* and other functions in Ramzan, in Muharram, . . . it just kept accumulating. I went to London, to so many places. Still it keeps accumulating. I've used it like this and still there is money left for the burial [she laughs]. This is my story. I can't speak for others. (Interview, Hyderabad, 18 February 2000).

Jamila's refusal to ask for a fee is typical, for leaders tend to see themselves as performing a religious task and most do not feel comfortable negotiating a fee. Although her social and economic position meant that she did not have to depend upon this money to meet her living costs, others support themselves and their families with their earnings. The money one earns in offering ritual leadership is a gift one can happily accept, as Jamila implies. It is "good money" which is specially blessed, since it is received for performing an important religious service. She and most women who pay or receive *hidayat* see the money as a tangible demonstration of the favor of God and those beloved to God—the *Ahl-e-Bayt*—for the work she performs.

Summary

The *zakira* is the "rememberer," the one who assumes responsibility of keeping alive the founding stories of the faith. She also provides the community's link to that epic period, her oration helping believers go back in time to experience the sorrows and joys of the beloved family of the Prophet. Inherited religious knowledge tells women that *zakiras* can also be an important force for change, for whoever takes on the role is linked through history to the strength and action of such early female figures as Zaynab. Women know this, as I discovered one day when I was making my way from a crowded *majlis* in the Old City. I started talking to a middle-aged women next to me, and when she heard that I was interested in women's religious practices she went on to tell me how "Shia women started a revolution." Zaynab mourning in the prison of Damascus, she explained, alerted local women to the fact that the family of the Prophet had been slain. When the women understood what had taken place, they responded by "going on strike": they refused to do housework until their men challenged Yazid on the matter. When the unrest grew and men started to ask Yazid difficult questions, he was forced to set the captives free. Thus, my companion asserted, women's actions set change in motion, laying the groundwork for revolt in the Umayyad empire (interview, Hyderabad, 26 June 1997).

The sense of female power that resides in Shia collective memory can be a potent force, as is demonstrated by a story related by one of Pakistan's Shia leaders, Agha Syed Hamid Ali Shah Moosavi. Agha Ali Shah tells of his father Syed Budhey Shah who, before the days of India's partition, lived in Sialkot during a period when Muharram processions had been outlawed. One year Budhey Shah's active lobbying against this prohibition resulted in the colonial authorities preemptively arresting all the male members of his family before the main mourning days. On Ashura the police were astonished to see women take the men's place: they processed into the streets leading an iconic symbol of Husayn's horse and beat their chests in time to chanted refrains such as "*Ya* Husayn!" The account concludes with a report that the police commissioner abruptly reversed his position and issued a license for the procession, noting that "no one could stop a nation the women of which carry such a spirit." The story vividly communicates the power of "rightly-guided women," and Agha Ali Shah clearly credits them with the fact that the Sialkot procession is now a regular Muharram event.*

What influence have female religious leaders had in Hyderabad, and what limitations have curtailed their power? When I asked women about how *zakiras* have impacted the community, I heard stories about how charismatic local leaders have changed religious practice. For example, Nawar, an elderly grandmother, tells how Latif al-Nisa influenced the style of women's mourning assemblies in the 1940s and 1950s. "'These are the mourning rituals (*azadari*) of Husayn,' she [Latif al-Nisa] would say. 'We should not have distinctions between the rich and the poor. We should have the *majlis* in its correct sense.' At that time the women used to wear lots of gold ornaments. What did they do during Muharram? They would wear silver rather than gold!" Nawar, today a respected local elder, shakes her head and laughs at the idea of wearing jewelry during the main twelve-day mourning period. Customs have changed dramatically from those days, and Nawar credits Latif al-Nisa with contributing to that change, including the shift to wearing mourning clothes of simple black. She narrates how as an unmarried school girl she had an unforgettable encounter with Latif al-Nisa when she came to her home one day for a visit. "I can still picture it: she was sitting right as you're sitting with me now. It was the twenty-fourth of Safar . . . I was wearing a black sari with a border and came with a tray to serve her tea. She asked me, 'What is this? Why are you wearing this border on your sari? Don't you have respect for the Imam [Husayn]? Take it off.' I had to tear it off right in front of her. She had that much strength, that much character. We'd do anything for her" (interview, Hyderabad, 4 April 1997).

Nawar's clear memory echoes a story orators sometimes narrate about how Zaynab chastised the women who came to attend the very first *majlis*. "The women of Damascus . . . thought that here was an opportunity for them to show off their ornaments, their pomp and splendour, and their great wealth. But they came in and saw Zaynab sitting on the floor. She lifted her head and said, 'Is this the way that you come to a *majlis* in your city?' They understood what she was saying, and so went back and put on black clothes and returned" (Howarth 2001, 190).

*See the article "Biography of Quaid-i-Millat Jafariya, Pakistan, Agha Syed Hamid Ali Shah Moosavi," by Syed Qamar Haider Zaidi; http://www.tnfj.org.pk/sec/bio.htm (accessed 11 November 2008).

With or without its echo in Shia founding stories, the anecdote about Latif al-Nisa reveals something about female religious leadership and the power to affect change. The charismatic *zakira* framed her ideals about appropriate dress in terms of her listener's personal relationship with a central figure of the faith: "Don't you have respect for the Imam?" she queried. The young woman responded to this question about dress because of her devotion to Husayn and her respect and love for the leader who asked it of her. Indeed, Nawar notes, "we'd do anything for her." Although Latif al-Nisa was undoubtedly only a part of a larger movement for change, her contribution was not insignificant. She was able to have an impact by drawing upon the power of her personality and the wide respect that women held for her role and position.

Around the same period leaders including Latif al-Nisa mobilized women to contribute money to build the women-only *ashurkhana* Yadgar Husayni. The role of *zakiras* was definitely important in spreading the word and encouraging women to construct (and later expand) Yadgar Husayni "for our Imam." As religious leaders, the *zakiras* had the respect of ordinary women, interacted regularly with the community during rituals, and had an accepted and established platform for addressing the community at religious gatherings. It is clear that female ritual leadership has had a substantial impact on the local community, particularly when women unite the power of their personalities with the power of their leadership positions.

Change seems to be most successful when it is tied to people's religious convictions, whether the issue be altering one's style of mourning dress out of respect for the *Ahl-e-Bayt,* contributing money to a cause rewarded and blessed by Husayn or the "Mistress of the Worlds" (Fatima), or even participating in demonstrations against political oppression (Hegland 1990, 189). I have been struck by how rarely women in Hyderabad use their status as orators and religious leaders to highlight progressive issues about which some feel strongly. *Zakiras* seem to be selective about issues they choose to raise publicly. For example, I have talked with leaders who are critical of current ideas about purity and women's religious participation or about certain aspects of the practice of veiling (*hijab*). Despite their private views, they rarely address these topics directly from the pulpit. When I asked one *zakira* about this, she justified a quietist approach by saying that the pace of change is slow—and that things eventually will shift because the current state of affairs is not according to God's intention.

But women also are aware that a *zakira* can be marginalized if she gains a reputation for being too "radical." As Howarth (2001, 264) has noted, the community can exercise a subtle control over what a leader can and cannot say. Audiences occasionally have challenged an orator's position or, in extreme cases, barred her from leading local gatherings. Although this happens very rarely (and most often involves male leaders), most *zakiras* are careful in choosing the causes around which they rally, for an unwise position might jeopardize their reputation as leaders within the community. There thus seem to be limits to how far most women choose to use the influence and power of their position. It can be much less risky to place one's weight behind changes such as shifts in the custom of mourning dress or the construction of a religious shrine than to lobby for changes having support within entrenched power structures.

We get a sense of the furor that can arise when one adopts a stance which contradicts popular perceptions in Toby M. Howarth's brief anecdote about a *zakir*'s remarks on women and purity (2001, 141, note 14). Zaki Baqri, a popular orator, especially among young educated Shias, touched on this topic during a 1997 Hyderabad *majlis,* at which he addressed the topic of "women's rights." In his talk before an assembly of nearly one thousand men and women, he stated that menstruating women could join the community to offer special prayers (*zikr;* here meaning the repeated remembrance of God) during the time of ritual prayer (*namaz*). His position was not wildly radical, for he did not suggest that menstruating women could offer the *namaz,* only that they could pray in an alternative form at the same time. In saying so, however, he stressed that a menstruating woman was not impure and that "no one can take away her right to pray." This point proved to be so controversial that it was immediately brought up with the *zakir* after his talk and was discussed widely in the community after the *majlis* was over.

While Zaki Baqri may have alienated a portion of his audience, his role as ritual leader was not jeopardized because of his wide support by young educated Shias who would continue to invite his leadership. A female orator's situation is different, for her popularity is dependent not just upon her immediate audience but also to some degree upon the wider community of men who can exert control over whether or not the women in their families attend her events. A *zakira* who gains a reputation of being radical can thus be isolated from her base of popularity and lose her impact on the community altogether. Ironically this means that it may be easier for men to raise controversial issues about women's purity or veiling than for women to spearhead direct efforts to bring about community change.

In looking at the impact of women orators, however, it seems clear that even within a restricted arena of power, strong and visible female leadership provides an inspiring role model for girls and women in the community. Drawing upon her research in the Pakistan Shia context, Mary Hegland (1995b, 1995a) has confirmed that women's leadership in the *majlis* is directly tied to feelings of confidence, competence, and self-worth and, consequently, to women's success in the world. Erika Friedl (1994, 166) has echoed this point in her analysis of sex-segregated schools in Iran. In her view girls gain self-confidence in an all-female environment where leadership and decision making are in the hands of women.

In contrast, when girls inhabit a space dominated by male students, leaders, and authority figures, even subjects of study and models of learning reflect masculine emphases and female self-esteem declines. The same is true of the *majlis* environment. Female religious leadership not only offers visible role models; it also shapes the very character of the ritual, for a *zakira* expresses a feminine worldview even through the topics she chooses for her oration. A middle-aged woman described the gender difference this way: "Often women are very practical in the way they address the topic. For example, relating *hadith* which are very family-related, interpersonal. There is one [which says] that the smile of a parent for her child is worth a thousand of the spiritual rewards (*sawab*) of doing the pilgrimage. And the smile of a child for a parent is worth a thousand *sawab* of the pilgrimage. Like that. We didn't hear these things earlier [in *majalis* led by men]" (interview, Toronto, 6 April 2001).

Female religious leadership has no single face but is inhabited by a large informal network of women ranging from those who make careers of oration to those who act as *zakiras* only from time to time. Yet whoever plays the role is linked through history to the strength and action of early figures such as Zaynab and Fatima. Female religious leaders, whether acting in history or in contemporary ritual, offer women inspiration and a point of reference in their lives. As the sociologist and activist Farida Shaheed (1995, 87–91) has pointed out, this is crucially important, with women's emotional health being linked to the presence of powerful and affirming models of feminine leadership, initiative, and strength. In Shaheed's opinion positive role models offer women the chance to dream of alternative lives or potential change. She identifies the absence of such role models in Pakistan (Sunni) society as a key factor in the lack of public mobilization on women's issues, calling it one of the most debilitating forms of oppression. In the Hyderabad Shia community, strong female leadership rooted in sacred history has catalyzed vibrant and active female participation in religious rituals. It has also contributed to the obvious confidence of many local women, most visibly expressed in the accomplishment of founding and running Yadgar Husayni.

· CHAPTER 5 ·

The *Alam*—A Symbol of Presence

Of all the religious symbols that carry meaning for Hyderabad's Shias, the most ubiquitous is the ritual object known as the *alam*. As we have seen, this emblematic crest or metalwork "standard" is closely associated with sacred spaces (such as Yadgar Husayni) and ritual performances (such as the *majlis* or *jeshn*). Moreover, Shia children are taught the primacy of this symbol from the very beginning of their religious education. The popular Indian religious primer *Imamiyah Dinyat* (2001, 1:8), for example, teaches that "Allah is our God," "Islam is our religion," "the twelve Imams are our guide," and "the *alam* is our sign (*nishan*)." The popularity of the *alam* is not limited to South Asia. As Peter Chelkowski (1986, 212) noted in his survey of popular mourning rituals, the *alam* is the most important object in Muharram processions worldwide.

David Morgan (2005, 50) has reminded us that religious images often serve as a type of "external scaffolding" for a concentrated interior experience. In other words, seeing is a practice that allows the viewer to bring a focused consciousness to central internalized realities. This is especially true when the believer intermingles seeing with other sensory activities including reciting, praying, singing, eating, drinking, or even suffering. Yet seeing cannot function as a religious practice without an imaginative vision that brings the symbol to life. To put it another way, a person lacking ties to the imagination or beliefs of a given community would find it hard to see an image's religious meaning in the same way that people from that culture and time would. To study visual culture, then, involves studying not only an image but a community's ways of seeing and imaging that symbol as well.

Women use the *alam* to enliven and intensify their inner religious experience. In order to understand the great popularity of this revered icon, it is useful begin with an exploration of its history and symbolism.

History and Symbolism

In both Arabic and Persian the word *alam* conveys various senses related to a distinctive sign or mark, such as a flag or signpost. J. David-Weill (1960, 1:349) has pointed out that in pre-Islamic Arabia a white cloth attached to a lance functioned on the battlefield as a symbol of the Quraysh tribe. During the Prophet's time such flags representing tribes or groups were known by several names, including *alam*. Their chief purpose seems to have been martial, providing a marker of group identity during times of war. They probably also functioned as rallying points for the warriors or signaled defeat when they fell. Although originally the word *alam* seems to have referred to the flag or banner of a particular group, significant meaning also has been invested in the emblematic crest which either topped the pole to which the flag was attached or was borne on a separate pole. The scarcity and heterogeneity of sources, however, make it difficult to trace definitively the early use and development of these objects. J. Calmard and J. W. Allan (2000) have offered a summary of what is currently known in their article "'*Alam va 'alāmat*" in *Encyclopaedia Iranica*. They point to a 1237 C.E. / 634 A.H. manuscript from Baghdad that shows the use of a broad-bladed metal finial affixed to the top of a wooden shaft adorned with flags or tassels. This kind of device was used in Egypt and Syria throughout the Mamluk period. The second half of the fourteenth century C.E. / eighth A.H. marks the emergence of a design incorporating dragon heads (associated in Assyrian or Persian culture with divinity, strength, and power) paired on either side of a spearhead-shaped center emblem. Finial designs further developed, incorporating a variety of symbols and range of forms, although almost always combined with a flag of some kind. These devices soon became a striking feature of warfare and parades.

From its largely martial origins the *alam* developed into a symbol to convey Shia religious identity. The earliest record indicates the use of *alams* of some kind in Muharram ceremonies under the Buyid rulers (945–1055 C.E. / 339–447 A.H.) of Persia (in present day Iran Iraq). *Alams* became more widely used once Shia beliefs were adopted as the state religion under the Safavids (1501–1732 C.E. / 907–1145 A.H.). The passage of *alams* into North India has been attributed to the Iranian mystic and missionary Sayyid Muhammad Ashraf Jahangir Simnani (d. ca. 1436 or 1437 C.E.), who arrived in India about 1380 C.E. (Rizvi 1986, 2:293, 347–48). In South India it is most likely that they were introduced, along with other mourning rites, by Shia immigrants during the Bahmani period (1347–1422 C.E.). By the time the Qutb Shah dynasty began in Golconda (1518 C.E.), Shia rituals were well established and *alams* were in regular use. In fact, the *alam* is a distinctive feature in architecture from that period, with the Qutb Shah rulers incorporating the image of the metalwork crest into the façades of most public buildings. The best-known examples are found on the Charminar, the Old City monument that symbolizes Hyderabad and that is itself shaped in the form of another highly revered Shia symbol, the tomb replica (*zari* or *taziya*). During this same period pilgrims brought relics from Karbala that were incorporated into *alams* and housed in specially constructed *ashurkhanas*. For example, a piece of the wood on which Fatima is believed to have been given her funerary bath was incorporated into the famed *Bibi ka alam* (*Alam* of Her Lady). These well-known relics and the sites that house them continue to be popular centers for pilgrimage and ritual activities today.

According to Muslim tradition, it was Ali, the cousin and son-in-law of the Prophet, who generally carried the *alam* into battle during the lifetime of Muhammad. Shias name Abbas, the half-brother of Husayn, as the brave standard-bearer during the epic fight at Karbala. It is these *alams,* particularly the one carried by Abbas for Husayn, that are believed to be the prototypes of the present Muharram icons. Even though it cannot be conclusively demonstrated whether Ali or Abbas carried a flag, an emblematic crest, or some combination of the two on the battlefield, Shias today clearly identify the metalwork crest as the primary symbol of Husayn and his followers. In fact, the actual standard is believed to be enshrined in a Lucknow *ashurkhana* (Ali [1832] 1917; 12. 35).

It seems likely that, for Indians, the primary locus of meaning in this powerful symbol of identity has evolved over time from flag to crest. In Mrs. Meer Hasan Ali's ([1832] 1917, 38, 48) description of nineteenth-century Lucknow, there are references to both the flag and crest as essential parts of the Muharram "banners of Hosein." John Norman Hollister ([1943] 1953, 168–69) wrote later that "the term *alam* is used for the crest and the standard [that is, the staff], or for the standard alone, to which streamers and pennants may or may not be attached." In contemporary Hyderabad, however, the use of the flag has been almost totally eclipsed by the use of the decorative crest; it is the latter alone to which the term *alam* refers. For the Hyderabad community the most meaningful occasion of flag symbolism occurs quite apart from the use of *alams.* It takes place at the beginning and ending of the mourning season, when a flag flying over the imposing gateway to Dar al-Shifa, the main Old City gathering grounds for Hyderabad's Shia community, is taken down and changed to either red (celebratory) or black (mourning), depending on whether the season is starting or concluding. In rituals organized by women small green flags—usually bearing the names of the *panjatan* (Muhammad, Fatima, Ali, Hasan, Husayn)—are sometimes carried in processions, but their use seems almost perfunctory when compared to the highly emotional ambience generated by the *alam* or other iconic symbols such as the cradle (*jula*), tomb replica (*zari*), or bier (*tabut*).

In the present Indian urban context, then, an *alam* most often consists of a metalwork crest decorated with calligraphy or other embellishments. The type of metals and other materials used and the quality or complexity of craftsmanship vary, conveying something of the socioeconomic position of the one for whom it was made, as David Pinault (1992, 81–82) has observed. The most popular design is the raised palm or *panja* that symbolizes the *panjatan.* Craftsmen who make these icons attest to the meaning with which they are constructed. Sayyid Taqi Hasan

Wafa (2000, 108–11) interviewed one of Hyderabad's hereditary *alam* makers to describe the style of the traditional *alam* and the meanings of some of its parts:

> On the top is the calligraphy of Allah in Arabic script. Below that is the shape of Zulfikar, the double edged sword—the sword which always worked in the cause of righteousness. Then there are the Jeeban or the tongues which symbolize the expression of the truth. The Sharjah symbolizes an animal which the artist makes as a symbol which overpowers evil. The circle of the Alam is called the Petha and its center is known as Hatheli. These are generally the areas where the craftsman puts in all his skill. In the Petha the names of the Imams are engraved and in the Hatheli intricate calligraphy is done. If the name of only one Imam or that of a particular martyr is engraved, the Alam symbolizes the commemoration of that particular potentate. In the Hatheli sometimes verses of the Holy Quran too are calligraphed. Sometimes the name of the person who gets the Alam made along with the date of manufacture is engraved at the bottom. . . . Sometimes precious stones are studded in the Petha and the eye of the Sharja. Sometimes ear-rings too are placed on the jeebs. This symbolizes that the Alam is to commemorate Bibi Sakina [the daughter of Husayn]. The Bibi ka Alam [dedicated to Fatima] too carries precious stones on the two Jeebs.

The artist tries his best to create a feeling of reverence in the minds of the beholders. This means incorporating symbols that are linked to the religious imagination through the gaze of the faithful viewer. As the craftsman pointed out, the topmost place is reserved for God, who stands above all. The stylized word *Allah* rests upon the double-pronged sword of righteousness, the legendary Zulfiqar, the "best of all swords." This is the weapon that was won by Prophet Muhammad in the battle of Badr, passed on to the valiant and courageous Ali and through him to others of the imams. In the symbolism of the *alam* the sword springs from the tongues of truth, a visual combination that connects the devout viewer to the central stories of Shia faith: Husayn and his companions dying because of speaking the truth in their uncompromising stand for the right path; Zaynab, the bold sister of Husayn, courageously addressing the court of Yazid and upbraiding the ruler for leaving the path of righteousness. The *alam*'s iconography also reminds faithful Shias that evil is ultimately overpowered by divinely associated protecting forces—even if that triumph comes only at the end of time. This theological concept is sometimes symbolized by traditionally powerful animal figures, dragons, snakes, and lions being the most popular (Naqvi 1993, 159; Calmard and Allan 2000, 786–87). Within the acknowledged heart of the *alam*, the central flat face usually bears calligraphy that recalls the names of the beloved *masumeen* (the pure ones): Muḥammad,

Fatima, and the twelve imams. Even the most simple metalwork *alam* will have woven into the design the names of the *panjatan;* the more intricate ones often contain one or more verses from the Quran or the name of the holy soul being commemorated by the icon. The *alam,* then, is a potent "imagetext," to use David Morgan's term. It juxtaposes highly evocative names, phrases, or passages with symbols such as the righteous sword, the mighty tongues of truth, and the martially derived battle standard itself to create a symbol greater than the sum of its parts. In the faith-filled gaze the design of the *alam* is replete with Shia theology, offering links to central religious concepts and key personalities in ways that increase the viewer's perception of the holy.

For the outsider it is hard to overlook the anthropomorphic character of the *alam.* Jewels or stylized earrings may be incorporated to link the icon to personalities and stories that are part of an inherited Shia worldview. These are elements that, in the craftsmen's eyes, help to "create a feeling of reverence" in viewers.

A display of alams *at a Hyderabad* ashurkhana. Alams *are more than a reminder of battle or martyrdom; they link the faithful to the revered family of the Prophet.*

These additions are only part of what contributes to the *alam*'s anthropomorphic character, however. Hanging from its base is usually a *dati,* a rectangular length of cloth that is draped to cover the staff. The *dati* can be of simple material or fine, highly embellished cloth such as brocade and silk; it is sometimes embroidered with the names of the *panjatan or* other imams or martyrs or with verses from the Quran. At times the *dati* almost looks like a cloak; in fact, in Kashmir it is sometimes referred to as a *dupatta,* the word used for the veil women commonly drape over their heads and chests for modesty (Khatoon 1990, 23). When combined with the shining emblem of the *alam,* the effect is regal, as Shebhaz Safrani (1992, 77) described in his edited book on Hyderabad and Golconda: "Metaphysical to the faithful, overwhelming to zealots, simply moving to the poetic, the Qutb Shahi *alums* have a transcendent power that is still awesome. . . . The calligraphy, shaped to take the fullest advantage of the Arabic words Muhammad, Ali, Fatima, Hasan and Husain, has circular bases with hollow ends for wooden staffs. It is this calligraphic transmission, the polished metal, the *alums* decked with flowers that ordinarily adorn the necks of the living—that creates an impact."

Safrani points to several elements that combine visually to inspire most believers, including garlands of flowers. During major remembrance anniversaries some *alams* can be so laden with flowers that it is impossible to see the well-polished crest. These decorations are not just visual components of the *alam*; they are the product of acts of religious devotion. Believers make use of flowers to "greet" or acknowledge an *alam,* their behavior echoing traditional ways of greeting or honoring elders or respected guests. These faith-inspired actions contribute to the sense of *alams* as living personalities, a point that some Shias find troubling, as we will see. Before discussing Shia perceptions about the veneration of the *alam,* it is useful to review other faith-filled behaviors associated with this important symbol.

Remembrance and Performance

In *Reliving Karbala: Martyrdom in South Asian Memory,* Syed Akbar Hyder's fascinating 2006 account of South Asian Shia engagement with the Karbala metaphor, the Hyderabad born and raised author recalls how his grandmother had a silver *alam* built for each of her children and grandchildren. The icons represented Husayn and Abbas, Zaynab and her sister Kulsum, Husayn's nephew Qasim and his children Ali Akbar, Ali Asghar, and Sakina. While he was growing up, Syed Akbar would join the other household children during Muharram in helping to erect the *alams,* the name and personality associated with each conjuring up images and stories that filled their imaginations. Household *alams* like those of Syed Akbar's family tend to be kept on display in a room permanently or temporarily dedicated to that purpose; if the family's space or resources do not permit, they are kept in a sanctified space in a cupboard or on a shelf. The *alam* is held erect by a supporting staff or pole and is generally positioned so that when one stands or sits in front of it, one faces the direction of Mecca (most *ashurkhanas* are constructed with this directionality in mind). This alignment locates the *alam* within the wider coordinates of sacred space. The physical orientation of the *alam*—whether it is prone or erect—also has meaning for the believer. The crest lies prone when not in use, or sometimes it is laid down at a particular performative moment to convey death. At all other times the *alam* remains erect. In fact, Shias generally believe that if one owns an *alam* one has the responsibility to see that it is displayed upright during Muharram. Many also will agree that one has an obligation to hold a *majlis* in honor of the personality in whose name the *alam* is dedicated. Lighting incense and candles and saying special prayers also tend to be part of what one does in keeping an *alam* on display, at least during the main mourning period.

Many women visit *alams* as part of their regular religious practice. For example, when a commemoration gathering is held in a place where one or more *alams* are present, it is common for participants to take at least a moment to visit the icon or icons either before or after the event. Sometimes they bring strings of jasmine and roses to tie to the crest. Faithful believers visit the *alams* at other times: as part of weekly or seasonal routines or during times of stress or difficulty. Some *alams* are visible only during certain times of the year, usually being raised on the first of Muharram (or sometimes on the martyrdom anniversary day) and lowered at the end of the mourning period. The exact day on which an *alam* is lowered varies. It is sometimes the third day following the tenth of Muharram, but more commonly, at least in Hyderabad, it is on Arbain, the fortieth day following the death of the martyrs at Karbala. This seasonality of display means that *alams* are vividly present during the most highly emotional period of the year, helping to define the boundaries of this special time in the same way as the wearing of black clothes or the holding of commemoration gatherings do. The highly emotive rituals of installing and putting away *alams* have led many scholars to mistakenly assume that a seasonal display is the norm for all *alams*. However, if it was at one time standard to restrict *alams* to the first ten or twelve or forty days of Muharram, the custom seems to be changing. In Hyderabad one can visit *alams* dedicated to Zaynab, Sakina, Zayn al-Abidin, and Husayn at community *ashurkhanas* throughout the year. *Alams* dedicated to the Twelfth Imam also are kept on perennial display since Shias believe that this final guide is always present in the world. As one popular *zakira* remarked, "It makes us feel good to go and see the *alam*. It reminds us that he [the Twelfth Imam] is with us" (interview, Hyderabad, 18 March 1996). *Alams* are also on display year-round in some homes. A woman explained to me that she keeps the family's *alams* visible throughout the year because the Umayyad ruler Yazid "succeeded once in lowering the *alam* of

Husayn. Why should we allow him a larger victory by lowering and putting them away each year?" (interview, Hyderabad, 21 June 1995). Thus, for believers, the timing of the display of these iconic symbols is loaded with meaning. The devout may see an *alam*'s permanent display as a testament to the abiding presence of one of the descendants of the Prophet or as a symbol of the victory of truth over injustice. Or the pattern of rising and falling may help to signal the boundaries of mourning for those who remember and grieve the losses of the Prophet's family.

The following more detailed description of how Shias engage with these sacred symbols is based on my 1995 visitation to a half dozen Old City *ashurkhanas* on the last day of the main mourning season. The neighborhood streets carry an air of expectation on this special day as people prepare for a major procession and dozens of commemoration gatherings, large and small. The main roads are clogged with rickshaws and black-clad people on bicycles, motorbikes, and foot. Melodic elegies float out over the crowds from loudspeakers rigged on utility poles and shop fronts. Roadside stands offer water to the thirsty, while a plethora of black banners announces recent and upcoming *majalis*. This anniversary day, Arbain, commemorates the burial of the martyrs of Karbala; it is also the day when a majority of the seasonal local *alams* are put away until the following year.

The catalyst for the day's small pilgrimage is Chandapa, an elderly woman who regularly spends many hours at Yadgar Husayni. A childless widow both wrinkled and frail, she lives with her brother, on whom she is dependent. Her simple worn black sari and dusty sandals and the rubber band carelessly holding back a thin braid testify to the poverty in which she lives. Because of a heart condition she can no longer walk great distances. This limitation frustrates her, for it makes it difficult to visit regularly the shrines she has known all her life. When Chandapa learns that I have a motor scooter, she leaps at the chance to visit all her favorite icons and offers to escort me as a guide. Like most Hyderabad Shias, Chandapa is well acquainted with the locations of the major *alams* and the stories associated with them. This is part of the collective knowledge of members of the community of faith. She also knows that by evening a good number of these treasured symbols will be put away and that to visit them on Arbain brings great blessing (*barakat*). There is, thus, a great personal impetus for her to act as guide. It is possible that Chandapa also believes that she will receive a measure of spiritual reward (*sawab*) for assisting me, an outsider and potential Shia, to visit the *alams*.

We meet at Yadgar Husayni where about fifty women are gathered in the hall, and a steady trickle is arriving through the main doors. The organizers expect more than a thousand women at their *majlis*, due to begin within an hour. Inside the shrine's inner room (*sher nishin*) women are tying flowers to the staff of each of the three *alams*. Photos on the walls that depict the tombs of the *Ahl-e-Bayt* have been covered with small black drapes to convey mourning. Chandapa and I set out, our first stop being nearby Alawe-e-Sartoq, the *ashurkhana* housing the *alam* associated with the fourth imam, Zayn al-Abidin. Black awnings have been erected in the vast courtyard surrounding the *ashurkhana* to provide shade for the anticipated crowds. Inside, the *alam of* Zayn al-Abidin stands almost totally obscured by heaping garlands of jasmine and rose. One can catch only a glimmer of its brass body, renowned to art historians for of its elaborate dragon-head design and to scholars of religion for the relic it contains from the manacles that bound Zayn al-Abidin after his capture at Karbala.

Like the other women and men who come to visit this icon, Chandapa offers tangible signs of her love and respect. She presses her face against the stand, fingering and caressing the flowers, then brings her hands to her face in a gesture that indicates the appropriation of blessing. Beside her another woman kisses the bedecked *alam,* then takes a rose petal from one of the garlands and puts it into her mouth, ingesting its blessing. Many of the people in the small room are sobbing; some stand an arm's length away from the *alam,* fully engaged in the moment, their lips moving in silent prayer. Children come with their mothers and reach up to touch the flowers, or they are lifted to kiss the *alam*'s covered surface. Some of the women raise one of the garlands or the brocade cloth tied to the stand and bring it to their faces: touching first one eye, then the other, then the forehead, and finally the lips—a fluid gesture of greeting or parting that one traditionally extends to the hand of a respected elder.

When she finishes her reverential greeting and prayer, Chandapa heads across the dusty grounds to another *ashurkhana* on the large Dar al-Shifa premises. Before entering the shrine she bends to touch the threshold. Inside she takes a bit of the earth of the courtyard and puts it on top of her head. When we leave, she repeats the same motions, appropriating the blessing of what she considers sacred soil. Inside the *ashurkhana* a dozen women and girls are sitting cross-legged, chatting. A short distance away stands the *alam* of Zaynab. It is mounted on a tall wooden staff fixed to a low stool and is about five feet high, the size of a small person. The detailed calligraphy on the metallic crest is masked by a veil of black cloth, mimicking a woman's outer modest covering. As is the case elsewhere, the *alam* is surrounded by other iconic symbols: two glass-encased tomb replicas (*zaris*), photographs of the tombs of martyrs, and a lovely wall tapestry of the Kaba. Chandapa greets the *alam,* then steps back to stand before it, eyes closed, lips moving. After a few moments she continues across the room, travels down a short flight of stairs, and passes through a low door. Turning a corner, she enters a hidden and cramped alcove, the *ashurkhana* of young Sakina, the daughter of Husayn. A beautiful brass *alam* glows softly in the dim corner, and a small *zari,* possibly a replica of Sakina's shrine, stands before it. The faint light and cramped space imaginatively recreate the atmosphere of the prison in which believers know Sakina died.

The popular *ashurkhana* dedicated to Husayn's stepbrother Abbas is privately owned, and one must enter through a gate in a high compound wall surrounding the family property. The covered verandah that stretches across the front of the house overlooking a large courtyard functions as the main *ashurkhana.* A group of ten women are taking rest in the shade, while two others from the caretaker family sit on the verandah eating. An *alam* of Abbas, wrapped in an aged embroidered cloth, is resting prone on the floor, supported by pillows. Only the crest is exposed. The created effect is that of a body left for viewing before its burial. On the verandah walls hangs a wealth of evocative artwork, including beautiful paintings depicting Karbala scenes: the riderless and arrow-pierced horse of Husayn, the huddled veiled figures of the women. A small room branches off from the main *ashurkhana* area. Inside resides another *alam,* a tall rack of vertical wooden dowels set before it. Dozens of locks are affixed to the dowels, left by supplicants who made a vow before the *alam.* Those who participate in the ritual say that the lock is a reminder to Abbas; they remove it only when he has intervened to meet their stated need.

This brief account offers several insights. First, it conveys something of the familiarity and ownership with which devout believers engage with popular *alams.* Despite her apparently limited social station, Chandapa moves easily through the shrine spaces, identifying and talking with individuals who oversee some of the sites and taking apparent pride in introducing and explaining the displays to an interested outsider. Many of these familiar shrines are not only places for spiritual connection but also public sites where women can rest from household and other responsibilities, passing time with female companions. Devout men and women also see these spaces as ones where they can bring their needs before powerful intercessors. When Chandapa touches the threshold or lintel of the entranceway, then brings her fingers briefly to her lips, she is demonstrating an unspoken belief in the blessing of the site. This simple respectful action is also a way of appropriating the *barakat* associated with something perceived as holy. At one *ashurkhana* Chandapa even sprinkled a bit of the sandy dirt from the courtyard onto her head, her reverence for that earth being reminiscent of Shia reverence for the sacred soil of Karbala.

In almost all of the *ashurkhanas* described above, we find the *alam* embedded within a matrix of symbols, whether tomb replicas (*zaris*), photographs of holy sites, or visual depictions of key events from religious history. Just as the *alam* is a melding of symbols and texts designed to inspire the religious imagination of the viewer, the environment surrounding the *alam* is rich with connections to Shia faith. These connections are not simply iconic, for the very atmosphere surrounding the *alams* is for the faithful an evocative experience. Thus the dark subterranean corner that houses Sakina's *alam* leads the believer back to the dungeon where Husayn's daughter lost her life. Similarly, the reverently wrapped *alam* of Abbas "lying in state" on the verandah evokes a prefuneral wake familiar to Indian Muslims, with family and friends gathering in vigil to mourn, pray, and share comfort in a last respectful tribute to the deceased. Such associations become especially powerful when the *alam* is used performatively to help recall or reenact events connected with the lives of the Prophet's family. For example, at a *majlis* dedicated to the memory of a particular member of the *Ahl-e-Bayt,* a passionate oration is sometimes followed by one or more *alams* being brought out before the bereft assembly. Participants may process the icons around a given circuit and then ceremoniously lay them down to be covered by a shroud flecked with red, symbolizing the death of the martyrs. Most often the procession is accompanied by the recitation of mournful dirges (*nauhas*), the cadence of which is kept by rhythmic chest beating (*matam*). The sanctity of the moment is sometimes heightened by burning incense; in fact it is occasionally around a smoking incense pot that an *alam* is processed. The devout often crowd forward, trying to touch the sacred symbol to gain a measure of blessing. In Shia communities elsewhere the devout sometimes reenact a burial by taking annually constructed icons in procession to be buried on land designated as Karbala (Fernea [1965] 1989, 210–15) or to immerse them in the sea (Pelly 1879, xvii–xxiv). Whatever its form, the performative use of the *alam* is much more than a pageant of symbols; it helps the believer create an embodied spiritual experience that goes beyond the rational articulation of faith.

Yet the *alam* is not simply a tool for remembering—or reentering—the past. The believer does not return to events in religious history simply to view or experience them. One enters the past in order to stand alongside the souls who lived through those critical formative times. In other words the *alam* provides many of the faithful with a powerful point of connection in their ongoing relationship with the Prophet's family. People demonstrate their respect, love, and reverence for members of the *Ahl-e-Bayt* through the ways they engage with the *alams:* some kiss the crest or the flowers draped around it; some greet the *alam* with the gestures used locally to greet elders; others stand weeping or in silent or half-audible prayer. When the *alam* is part of a performed ritual it is especially evocative, inspiring the engaged believer to look beyond the symbol to see the body of Husayn, Abbas, Zaynab, or another of the beloved family of the Prophet. I recall, for example, one black-clad woman, a grandmother, who was at a *majlis* to mark the death of Sakina. She had the responsibility of holding the family *alam* dedicated to Husayn's daughter. All around her the tragedy of the child's passing was being evoked: first through a powerful sermon, then by the carefully crafted words of a moving *nauha,* punctuated by the small crowd's sobs, cries, and the accompanying sharp slap of the *matam.* The grandmother stood before other participants with the symbol of Sakina before her, leaning her forehead against the glinting metal as tears coursed unchecked down her cheeks, her body swaying with grief. Immersed in the tragic death of Husayn's beloved daughter, she was totally lost in the moment—a moment that was personal, profoundly intimate, and almost impossible to penetrate or communicate.

Mohammed K. Fazel's (1988, 45, 46) description of his participation in Muharram performance rituals while growing up in the Indian city of Bombay is useful in trying to understand what can be for the believer a truly transformative experience: "Suddenly the doors would be flung open. Instantaneously, the drum and the cymbals would begin their dirge. And Imam Hussain, in a blood-smeared shroud, astride his steed Zuljenah would enter. For the crowd, there was no building up to a climax. The instant Hussain appeared, frenzy spread. We would slap our chests with open hands and slash our backs with the *zanjir* [a flail made of knives], chanting *Vai Hussain kushte shod*—Woe betide, Hussain is slaughtered." Although the context is different—here the Bombay *taziya* enactment, with the martyr Husayn symbolized by a living actor rather than a metal emblem—the feeling of immediacy and consuming grief is the same. Note Fazel's identification: "the instant Hussain appeared," not "the instant the actor portraying Hussain appeared." Although some might be dismissed as mere literary style, it seems clear that Fazel is accurately communicating his own experience at the time. For him and for others it *was* Husayn who appeared blood-smeared and weary, just as, for the grief-stricken grandmother in the description above, it *was* the body of Sakina that she held in her trembling arms.

These observations offer an important corrective to academic assumptions in many writings on Shia iconography and ritual in which the *alam* is described as a symbol having martial connotations or as a representation of sacrifice for the cause of justice. Although, as we have seen, the *alam* has its roots in the battle standard of the fourth imam, most women—perhaps to a greater extent than men—do not relate to it primarily as a symbol of the battlefield flag or the "standard of Truth carried by Imam Husayn" (Lalljee 1977, 85–86). Rather, for the majority an *alam* has its deepest connections as a sign of the empowering presence of the *Ahl-e-Bayt.*

The Power of Blessing and Grace

It is hard to separate the meaning of the *alam* from people's sense that there is blessing or grace (*barakat*) associated with it. The Urdu word *barakat* is adapted from the Arabic term *barakah,* the nominal form of the root *brk,* and connotes "increase, abundance, prosperity, blessing; good fortune, auspiciousness" and "inherent prosperity which produces success or abundance" (Platts [1884] 1977, 148). The word *tabarruk*—the blessed gift given to guests at remembrance gatherings—comes from the same Arabic root. *Barakat* can be best understood as a beneficial power that has its ultimate source in God or, as one author put it, "the manifestation of God's grace on earth" (Rabinow 1975, 25). The flow of this grace is limitless and has the power to bring benefit, protection and transformation. This grace differs from the spiritual benefit or reward gained by performing a good deed or action (*sawab*), because it has its effect in this lifetime rather than in the next.

Barakat is generated when people of good intention perform pious acts such as praying, reciting the Quran, making a pilgrimage, fasting, making vows, and doing good deeds. However, *barakat* does not spring from the action itself; rather the source is the performer's contact with an entity that is so closely associated with God that it embodies divine grace. The Quran, the Kaba, God's holy names, the *panjatan,* and the imams are all examples. The nature of each is indivisible from the holiness of God's blessing. *Barakat* is also present in a piece of hair or clothing or in other objects associated with a holy person, whether that person is the Prophet, a saint, or one of the imams. Some devout Muslims see *barakat* as intrinsic to whole groups of elements connected to the Prophet and used in ritual, for example, dates, olives, henna, and particular perfumes. Many Muslims drink or carry away *barakat*-laden water drawn from the Zamzam well during the once-in-a-lifetime pilgrimage to Mecca, water that is associated with God answering the prayers of Hagar, the consort of Prophet Abraham and the mother of Ishmael. The presence of *barakat* is thus a theological marker, a signal of one's religious belief. Shias see the earth of Karbala as filled with blessing because it came into contact with the blood of Husayn. Similarly such icons as the *alam* are grace-filled because of their association with one or more members of the beloved family of the Prophet.

As we have seen, periods of time can also carry special blessing. These include days such as Arbain or the birthdays of the *Ahl-e-Bayt* and days or months that have broader associations. Fridays or the the early morning hours of each day are times linked to the Prophet and prayer, and many Muslims see them as specially powerful. So, too, special annual days or months such as Ramzan, the month of fasting; or "the night of Power" (*Shab-e-Qadr*), when the Quran was revealed; or the full-moon night during the month of Shaban known as "the night of Mercy" (*Shab-e-Barat*), when Hyderabad Muslims pray for the souls of the dead and the year to come (D'Souza 2004). The *barakat* associated with particular points in time makes especially blessed any religious rituals conducted during those periods.

Part of the characteristic of *barakat* is that it is passed to objects, people, places, actions, or times without the original source being depleted. Thus, for example, a string of prayer beads (*tasbih*) contains tangible grace or *barakat* because the Quran is recited as the beads pass through the believer's fingers. Yet the words of the Quran never lesson in their miraculous power. Shrines dedicated to Zaynab, Fatima, or one of the *Ahl-e-Bayt* are rich with *barakat* because of their connection to souls beloved by God; yet their holy power is never depleted no matter how many devout pilgrims visit and absorb the *barakat* of the holy site.

It is not surprising that people vary widely in their beliefs and understandings about this kind of divine grace. The spectrum runs the gamut from Muslims who are keenly aware of and actively seek out sources of blessing and power to those who dismiss as irrational superstition the idea of passively acquiring grace. To give some examples, a women who regularly prays at Yadgar Husayni described how the *barakat* of blessed water gave her peace and released her from headaches and tension. She found divine grace to be such a basic part of life that it was hard for her to understand my questions about it. It was like trying to explain the wind: it simply *was*. Quite a few of the women I met who held strong beliefs about *barakat* felt similarly. Many of these believers had limited formal education. Some quickly grew impatient with trying to answer questions, while others were amused and incredulous at my lack of understanding about something so obvious. On the other side of the spectrum are Shias such as the university professor who rolled her eyes and laughed when I asked about the practice of blowing on water after reciting a litany of prayers (a widely followed way of bringing a tangible blessing to water). She did not believe that water changed through contact with breath that had carried God's holy word, although she did have tremendous faith in the power of prayer as a method of intercession. Another well-educated woman with whom I spoke implied that belief in *barakat* is a stage in people's faith: as people became more knowledgeable, they leave it behind. Although she herself did not have a strong belief in the power of things that are blessed, she felt that there was little harm in holding such a belief, for anything that brings a person closer to God is basically good.

Although people's ideas about *barakat* vary, quite a few Shia women believe that tangible blessing is part of what makes the *alam* special. For them, like Chandapa who sought to visit as many *alams* as she could on the anniversary of Arbain, the icon is more than just a reminder of the family of the Prophet or the losses of Muharram. It is an object that, through its association with God's beloved *Ahl-e-Bayt,* has the ability to bless, heal, and transform. This belief is expressed in such faithful actions as kissing or reverently touching the icon or even ingesting petals from the flowers that are draped around the crest. The appropriation of blessing is also demonstrated by the popular practice of tying to a person's wrist a thin red string that has been touched to an *alam*. Syed Akbar Hyder (2006, 15) describes his grandmother's tying such a thread on his and his cousins' wrists each Muharram season. "She told us that for the rest of the year we were under the protection of these [Karbala] martyrs."

Some of Hyderabad's *alams* are highly revered for the power of their blessing. In his study of Hyderabad Muharram observances, T. Vedantam (1975, 14) has described one that has been renowned for hundreds of years: "Even the Emperor Aurangzeb, said to be bitterly anti-Shia, and who had prohibited installation of Alams in his realm, later issued the charter . . . mentioning Miracles of the Alam of Sar-touq-Mubarik and ordered its shifting from Atebar Chowk to the present premises . . . so that larger numbers of people have the benefit of the blessings of the Alam. He also made a daily grant of '*Huns*' (gold coins) for the '*Ood-O-Gul*' (incense and flowers) of the Alam." The miracles associated with the *alam* dedicated to Husayn's son, the fourth imam, were so widely reported that even a conservative Sunni monarch like Aurangzeb could not overlook evidence of divine blessing. In fact, the ruler not only preserved the relic; he also moved it to a more fitting location and extended regular support for its ritual upkeep. People's close attachments to the *alam* are clearly fed by their perception of its ties with divine grace, most tangibly manifested through healing and answered prayer.

Purity and the Maintenance of Sacred Symbols

A strong sign for women of the sacred *barakat*-laden nature of the *alam* is the fact that one should not touch it if one is menstruating or experiencing postpartum bleeding. According to popular Muslim understanding (based on Quranic verse 2:222), women become ritually unclean through contact with menstrual or postpartum blood. This is the main reason that bleeding women are excused from their religious responsibilities for ritual prayer (*namaz*), fasting, and circumambulation of the Kaba during pilgrimage. It is only after performing religiously prescribed ablutions (common to male and female bodies that have been in contact with impure substances) that a woman's body is restored to a state of ritual purity. The focus on purity in religious practice has its roots in the words of Prophet Muhammad, who is reported to have said that "purification is half of faith" or, according to another popular tradition, "the key to Paradise is worship [*salat, namaz*]; the key to worship is purification" (Ali 1944, 41).

Purification is perhaps best understood as a symbolic cleansing before an intimate encounter with the holy. As Julie Marcus (1992, 75) has described it in her insightful study of gender hierarchy and pollution laws, it is the removing of invisible dirt from the imagined body. A person who has been in contact with defiling substances regains ritual purity by performing either a full bath known as the *ghusl* (the greater ablution) or a partial washing (of hands, forearms, head, and feet) known as the *wuzu* (the lesser ablution). Whether one requires a *ghusl* or *wuzu* depends upon the type of defilement that has taken place: a *ghusl* is necessary after exposure to "major" impurities: ejaculation, sexual intercourse (with or without ejaculation), menstruation, childbirth (affecting both mother and child), and death (or touching a dead body). *Wuzu* is sufficient if one has had contact with "minor" impurities, including dust or mud from the roads (and hence also the soles of shoes), any traces of urine or fecal matter (assumed present after urination, excretion, or the expulsion of bowel gas), vomit, and blood, pus, or yellow liquid issuing from the skin. The *wuzu* is the regular ritual purification undertaken before performing the daily ritual prayers.

Over the centuries theologians have elaborated on the practical steps necessary to make an object, place, or person ritually pure. Believers who follow their injunctions must be vigilant on multiple fronts, seeing to the purity of their bodies, their clothing, and ritual objects, and to the place where religious rites are performed. This emphasis has carried over to wider practices, with many Muslim women believing that a state of elevated purity is required to engage with the revealed word of God. Consequently in India and other parts of the Muslim world, many menstruating or postpartum women will not touch the Quran or even recite its words until they return to a "clean" period. The same thinking about clean and dirty and the experience of the holy is reflected in women's tendency to refrain from touching an *alam*—or entering the purified room in which it is kept—during cycles when their bodies emit what is seen as an impure substance.

Marcus (1992, 70–90) has argued that gender differences in control over one's state of ritual purity are central to the construction of gender hierarchy in Islamic societies. Women, unlike men, have little control over the most common processes that keep them from a state of elevated purity, particularly menstruation and postpartum bleeding (the latter rendering a woman ritually unclean for forty days after the act of giving birth). As Anne H. Betteridge has noted (1986, 405), the combination of women's physiology and the fact that caring for the home and family often puts women in contact with children who are regularly soiled by urine, feces, or vomit has been an important reason why some male leaders exclude Muslim women from certain rituals and ritual spaces. In the Shia case gender differences are even more stark, since feminine blood is defined as defiling, while masculine blood—shed through martyrdom or its ritual reenactment—is widely understood to be pure.

How do these experiences and beliefs impact women? Based on my interactions in Hyderabad, it seems that most women tend to accept their ritual exclusion, viewing it as the result of a betrayal by their bodies rather than of questionable interpretations by religious scholars. Female perceptions of their own physiological limits, when compared to normative male standards, undergird women's acceptance of gender-based religious hierarchies. These established beliefs may also help women come to terms with the experience of marginalization in mixed-gender environments, since most are already familiar with a physiology-imposed pattern of limiting their religious participation. Finally, female notions of purity/impurity and its restriction on ritual engagement serve to demarcate "religious" actions, occasions, and objects from "holy" ones. The female is never excluded from commemoration gatherings (excepting in the leadership role of *zakira*), from the reception of *barakat*-laden *tabarruk* (although she may not prepare it), or from prayers and other nontactile forms of communion with God or the family of the Prophet (although she may not participate in ritual prayer, with its implication of prostrating before the divine, or have physical contact with the revealed book or the *alam*). Thus the implicit theology around impurity and exclusion seems to distinguish the mysterious encounter with the holy from less-numinous acts of religiosity and the passive receipt of God's blessing.

People's perceptions of the divinely associated character of the *alam* mean that most Shias handle it, like other sacred icons, with great care and respect. This includes keeping the revered symbol in a ritually pure place. The majority of Shia families in Hyderabad do not have a permanent *ashurkhana* in their homes; those with sufficient space traditionally set aside a room for the display of the family's *alams* during Muharram. To prepare the space the family thoroughly washes and cleans the room, sometimes whitewashing the walls or hanging sheets to section off a ritually purified area. Once the room is prepared, the *alams* are removed from the boxes or trunk in which they were stored during the year. They are cleaned and polished and then ritually installed in the temporary *ashurkhana*. Family members generally see the sanctified space in which *alams* are kept as being off-limits to those not in a state of ritual purity. As Jamila Jafri explained, these requirements have particular relevance for women who wish to keep an *alam* at home:

> See, there is this thing called *najis* [dirt, impurity]. Things like urine, blood, the menstrual period, excrement, any dead animal . . . all these are *najis*. There are so many things. Now most homes have children in the house. They pass urine here and there; the place then becomes *najis*. If there is an *ashurkhana* in the house, children are forbidden inside, women who are menstruating are forbidden. But if there is no *ashurkhana* [that is, no separate room], then the whole house becomes *najis*. If you have to make it pure (*pak*), you have to clean the whole house with water three times. There are so many rules about this. How many times you need to do it, how much

> water to use. If, for example, there is a birth at home the whole house must be white-washed. There are so many do's and don'ts. (Interview, Hyderabad, 15 February 2000)

A person, place, or object loses ritual purity through contact with impure (*najis*) elements, including certain body fluids and excretions. Since impurity can be transmitted, a purified space becomes ritually impure when a polluting element enters it, and elaborate rules of Islamic law govern how to restore its ritual purity. This issue is strongly gendered because of women's experiences of menses and childbirth and their proximity to infants and children. Female physiology and life circumstances and the rules surrounding ritual cleanliness make it challenging to ensure a pure environment for the *alam* at home—especially when there are young children. In most homes, in Jamila's words, "it's easy for things to become *najis* and so difficult to get things *pak*."

When faced with all the responsibilities associated with keeping and handling an *alam,* many women today feel it is just too hard to keep these powerful icons n the home. One woman in her sixties who lives part of the year in Canada with her daughter reflected that "it is difficult these days for everyone to keep *alams*. You can't touch them during your menses—how can you keep them or take care of them?" (interview, Hyderabad, 20 June 1995). Another woman who lives in a house her father built more than fifty years ago noted that modern homes have little space for a separate *ashurkhanas* to keep *alams*: "An *alam* should really have its own room. But these days, with people living in modern flats, who can spare a separate room for a shrine?" (interview, Hyderabad, 26 March 1997). The care involved in keeping an *alam* is also difficult because of changes taking place in the structure of contemporary families. One young woman who received her doctor of philosophy for work on Shia lamentation poetry put it this way: "Before, women used to be at home. Their only job was taking care of the home, of the family. Now so many are working. How can they find the time to do all these things?" (interview, Hyderabad, 18 March 1996). Many women voice similar sentiments: women are so busy these days that it is hard to keep up with work at home, including doing all that necessary to care for and honor these sacred objects properly. As family size shrinks, emigration increases, and the traditional joint family system breaks down, there are fewer people in the household to care for a private *ashurkhana* or to organize a regular *majlis* to honor the martyrs represented by one's *alams.* One full-time housewife, a devout Shia with four teen-aged children, shook her head when I asked if she kept an *alam* at home. "We don't have our own *alams.* You must be so careful. Keeping them is a lot of work" (interview, Hyderabad, 12 June 1995). People's perceptions about the demands of keeping a sacred object such as an *alam* are part of the reason sites like Yadgar Husayni have gained tremendous popularity among the community of women.

The Nature of Veneration of the *Alam*

As earlier noted, Shia engagement with the *alam* is intrinsically tied to the community's imaginative vision. To those who stand outside the boundaries of faith and do not have access to that vision, the devout veneration of the *alam* may appear to be worship of an object or idol, an idea that horrifies most Shias. A good example of this misconception is found in the comments of the orientalist missionary G. E. Brown (1912) who noted the "surprising Moslem idolatry" visible in Muharram rituals. The outsider's perception that believers are worshipping the *alam* is fueled by popular expressions of faith, such as garlanding the icon or placing before it tangible reminders of a vow. The conflation of ideas of veneration and worship is further fed by the fact of Hindu participation—and sometimes even leadership—in some Muharram activities (Naqvi 1984, 219–20). In his classic study of Shia faith in the Indian context John Norman Hollister ([1943] 1953, 179) cited the following 1940 newspaper report of Hindu participation in Shia religiosity: "Hindus from all castes, excepting Brahmans, call the *alams* pirs [saints or spiritual guides] and have incorporated them into their religion. The *alam* of Ali is called 'Lal Sahib' and the other two are known as riders; . . . these three *alams* are 'looked upon and treated with the same reverence as the village Goddesses.'"

In his article on Indian *ashurkhanas* in an edited volume on Shia belief and practice, M. L. Nigam, director of the Salar Jung Museum in Hyderabad, sought to clarify the differences between Hindu and Shia believers by comparing their ways of engaging with *alams*. He began by noting the reasons some Shia rituals have resonance for Hindus:

> The offerings of *agar* [incense] and flowers, distributing alms to the poor (*lungur*), the reading of emotional verses, *marsiyas* [elegiac poetry], in honour of Husain, and *nazr* [offering] to help the maintenance of the shrine echoed the similar ceremonies held inside a Hindu temple. The *udi* or ash, applied on the forehead by the devotees, reminds us of the *vibhuti* of Hindu temples. The offerings of rice, jaggary [raw sugar] and coconut to *alams* is again a typical Hindu custom, popularly known as *prasadam* in temples. The *alam* which contains the relics of Husain was not a new phenomenon to the Hindus. The placing of personal relics of the Jain, Buddhist and Hindu saints inside the religious shrines had been an ancient practice in south India. The *panjetan* representing the "palm of a hand" . . . provided a fresh imagery to the eyes of the Hindu devotees, who had a long-standing

> tradition in India to worship the feet "*padas*" and "palms" of the Hindu divinity. (1984, 120)

According to Nigam, it is the familiar imagery and similarity in practice that attracts Hindus to Shia ritual gatherings. The difference between the two groups is that while Hindus consider an *alam* to be a divine object of worship, Muslims see it as an inspiration to recall members of the family of the Prophet and a means through which to pay respect to them. In Nigam's words, for the Muslim "the element of worship was not there, as a Muslim is supposed to worship only one God as per the canonical injunctions of the Holy Quran" (121).

The question of the influence of Hindu culture on Muslim beliefs and practices has existed as long as scholars have studied Islam in its Indian context. Comments have been raised about the syncretism of the Mughal ruler Akbar, the nexus between Muslim mystical expression and the *Bhakti* (Hindu mystical) movement, the cult of saints, and various aspects of popular practice. Criticism has also flourished within the Muslim community and has fueled tensions between Sunnis and Shias. It is not unusual for the *alam* to be a lightning rod for these kind of debates, as seen in this sixteenth-century report from Bijapur: "As a clamorous procession of five hundred Shiʿas approached Shah Sibghat Allah's *khānqāh* [a dwelling or retreat for Muslim mystics], the Sufi sent one of his followers out to destroy the *Shiʿa symbol* [emphasis mine] being carried at the head of the procession. This was done, touching off a bloody riot between the Shiʿas and a number of Sibghat Allah's *murīds* [disciples]."*

Although tension has not remained constant between Sunnis and Shias in India, it is almost always accusations of idolatry that have fueled the intermittent flare-ups through the centuries. One fallout has been the rise of an apologetic that asserts the Islamic roots of certain symbols and rituals. As Annemarie Schimmel (1987, 455) has noted, the rhetoric of Indian Muslim reformers usually aimed to distance Muslim practices from those of Hindus. In the introduction to his translation and of the Quran, Ahmed Ali (1997, 136) gives a good example of this type of apologetic in his comments about people's reverence for the *alam*:

> Every thing in the Universe is a Sign of God particularly those associated with godly objects and the men of God:
>
> "Verily, 'Safa' and 'Marwa' are among the signs of God; whoever therefore maketh a pilgrimage to the House or performeth 'Umra.' Therefore it shall be no blame on him to go round them both; and whoever of his own

*From Malfuzat-i Shah Sibghat Allah (1606–1607), fols. 4b–5a, compiled by Habib Allah Abd al-Fattah, translated and quoted in Eaton, *Sufis of Bijapur: 1300–1700* (1978, 16).

> accord doeth anything good in deed, verily God is Grateful, All-Knowing." 2:158
>
> "As (as for the Camels) We have made them for you, of the Signs of God." 22:36
>
> "That shall be so, and whosoever respected the Signs of God, then that verily is the outcome of the piety of heart." 22:32
>
> Mere common sense is needed to know that if the mound of *Safa* and *Marwa* and the animals of sacrifice are worthy to be the Signs of God, [then] the token of the Emblem or the Standard of Islam with which Husain fought and established the Truth will be the greatest sign of God, i.e., the Sign of the Religion revealed by the Lord and respect and reverence to it cannot be but the Sign of the piety of the individual. Be it known that the Shias, the followers of the Quranic faith, the Islam-Original, are more careful against '*Shirk*' [equating a person or thing with God] than any other school. They regard the '*Alam-e-Husainy*' neither as God nor as Husain but as a token of the Standard of Islam.

Ahmed Ali tries to counter criticism against the *alam* by pointing out that the Quran itself draws attention to certain "signs of God," including the camels and hillocks (*Safa* and *Marwa*) that are part of every Muslim's pilgrimage to Mecca. If God identifies these objects as divine signs, then certainly the standard under which Husayn gave his life to defend his religion would be "the greatest sign of God." This exegete is clearly trying to correct popular Sunni misconceptions by noting that a person's reverence toward an *alam* is only a sign of their piety, not a sign that they are committing the sin of equating something or someone with God (*shirk*). In a remark directed as much toward his fellow Shias as toward Sunnis, he further stresses that the *alam* of Husayn is merely a token of the standard that represents God's religion; it is neither God nor Husayn.

Yet as we have seen, the most important significance of the *alam* for many women is its role as a symbol of the connection with sacred personalities. One fifty-year-old Indian woman who left for North America as a young bride describes the development of her thoughts and emotions around this point:

> I went through a phase of deeply questioning certain of our practices. I don't know what kissing the *alam* means for me; . . . why do I have to kiss a piece of fabric [the *dati* which hangs from the metalwork crest]? So for several years I didn't. But then I changed. I came to believe that it stands for something. It's not the physical thing itself, it's the things I say in my head as I kiss that fabric and touch it to my eyes. My remembering, my honoring, it all takes place in my head. These are living spiritual teachers. Friends who

> are there just as we have physical friends. If I ask my friends to come over to my house and help me prepare for a party, they help me. In the same way we can ask for help from these friends. It doesn't mean that we are taking something away from God. You can develop relationships with them, very deep. But it takes time; it depends on how much time you invest, how much you can invest. (Interview, Toronto, 6 April 2001)

This successful businesswoman from a well-respected family of educators was troubled by what seemed to be an anthropomorphizing of an object. Gradually, however, she came to see the *alam* and her own rituals of respect as representing a deeply felt connection with the "living spiritual teachers" who stand behind the symbols, a relationship with cosmic friends that does not take anything away from the primacy of God.

Still, there are some Shias for whom the similarity of *alam* rituals with Hindu practices is just too uncomfortable. I once asked an educated and forthright friend whether the *alam* in her home had any special personality associated with it. She gave me a long look before warning me against such inquiries. "You know we must be cautious about this; there is a danger for us here. These are simply symbols." She later confessed what she called her own "radical thinking" about *alams*, namely, that "they are fast and dangerously becoming close to idols." The very fact that *alams* have "distinct personalities" attached to them, she pointed out, puts them at a particular risk. In her opinion the connection between the *alams* and the *Ahl-e-Bayt* has become so strong that some Shias feel "their personality is missing" unless there is an *alam* present. The question this woman asked was, "Do we need *alams*?" Underlining the importance of Muharram for her own spiritual balance, she pointed to the strong history of oration of the martyrdom events, the evocative poetry of lamentation, and the value of clarifying one's knowledge and philosophy in light of the tragedy at Karbala. These components were sufficient without the presence of a potentially problematic icon. Yet my middle-aged friend felt uneasy sharing these thoughts with others, particularly members of the "older generation," many of whom are deeply attached to certain rituals and to *alams* that have been in the family for generations (interview, Hyderabad, 24 March 1996).

This woman's warning was certainly not the only one I heard; time and again, particularly among educated Shias, I encountered a hesitancy to discuss the details of belief and practice involving *alams*. Many people are sensitive about the fine line separating veneration of a symbolic object from worship of a power-filled one and are especially cautious when discussing these matters with an outsider who may misrepresent their faith. Yet, as my friend observed, the connection between remembrance gatherings and this symbol of the *Ahl-e-Bayt* is strong for today's believers, and few will voice objections about an icon that occupies such a central ritual place for the majority of Hyderabad Shias.

Summary

The *alam* is one of the most popular symbols in Shia ritual worldwide, and its use helps to create and nurture a unique Shia culture of belief. Although many writers—Shia and non-Shia—have stressed the symbolism of the battle standard when writing about these icons, most women see the *alam* not as a symbol of war but as the empowering presence of the martyr in whose name it stands. In other words, something is missed in Peter Chelkowski's (1986, 220) description of the *alam* as "a symbol of fighting for the uncompromising cause of right and justice," giving Shias the feeling "of actually fighting at Karbala." Chelkowski is not alone in making such gendered associations. In his book describing the martyrdom of Imam Husayn for an Indian audience, Yousuf N. Lalljee (1977, 85–86) has made quite explicit his claim that the *alam* is "a replica of the Banner or Standard of the Holy Prophet and the Holy Imams" and "is symbolic of the Holy Standard of Truth carried by Imam Hussain." In the same vein M. Abdulla Chughtai (1936, 59) noted in the context of his discussion of the motif of the *alam* in mosques of the Quli Qutb Shah period: "Perhaps its aim was that the *Alams* would always be considered present even in the mosques *as an emblem of the war of Karbala*" [emphasis added]. William Knighton ([1855] 1990, 143) used the word *arms* to convey the meaning of *alams* to his Victorian English audience. David Pinault (1992, 140), while describing Muharram rituals in Hyderabad, repeatedly referred to *alams* as "battle standards" or "battle crests," perhaps to buttress his interpretation of the fervent dedication of young men to self-flagellation (*matam*) and the cause of Husayn.

Although this martial emphasis may be true for many Shia males, especially those engaged in injury-inducing *matam*, it fails to capture the fullness of the meaning of the *alam*, particularly as experienced by women. As we have seen, the most powerful meanings of the *alam* for many believers (male and female) comes through its close connection with the personalities of the beloved *Ahl-e-Bayt*. In front of the *alam* one can express empathy and grief at the pain that the family of the Prophet endured; one can demonstrate one's respect, loyalty, and joy at times of anniversary celebration; and one can pour out one's own story, gaining comfort and hope from an assured listening presence.

The *alam*, then, is a symbol that the relationship between believer and revered soul is intimate and accessible. As the anthropologist Azam Torab (1998, 318–19) has pointed out in her study of urban Iranian women, the family of the Prophet is a living and vital part of the believer's social world. This assertion echoes the findings of Nancy Tapper (1990), who in her study of Sunni pilgrimage in

Turkey found significant parallels between women's visits to the shrines of saints and their formal visits to senior relatives (both known as *ziyarat*). Women saw both visitations as a tangible way to demonstrate their respect for people—past or present—whom they or their family members regard highly. In the case of pilgrimage, seeking intercession from the "friends of God" was a secondary motivation for the women's visit; maintaining and honoring the relationship was the primary purpose. To understand Shia women's rituals, then, is to understand that for many women ties with the family of the Prophet are part of a presently existing and mutually supportive network of relationships. As Mary Hegland (1995c, 52) has pointed out, "Relationships with the *ahl al-bayt* are intense and highly personal. Time and space are eliminated as believers think of the *ahl al-bayt* as their own brothers, sisters, mothers, fathers, sons and daughters. In sharing their sorrows through intense repetitious interaction and demonstrations of loyalty, believers become related to them and thus expect their consideration."

Hegland is correct in noting that there is a certain degree of mutuality in what many experience as a vibrant relationship. A devout woman faithfully remembers and honors the family of the Prophet while at the same time knowing that she enjoys the blessing, presence, and protection of these special souls. She can open her heart and expect to be heard. This mutuality in relationship is true not only in how many women relate to the *alam,* but also in their experiences of remembrance gatherings and supplication rites. Thus, for example, believers know that Fatima draws comfort from the love, loyalty, and devotion she witnesses at every *majlis* and supplication ritual dedicated to her name and that she also intercedes for the faithful in helping to meet their immediate needs and in her intercession with God on the Day of Judgment.

This feminine emphasis on relationship may be why Toby M. Howarth (2001, 262) has observed that women's ritual gatherings have a "subtly different" feel from those led by men. Part of the difference he identifies is that many women's *majalis* frequently include only mourning poetry (*marsiya* and *nauha*) without an oration. He observes that when women do deliver talks, these usually consist of recitations of the sufferings of the martyrs told to elicit crying and other expressions of mourning from the listeners. What draws Howarth's attention is the comparatively greater value given by men to the discursive portion of the oration, the intellectualized presentation that seeks to educate people about their faith and the world in which they live. What Howarth may, however, be observing is a subtly different emphasis in the purpose of remembrance gatherings. For many women the primary aim of the event is to express one's support of the *Ahl-e-Bayt;* to stand loyally at the side of the family of the Prophet just as one would stand beside a friend during a crisis. To mourn with the family of the Prophet is of prime importance; offering or listening to a broader educational talk is a secondary matter.

Although male leaders seem to give higher priority to intellectualized discourse than do women, this gender difference is not absolute. Honoring the relationship with the *Ahl-e-Bayt* is also important for men; as Howarth has noted, when time is short it is the recitation of the sufferings of the family of the Prophet that takes precedence for both men and women.

This perception of gender differences is supported by psychological research that suggests that male and female views of the world are sometimes substantially different. In an important challenge to established theories of human development, respected clinical psychologists Jean Baker Miller and Irene Pierce Stiver (1997, 16) noted that, "if we observe women's lives carefully, without attempting to force our observations into preexisting patterns, we discover that an inner sense of connection to others is *the* central organizing feature of women's development. . . . Women's sense of self and of worth is most often grounded in the ability to make and maintain relationships."

Miller and Stiver's thesis is that experiences of mutual engagement and empathy shape psychological growth and overall health to a greater extent than personal independence does. They drew upon decades of research and clinical practice to dispute the notion—rooted in Western philosophy and sciences—that the goal of human development is to become an independent and self-sufficient individual. Using women's lives to redefine the norm, they found that the central and powerful experience of relatedness, and the pain that results from breaks in that relatedness, is the most crucial factor in the way people see and act in the world.

Miller and Stiver's work is part of a larger body of literature that builds on the ground-breaking research of Carol Gilligan, first published in her book *In a Different Voice: Psychological Theory and Women's Development* (1982). Gilligan learned that women tended to score lower than men on tests of moral development. When she examined this fact more closely, she discovered that women were reasoning from a perspective that sees the world in terms of a network of relationships. In other words, women favored a different decision-making framework from that of most men when solving moral dilemmas. Gilligan called this orientation an "ethics of care," in contrast to the already known "ethics of justice." Both ways of reasoning are valid in framing personal morality and, she asserted, need to be equally acknowledged and respected.

My experience of Shia women's ritual practices suggests that the framework of relatedness and care is primary in guiding women's religious practices and priorities and may also be helpful in explaining certain aspects of male religiosity. It is foundational to women's meaning-making surrounding the *alam* and other potent religious symbols. Ultimately, however, the meaning of the *alam* icon remains personal, complex, and highly individual. Few, however, in the community would disagree that the *alam* is—at the very least—a sacred emblem that must be treated with respect and reverence. It thus remains a commanding and, for some, a transformation-inspiring presence through which men and women physically demonstrate their great love and respect for and solidarity with the long-suffering family of the Prophet.

· CHAPTER 6 ·

Rituals of Intercession and Blessing

Popular Shia rituals include the rites of intercession known as *amal* and *dastarkhan.* The former is a litany of prayer that involves the repeating of a powerful phrase or scriptural verse, while *dastarkhan* (known as *sofreh* in Pakistan and Iran) is a special female gathering to commemorate the fulfillment of a vow. Most home-based supplication rites are led or organized by women, even when men participate in them. In fact, males are sometimes displaced from their homes for the duration of female-only rituals such as the *dastarkhan.*

Supplication rituals are a regular activity at *ashurkhana* Yadgar Husayni, with women sponsoring an average of three a week at that public venue. Given that this number does not reflect rates of domestic performance and that most *amal* and *dastarkhan* take place in the home, it is obvious that these rituals are an important part of the religious life of the Shia community. Yet supplication rites do not figure in any religious syllabus, including that of the weekly school run by the women at Yadgar Husayni. Unlike fundamentals such as daily prayer (*namaz*) or even remembrance gatherings such as the *majlis,* this aspect of female spirituality falls outside traditional curricula, which generally emphasize rational, establishment-endorsed precepts of faith. While formal study may give girls the theological framework in which such practices are rooted, including belief in the power of God, the efficacy of prayer, and the intervention of the *Ahl-e-Bayt,* it is the sheer popularity of these rites that brings them into women's lives, and it is personal experience and social performance through which they are passed on.

While it might be tempting to interpret the extracurricula nature of *amal* and *dastarkhan* as a signal of their relative unimportance, or at least lack of legitimization, this absence more accurately reflects the limits of codified explicit knowledge and the gendered nature of formal religious education. By situating these rituals outside the definitions and structures controlled by the religious hierarchy, individuals have greater autonomy and flexibility in determining their shape and meaning. In addition, using performance and example to pass on religious knowledge allows women to retain ritual ownership and power in a society where the religious establishment is equated with the world of men. To help understand how intercessory rituals have meaning for women, it is useful to begin by examining the larger context in which they are embedded.

Supplication and Blessing

Since the beginning of Islamic history faithful believers have cried out for divine help in times of trouble and anxiety. The scripture testifies more than once to the rightness of this act and to God's faithful listening: "And when My servants ask thee about Me, then [say unto them] verily I am nigh; I answer the prayer [*dua*] of the supplicant when he beseecheth unto Me" (2:186). Prophet Muhammad encouraged his followers to petition God, for "nothing is more honorable in God's eyes" (Padwick 1961, 211). The fifth imam added that "there is nothing more loved by God than man's asking and beseeching Him for His bounties and there is nothing which is disliked by God more than one who refrains from such devotion and does not beseech for His bounties" (Ali 1997, 1419).

Supplication often takes the form of a verbal plea or *dua*. Many believers incorporate this form of "crying out to God" into their regular daily prayers, for there is space for it at each prayer's conclusion. People also recite *dua* as a separate and independent petition outside the established prayer times. A believer may use her own words to formulate a plea or she may rely on one from a large body of already established texts. Many people have great faith in the power of particular formulations to address specific needs—recovered health, economic security, love and partnership, or other desires. The popular prayer manuals that abound in local book stalls and at many shrines are filled with carefully worded supplications and recommendations on how to use them. One small book typical of this genre is *Prayers for All Occasions* (n.d.), compiled and annotated by Bilkiz Alladin, a Hyderabad Shia. In her book we find Arabic prayers to meet many occasions and circumstances. Let us look at a specific example to become acquainted with some of the elements common to the understanding and practice of supplication.

Alladin presents two prayers thought to be helpful in overcoming indebtedness. She explains the origin of each one, starting with the account of an unhappy man who was burdened by debt and came to Prophet Muhammad for help and advice. After listening carefully to the man's tale of suffering, the Prophet suggested that he offer a prayer for divine assistance: "Oh God! Behold verily, I seek refuge in Thee from anxiety and grief. I seek refuge in Thee from inability and sloth. I seek refuge in Thee from niggardliness and faint-heartedness. I seek refuge in Thee from the burden of indebtedness, and the coercion of men" (26–27). Alladin notes that as the man faithfully recited this daily prayer, his debts diminished and his happiness was eventually restored.

The author relates a second story about a slave who came to Imam Ali crying that he did not have the money to pay his ransom and buy his freedom. Ali told him not to despair and gave him a prayer that the Prophet had taught him: "Oh God! Let thy lawful sustenance suffice me against thine unlawful sustenance, and make me by Thy grace dependent on none but Thyself" (27). The imam told the despairing slave that anyone who offers these words will find divine help and the ability to overcome debt—even a debt as large as a mountain. Having explained the origin of these prayers, Alladin concludes by recommending that a person recite the prayers daily to relieve economic woes.

This example demonstrates several common elements in the popular approach to supplication. First is the tie to the origin of the recited words—which is almost as important as the plea itself. Through the use of recorded tradition, Alladin places the prayers in a context, reassuring her readers that the words come from the Prophet. She also draws on tradition to provide encouraging examples of the prayers' successful use. These are important sources of authority and thus crucial in helping a believer have faith and confidence in the suggested entreaty. The author also suggests a petition process, which in this case is simple: to recite both formulations daily. For other prayers and in other manuals there are more elaborate instructions, including reciting the prayer along with Quranic verses, blessings on the Prophet, praises of God, and other well-known phrases of grace and power. Prayerful supplication, then, is usually tied to a known lineage—most often that of the Prophet, the imams, or the *Ahl-e-Bayt*—and has a specific form which the faithful believer knows to be effective.

Supplication is not only about words; a believer may also testify to her faithfulness and sincerity of purpose through meritorious action. The popular belief is that since a good deed pleases God, God will regard a prayerful request more favorably when it is accompanied by good works. When such actions are performed as the result of a vow, the practice is known locally as *nazr* (Arabic, from the verb *nzr,* "to vow") or *mannat* (Persian, from the verb *mnn,* "to confer a favor"). A vow, then, is a self-imposed promise made before God to undertake a stated act of piety when a specified circumstance comes to pass.

It is clear that Arabs made vows even before the advent of Islam. We have, for example, the Quran pointing to "righteous servants of God fulfilling their vows" (76: 5–7) and Umar bin al-Khattab asking the Prophet if he should fulfill a vow made before his conversion (al-Bukhari, no. 6697; quoted in Heck 2004, 449). Generally the practice was to offer a sacrifice in order to obtain good fortune; thus a man might vow to make an offering of fifty sheep if his wife bore a son or to refrain from eating meat until rain broke a drought. With the coming of Islam, however, the Prophet sought to make vows more intrinsically religious. The supplicant might pledge to perform extra daily prayers or to go on a special pilgrimage to Mecca. Prophet Muhammad also took care to clarify that if one did petition God and one's need was met, it was because the outcome coincided with the foreordained decree of God, not because the vow caused God to carry out the change (Heck, 2004, 450). In other words it is God's sovereignty, not human agency, which is paramount. This view reflects a conservative position on the taking of vows that still exists within the Muslim community today.

Over the centuries religious authorities have used the sayings and actions of the *Ahl-e-Bayt* to identify other legitimate acts of supplication that go beyond familiar religious duties. These include giving alms, praying through the night, helping people in need, reciting from the Quran, and offering particular sequences of recited prayer. Shias today include other meaningful acts such as sponsoring a *dastarkhan,* making a pilgrimage to Karbala, and presenting gifts to sacred sites. For example, at an annual ritual in Hyderabad women make vows while eating lemons they have pierced using an *alam* dedicated to Abbas, the half-brother of Husayn. When their prayers are answered, they craft a lemon from silver or gold and present it to the *ashurkhana* (Bilgrami 1995, 37).

A person may prayerfully cry out for her own needs and desires, such as getting married, having a child, doing well on exams, or obtaining a job or university berth (to name some of the most popular). She may also request divine intervention for the needs of friends, family members, the community as a whole, or people facing challenging circumstances. Islamic tradition underscores the power and merit of praying for others, reminding the faithful that angels join in the prayers of one who voices another's needs. A saying attributed to the seventh imam teaches that "whosoever prays for the believing men and women, and for the Muslim men and women, Allah will appoint for him on behalf of every believer an angel who shall pray for him" (al-Amili, *Wasa'il al-Shi`ah,* 4:1152, *hadith* no. 8893; quoted in al-Asifi n.d.). In other words, in lifting up the needs of others the faithful supplicant gains a host of heavenly supporters who intercede on her own behalf.

When petitioning God on behalf of others, one again has the choice of offering a verbal prayer (*dua*) alone or combining it with meritorious action. Performing meritorious deeds for another person's benefit is called *isla-e-sawab* (lit. "the comfort of reward"). As we shall see, it forms the foundation for the performance of collective *amal. Isla-e-sawab* involves redirecting to another person one's own earned reward (*sawab*). The tradition has its roots in the early years of Islam when a man asked the Prophet whether he could perform the pilgrimage (*hajj*) on behalf of his mother who had died before fulfilling her vow to perform it. The Prophet agreed that the man could do so; he simply had to state his intention that its reward go to the soul of his mother. *Isla-e-sawab* is popular among Muslims in South Asia, particularly in connection with death anniversaries. The family of the deceased often hosts an anniversary gathering three, ten, forty days, or one year after a person's death. As part of the occasion family and guests may gather together to perform a meritorious act for the benefit of the departed—reading the entire Quran, repeatedly reciting special verses, or holding a *majlis.* Occasionally one encounters a devotional book dedicated to a parent or other beloved person, in which the author redirects the heavenly rewards of the writing to the departed soul. It is thus possible to transform any act that is pleasing to God into a source of blessing for another.

Amal: An Intervention in Times of Need

One of the most popular forms of supplication among Hyderabad Shia women is *amal.* Locally the word *amal* refers to a ritual of seeking divine blessing and intervention through a prayer of petition. It comes from the Arabic verb meaning to work or to act (*aml*) and is best translated in a religious context as "practice" or "[righteous] deed." According to the classic Urdu dictionary compiled more than a century ago by John T. Platts ([1884] 1977), *amal* also means "mystical words or formula" and "charm," "incantation," and "spell." These terms do not accurately capture the believer's sense of the ritual, but they do confirm that Muslims in the nineteenth century used *amal* in a religious context and that orientalists such as Platts tended to see the practice as part of the realm of magic and superstition rather than religion.

In its broadest sense an *amal* is a sequence of prayers and actions that are performed to elicit blessing. The repeated recitation of fixed phrases in the form of a litany is characteristic and has a long history in Islam. One tradition records that Imam Ali asked the Prophet for the nearest and easiest way to God, to which the Prophet replied by teaching Ali a responsive litany using the words "There is no god but God" (*La ilaha illa 'llah*). The Prophet instructed Ali to listen to him recite the holy phrase three times, then offer his own triple recitation, then listen again, and so on, back and forth, in a long string of affirmation and praise. This technique of using repetition of particular phrases (often divine names) to deepen a connection with God flowered into the ascetic practice known as *zikr* (lit. "remembrance"), which Muslim mystics (Sufis) have used down through the ages as a form of meditation and spiritual enrichment (Padwick 1961, 13–20). Repetitive prayer is also known as *tasbih,* which has the meaning of glorifying God as well as being the popular name for prayer beads. Many Shia devotional books record the story of the origin of the best-known of these repetitive prayers, the *tasbih* of Fatima. The story describes Fatima as exhausted by the demands of preparing and caring for her home and family. She approaches her father to ask whether she and Ali can employ a servant to assist with the work. The Prophet replies by teaching her a prayer "more effectual than having a servant"; namely, to recite "[I proclaim] the glory of God" (*subhana illahi*) thirty-three times; "All praise be to God" (*al-hamdu illahi*) thirty-three times; and "God is greater" (*allahu akbar*) thirty-four times (Sayyid 1981, 16–17). This well-known sequence of one hundred acclamations is the most common recitation among people who pray using the *tasbih* and is popular among both Shias and Sunnis, although accounts of its origin often differ.

The assumption when one performs a litany is that people who desire something greatly will ask for it with repeated prayerful determination and that God will reward their faithfulness. This belief has been transmitted to the Shia community through a tradition recorded by the ninth-century-C.E. Shia religious scholar al-Kulini: "Never do forty men assemble together and make petition to God concerning some matter without God's answering them. And if there are not forty, then if four petition God ten times, He answers them. And if there are not four, then if one petitions God forty times, God the Mighty, the All-Powerful, answers him" (Padwick 1961, 260).

It is not clear when this practice of intercessory litany first became popular, but the tradition described above suggests hat it has a long history. The ritual is known by different names in different countries and cultures, even though scanty documentation makes comparative studies difficult. In Canada, Sunni immigrants from South Asia perform a specific variation which they call *ayat-e-Karimat* ("the verse of mercy"), named for the well-known Quranic verse (21:87) that believers recite. Women and sometimes men come together at home or the local mosque in order to repeat the verse 125,000 times, petitioning God's help in a time of intense need (Qureshi, 1996). In Iran, Pakistan, and parts of India the most common term seems to be *khatm,* meaning "end" or "completion" (although in Hyderabad the term in its ritual context is used almost exclusively to indicate a full recitation of the Quran in one sitting). In her study of the religious practices of Shia women living in Tehran, for example, Azam Torab (2006, 85–86, 234–38) describes three related *khatm* rituals that differ primarily in what is being recited: *khatm-e amman yujibu* is the repeated recitation of a single Quranic phrase (27:62); *khatm-e 'an'am* is the recitation of the whole long sixth chapter of the Quran which is regarded as specially blessed; and *khatm-e Qor'an* is the recitation of the full Quran. In all the *khatm* variations the female participants understand that the recitation generates a "cumulative power of blessing." They perform the ritual for specific intentions such as healing, a child's success in studies, the cessation of economic hardship, blessings on the dead, fulfillment of a vow.

In India people's needs are much the same. Women organize the intercession ritual to seek positive outcomes when a family member loses a job, in the aftermath of accident or sickness, when children are writing exams or need admittance to a school, and in situations of marital strain or divorce—to cite some of the most popular reasons for the ritual. The women perform intercessory litanies in their homes or at holy sites and shrines. Yadgar Husayni is a popular site to conduct this rite, for it offers a leader to organize and oversee the ritual as well as a pure (*pak*) setting for performance. What must a woman do when she decides to hold an *amal*?

First, one must select the text and the number of repetitions. A woman's choice depends upon her desire, her faith in specific formulations, and the situation for which she seeks intervention. The *amal* could be a particular Quranic verse or a well-known prayer (such as those attributed to or invoking Imam Ali). The number of times the words are repeated varies. In Hyderabad there are most commonly 125,000 repetitions; in other parts of India and in Pakistan 25,000 (*sawa lakh*) is a popular number, while Torab describes Teheran rituals with 14,000 repetitions. When I spoke to women about why they chose 125,000 as the number of repetitions, some said that such had always been the custom; others identified 125,000 as the number of prophets God sent to Earth (although most Islamic sources cite the number as 124,000); and still others suggested that 125,000 was the number of people present when the Prophet named Ali as his successor. In the Tehran rituals chronicled by Torab, women chose 14,000 because it represented one thousand repetitions for each of the *masumeen* (the "pure ones"; the Prophet, Fatima, and the twelve imams). Although the number may be meaningful through associations with Shia history, much of the number's meaning comes simply from its enormity: to repeat any recitation thousands or tens of thousands of times is a tremendous cry of faith. The longer the text and the greater the number of repetitions, the more people are needed to complete the recitation within a comfortable span of one to three hours.

The collective performance of an *amal* generally begins, as do all supplications, with the silent statement of intention (*niyat*). The intention may be offered by each person who has come to recite, as well as by the ritual organizer who speaks on behalf of the whole group. Most *amal* in Hyderabad follow with prayer, including people's performance of several *rakats* of *namaz,* although this is not the case everywhere. The assembled group then individually and quietly begins their recitation of the chosen text, keeping track of the number of repetitions with the *tasbih* (string of prayer beads) and some other counting device such as seeds, stones, or even tick marks on a piece of paper (Qureshi 1996, 52). The ritual leader or organizer of the event will have decided how repetitions are to be divided beforehand, usually after seeing the number of people present. For instance, if there are 25 persons and the recitation is to be performed 14,000 times, each person will have responsibility for 560 repetitions. Each person works individually toward her goal. When the task is finished, closing prayers are offered—again either individually or for the whole group. This commonly includes a prayer (*dua*) for the specific intention for which the event was organized.

To help the reader better understand how an *amal* precedes and how it has meaning for those involved in organizing and performing it, I have constructed the following narrative (and the subsequent example of *dastarkhan*) from my field research in Hyderabad. While the descriptions are of real events, circumstances and identifying details have been changed to protect the privacy of the women described.

Nur's daughter-in-law is pregnant, but the pregnancy has been difficult. She has been unable to keep much food down and often feels exhausted or giddy. The whole of the previous week she spent most of her days in bed. The doctor has said that if she does not get stronger she may have to come into the nursing home for a day or two and take some glucose intravenously. Nur is very worried. She remembers her own miscarriage as a young bride and does not want the same experience for her son's wife. She goes to the Yadgar Husayni *ashurkhana* and speaks with a woman named Ismat about what she wants to do. Ismat writes down the daughter-in-law's name and a few other details, then confirms that the rate for the requested intercessory ritual is a 190 rupees. After looking at the schedule for the week, she tells Nur that the *amal* will be held the next day at eleven o'clock. Nur leaves the *ashurkhana* happy and relieved.

The following day Ismat arrives at the *ashurkhana* before eleven. She greets a few women who sit chatting in the vast and airy main hall that opens onto the surrounding courtyard. As Ismat stops to remove the embroidered sheet (*chador*) with which she covers herself when going out, a woman with a young child carrying a garland of flowers crosses the hall to slip inside the *sher nishin* that holds the *ashurkhana*'s collection of revered icons. In the open courtyard three young women talk and laugh as they wash apples and grapes under a gushing tap. A faint smell of incense wafts from the room known as the *niyazkhana* (place for performing rituals known as *niyaz*), where a small group of brightly dressed women is busy cutting and arranging fruit in preparation for a celebratory *dastarkhan*.

It is nearly twelve o'clock before all ten women needed to perform the requested *amal* have arrived. Ismat is sitting with a friend who has stopped by the shrine for a visit and a chat and grumbles about people being late. She pauses to scold a woman who is sweeping and has overlooked a pebble under the mat Ismat uses for prayers. "What is this? What kind of cleaning is this? This is a shrine (*yadgar*)!" she reprimands. The woman grins in the face of Ismat's reproach and sweeps vigorously under the white sheet covering the mats on the floor. Eventually all ten women arrive. Most perform the ablutions (*wuzu*) in the courtyard as soon as they enter the *ashurkhana*; several take time to greet or talk with friends or to visit the icons housed in the *sher nishin*. Before arranging themselves in rows on the two long prayer carpets that are spread out in the front of the hall, most take a prayer tablet made of earth from Karbala (a *sajdaga* or *mohra-e-namaz*) and a string of prayer beads (*tasbih*) from plastic baskets that have been set out near Ismat. A few have brought these items from home, and they unwrap them from embroidered handkerchiefs or protective pouches before setting them down on the mat in front of them. The women also collect small piles of seeds from Ismat, and a few get a glass of water to keep by their side. Ismat sits cross-legged facing the two rows of women, her back to the closed door of the *sher nishin.*

As the ten women continue to settle, Ismat begins reciting from a small book in a clear melodious voice. She is reading *Hadith-e-Kisa,* one of the best-known traditions among Shias which describes an incident understood to confirm the sanctity of the Prophet's family. The Arabic recitation is familiar to the assembled women, and at key moments they punctuate it with invocations of praise (*salawat*) for the mentioned family of the Prophet. When Ismat has finished, the women stand and perform two *rakats* (formulaic sections) of ritual prayer (*namaz*), their foreheads resting on the earthen *sajdaga* with each prostration. Meanwhile, on directions from Ismat one of the women distributes money, placing a payment of twelve rupees in front of each woman. The participants know that by the end of this ritual the money will be grace-filled, containing the blessing (*barakat*) earned through performing a sacred deed. The women begin their recitations, some silently, others whispering in barely audible tones. All repeat again and again the words "Oh Ali, help [us]" (*Ya Ali madad*). Some of the women are reflective as they do this; some are lost in thought; a few rock gently as they say the words. When the noise in the hall ebbs for a moment, one can hear the slight whispering of their collective prayer. A young child races gaily across the hall, calling loudly, and all eyes move, heads turn, but lips keep moving, the recitation never stopping.

The women keep track of the number of times they repeat the phrase by deftly fingering the beads of the *tasbih.* When a woman has repeated the words one hundred times, she moves aside one seed from the small pile in front of her. When ten seeds have accumulated in a new pile, she sets aside a seed to mark one thousand repetitions and then starts the process again. In less than an hour the assembled women have called on the help of the revered first imam 125,000 times. As they finish, one by one most of the women touch the prayer beads lightly to each eye and then to their lips in a traditional and respectful gesture of greeting or parting. Almost all take a few moments to prostrate themselves with their heads on the *sajdaga* before kissing the stone lightly and either putting it away or rising to return it and the beads to the baskets at the front of the hall. The "*Ya Ali madad amal*" is now complete: together the women offered a litany of prayer, calling on the intercession of Ali to bring health and a safe pregnancy to Nur's daughter-in-law.

Ritual Components and Meanings

The *amal* just described has all the common elements of these popular rituals of intervention: the initial choices about holding an *amal* (including which type), the statement of intention, the initial prayer, the colossal litany of recited holy words, and the closing prayer. Faced with her daughter-in-law's deteriorating health and disturbed by painful reminders of losing her own baby years earlier, Nur made the choice to seek divine help. A practicing Shia, she performs her daily prayers, organizes a *majlis* once a year on the anniversary of her parents' deaths, and participates faithfully in commemoration gatherings during the Muharram season. In the past year she had been busy finding and arranging a suitable match for her only son, and she was pleased with the way the young woman is settling into their home. The news of the pregnancy was an overwhelming joy, for her elder daughter, although married, had not been able to conceive. This would be Nur's first grandchild. Returning with her daughter-in-law from the doctor's appointment where the pregnancy was confirmed, she had the rickshaw driver stop so they could buy three heavy garlands. They then visited Yadgar Husayni where the women garlanded the main *alams*. Nur was beside herself with excitement and gratitude. Two months later, however, she was distraught. Although the doctor seemed only mildly ruffled by her daughter-in-law's diminishing appetite and inability to gain weight, Nur feared the worst. She had been praying daily for the young woman's safe delivery ever since the doctor confirmed the pregnancy but felt that something more was required in this hour of pressing need. She decided to offer an *amal* invoking the aid of Imam Ali and went to Yadgar to seek help.

A woman who chooses to hold an *amal* during a time of crisis is often making a decision to "up the ante" in prayer. She perceives that a collective outcry will be more powerful than an individual act of supplication, however faithful the latter may be. Nur made the choice not to organize the ritual herself but to see that it was organized and performed at Yadgar Husayni. There were several reasons for this decision and several implications as well. First, as a resident of a Shia neighborhood in the Old City, Nur was familiar with the shrine and its workings and was comfortable there. She had participated in its gatherings and rituals and considered Yadgar Husayni a holy and blessed site. Moreover, she would gain benefits by holding her supplication there. First, she would have a person to organize the *amal*, relieving her of the burden of arranging and hosting the event herself. Having Ismat's leadership also meant that the performance is in the hands of a leader who could see that the ritual was conducted properly. When the event is held at home, the host usually invites a knowledgeable older women from an extended family or neighborhood network to assume the leadership. Most women consider this role vital, for they know that in order for a plea to be favorably heard the *amal* must be enacted properly.

Among the initial steps a woman takes in organizing an *amal* is to invite women who will participate in the reciting. At a home ritual women usually invite an extended circle of family and friends. At the shrine the participants are those who are known to the ritual organizer and sometimes one or more women from the family of the person requesting the ritual. For some types of *amal,* twenty to forty women may be required. The task of finding the right people can be challenging, for not everyone is able to participate. The ritual leader at Yadgar uses three criteria to guide her in this. First, for *amal* that involve the repetition of Quranic verses or chapters, performers must be able to read and recite Arabic clearly and correctly. This criterion is less urgent when the prayer involves calling on the name of one of the *Ahl-e-Bayt* or some other simple formulation. If Ismat is uncertain about a woman's proficiency in Arabic (for example, if a person who has requested an *amal* volunteers to take part in it herself), she will often invite the person to sit near her during the ritual so that she can keep an eye on her and be certain that the recitation is done "properly." A second important criterion for taking part in this prayer of petition is that the person be of "good character." In other words she should be a faithful practicing Shia who has refrained from the "wrong path" and who can stand respectfully before God without shame. Again, it is the efficacy of the ritual that is at stake. Ismat knows that to be acceptable, the prayers need to be offered by persons with pure hands, hearts, and minds. The third basic criterion for a woman's participation is practical: that she have enough time to devote to the ritual. A volunteer must have the flexibility to come to the shrine during the day on relatively short notice and spend up to several hours there.

Ismat has built up an extended circle of women who fill these criteria. The regulars are mostly women who have some education, limited family demands, and a need for extra money. Almost all are in strained economic circumstances because their husbands—the traditional income providers—are unemployed, dead, or out of the women's lives through divorce or separation (the latter sometimes initiated by the women). Participation in an *amal* brings these women a meager gift of money, an opportunity to engage in a respectable task along with other women, and the chance to gain a measure of grace (*barakat*) through the performance of a blessed task. Their participation in the ritual also gives the *amal* an added blessing. To recite words from the Quran or to call on one of the souls most beloved to God is a meritorious act. The main power of the *amal* is that women collectively apply the rewards they receive for performing this good work to the expressed need of another (*isla-e-sawab*). Yet since the *amal* at Yadgar Husayni also contributes to the welfare of women in need through a gift of money to performers, it brings the additional benefit of another meritorious act.

The donation (*hidayat*) given by the sponsor to the organizer is split among the performers, the ritual organizer, and the shrine. It is important to women and to the shrine's management committee that no profit be made on a religious act. All must be a voluntary donation. The performers receive the bulk of the gift, even though what they individually receive—twelve rupees in the example above—is minimal; enough to buy, for example, a kilogram or two of rice. Yet believers consider this donation specially blessed, just as they see all monetary transactions associated with the work of God (such as the *hidayat* received by a *zakira* in return for her services at a remembrance gathering). Moreover the choice to pay twelve rupees is itself meaningful, since twelve is one of several auspicious numbers in Shia belief, being associated with the imams Thus the payment and receipt of *hidayat* are designed to invoke a powerful religious symbol of presence and blessing.

The last matter to be decided by the sponsor and organizers is the type of *amal* to be performed. Nur chose the "*Ya Ali madad*" ritual because of her great faith in the family of the Prophet and, in particular, the Prophet's beloved son-in-law and chosen successor. Within the *amal* tradition there are established rituals involving different recitations, including *ayat-e-Karimat* ("merciful verse," 21:87) and *sura Ya Sin* (36:1–83), the two most popular at Yadgar Husayni. The most significant practical implications of the type of *amal* a woman chooses are the number of reciting participants and the time required. In the hour-long *amal* described above, for example, in which the recitation was the simple formula "*Ya Ali madad,*" ten women each repeated the prayer 12,500 times. When the repeated prayer is longer—a whole chapter from the Quran, for example—more women will be needed in order to perform 125,000 repetitions. For lengthier passages such as the eighty-three-verse chapter *Ya Sin,* there may be as many as forty women gathered so that the ritual can be completed in about two hours. For this reason the costs of this type of *amal* are higher, and organizers at the shrine request a larger donation.

Once the initial choices about venue, participants, and type of *amal* have been made, the performance may proceed. The first step is to offer one's clear, stated intention (*niyat*). When Nur first met with Ismat, the ritual leader asked for her daughter-in-law's name and the specific intervention being sought, noting them down in a notebook. Most women feel that it is vital to make a supplication specific. Ismat communicates Nur's intention for her daughter-in-law's safe pregnancy and delivery to the women volunteers. She knows that it is important for those who perform the *amal* to be clear about the intention for which they are praying. Most often participants offer the *niyat* silently before God at the start of the ritual, although it is sometimes the ritual leader who offers it silently herself on behalf of the group. While a clear knowledge of the intention of the prayer is crucial, the physical presence of the person for whom prayers are being offered—or even of someone connected to them—is not considered necessary. Sometimes the person requesting the *amal* resides in another country and sends a request for a ritual to be performed (along with money to cover the costs). In our example, although Nur sponsored the ritual, she was not there to participate. More comfortable at home with her ailing daughter-in-law, she had full confidence in the efficacy of the prayer being offered at Yadgar and did not feel that she needed to be physically close in order to partake of its power. Sometimes women who request an *amal* help to perform it; on other occasions, as with Nur, they are content knowing that people are praying in a concerted way for their intention.

The next performance step in the ritual is prayer. Purification, however, is a preliminary requirement. Thus, before the women assemble in the hall they individually perform the *wuzu,* the act of ritual purification that is an integral part of all daily prayers (*namaz*). Not only is purification "half of faith" according to the Prophet; Muslim legal scholars hold as well that failure to ensure purity can render a ritual unacceptable to God, negating the value of its performance. It is therefore of prime importance to the organizers and performers of the *amal.* Purity goes beyond cleansing body, clothes, and even mind; it also includes one's surroundings and the objects that are part of the ritual. This is why Ismat scolded the woman who was not thorough in her sweeping of the shrine. Her words—"This is a shrine!"—imply not just the holiness of the site but also the purity and cleanliness associated with a place that is close to God.

All *amal* at Yadgar Husayni formally open with the recitation of *Hadith-e-Kisa,* the "Tradition of the Cloak" which affirms the primacy, blessedness, and purity of Prophet Muhammad, Fatima, Ali, Hasan, and Husayn. While this faith-based account represents a statement of religious belief and Shia identity, it also contains a practical promise uttered by Prophet Muhammad: "By Him Who appointed me a Prophet, chose me as His Confident [*sic*], that no assembly of our followers and devotees, among which this event is narrated, shall spend a single moment but the mercy of Allah will envelop them, then and there; countless Angels of Allah shall pray for the remission of their sins till the group of faithfuls disperse" (Sayyid 1981, 44–45). In other words, the retelling of *Hadith-e-Kisa* will envelop the assembly of listeners in the mercy of God and will initiate a heavenly litany, with angels praying for the remission of the sins of all who have gathered. It is, thus, an auspicious beginning to the *amal.* It also provides an opportunity for group participation in blessing the Prophet and his family, as the women who have gathered repeatedly call out responsively: "O God! Bless Muhammad and the family of Muhammad!" (*Allahumma salla ala Muhammad wa-Ala Muhammad*). This formulation known as the *salawat* (lit. "benedictions") is a regular feature of both daily prayer and remembrance gatherings. Like *Hadith-e-Kisa,* it is a marker of Shia identity as well as a source of blessing since calling for God to bless another person—particularly those most favored and beloved by God—creates a positive reverberation on those who utter the call.

Following Ismat's recitation of the popular tradition, the whole group performs two *rakats* of prayer. *Amal* is often, but not always, linked with *namaz*-style prayer. Women use the recitation of these initial prayers to help create a blessed and holy setting, preparing the most favorable conditions possible for offering up a plea to God. The next step is to settle down to individual recitations in this collective call for help. In the example above each woman whispers or silently recites the words *"Ya Ali madad"* 12,500 times. Women use a combination of prayer beads and seeds or some other counting article to keep track of the number of times they repeat the litany. Their repetition is not loud; nor is it completely silent; some women whisper while others silently mouth the prayer. It is interesting to note that the words are physically enunciated even when they are inaudible. This contrasts with the silent *niyat,* when the recitation is done in the mind and one's lips remain still. The distinction between the words of intention and the words of prayer highlights the importance women give to the correct utterance of the words themselves. It is interesting to note that although proper enunciation is essential, undivided attention or trancelike meditation is not part of the practice. When there are distractions in Yadgar's hall, most women turn to look at what is going on—even though their litany (and the movement of their fingers on the prayer beads) does not waiver. While the ritual leader does not encourage inattention among the performers, there appears to be no harm if women are occasionally attentive to other things.

It is at the beginning of the women's collective recitation that Ismat has one of the volunteers distribute the money assigned for this prayerful work at Yadgar. Women consider the carefully selected amount (evocative of the twelve imams) to be blessed since, like all *hidayat,* it is associated with "good work." Some women believe that the money is also blessed by its presence at a place where believers are reciting prayerful words. Many women understand that holy words—including the names of imams or passages from the Quran—have inherent power and blessing (*barakat*) that can be passed on through their utterance or in other tangible ways. Reciting powerful prayerful words, then, blesses and transforms the objects involved in the ritual, including the *hidayat.* Some women demonstrate their belief in this transformative power by keeping a glass of water close while they perform the *amal,* then drinking it after the recitation is complete. The belief is that they are ingesting grace-filled water. I once saw a woman ask her fellow volunteers to blow into a bag after they had finished reciting. In it she had sweets, which she knew would be transformed by the grace-filled breath of women who had repeated thousands of divinely ordained words. Although not all women believe in the tangible passing on of blessing, for others it is part of what makes the ritual so powerful. Thus *amal* has an important dual nature: as a prayer of petition it is a vehicle for gaining divine help for the expressed need of its sponsor; as a power-filled ritual it also offers blessing to those who perform it.

An *amal* ritual at Yadgar Husayni has no clear and powerful ending but winds up gradually as women conclude their individual recitations. Each participant performs a final prostration, silently and individually bringing her own personal closure to the thousands of prayers she has just uttered. Often in home rituals women follow the individual completion with a final collective *dua* (sometimes more than one) that is recited by the ritual leader and formally places the good works before God in a plea for the desired cause. This is also a time when one may take advantage of the grace-filled atmosphere to add a prayer for one's own needs. If, as at Yadgar, there is no closing collective prayer, each woman respectfully puts away the prayer beads and the earthen *sajdaga.* Women often reverently kiss these articles before carefully placing them back in the basket in which they are kept at the shrine or in the special cloth or pouch in which their owner brought them. This simple reverent action palpably conveys a love and respect that goes beyond the symbol to what it represents: a connection to God and the beloved martyrs.

At a home-based event women tend to linger until all the recitations are finished, for it is not uncommon for the guests to join for refreshments or a meal. Conversations quickly return to earthly topics, as the women catch up on news and share the ordinary details of life. At Yadgar Husayni the volunteers leave one by one to continue with their day. Some stay at the shrine to talk with friends, others do their *namaz* or pay their respects to the holy personalities represented by various icons. Others rest, return home, or head out to run errands before returning to their families. Ismat remains until the last person has completed her recitation. If someone is particularly slow, she may help out with the prayers or request another woman who is finishing to sit beside the slower performer and help her to finish the required number of repetitions. She leaves only when all has been completed in this tremendous outcry of prayer.

Sources of Power

How do women understand the power they seek to engage through the *amal* ritual? What are their foundational beliefs in the "mechanics" of supplication? As we have seen, the core of any *amal* is the litany of prayer. In fact it is precisely the prayerful words that brand each individual type of *amal,* whether it is the *"Ya Ali madad,"* the *ayat-e-Karimat,* or another well-known version of the ritual. A particular *amal* gains popularity because people believe certain words are particularly efficacious in bringing one's needs before God. There are two main vehicles for this: the *Ahl-e-Bayt* and the revealed words of the Quran. Some women favor one form or another, but most make their choice depending on practical circumstances or their situation of need. For example, if one seeks healing for their sick child, one may invoke the intervention of Abbas, whom women know for his tender heart and deep affection for children, demonstrated most poignantly in his relationship with Husayn's daughter Sakina. At other times, or for other women, words of divine revelation are the vehicle of choice. Women's understanding of the family of the Prophet is one means to carry one's supplication to God.

In the example cited above, Nur requested a litany consisting of repeated cries to the first imam, a revered "friend of God." Her confidence in the prayer was deeply ingrained, for the practice of calling on Ali for help is an established part of Shia identity. It is also a visible part of the local landscape with various monuments and inscriptions from the Qutb Shah period upholding the power of the first imam. Typical is the tomb of Haya Bakhshi Begam, the wife of Sultan Muhammad Qutb Shah. Inscribed in black basalt, along with verses from the Quran, a prayer of benediction, and the date of the queen's death (1667 C.E. / 1077 A.H.), is a version of the powerful prayer known as the *Nadi-Ali* (lit. "Call Ali"): "Invoke Ali, the manifestation of wonders. Thou wilt find him a refuge in misery. All grief and sorrow will soon disappear by thy friendship [with God], O Ali. There is no soldier [*fata*, spiritually chivalrous person] like Ali, and no sword like Zulfiqar. Unto God" (Bilgrami 1927, 133–34).

The *Nadi-Ali* is familiar to most Shias, being not only a common prayer but also one whose story is told often by religious orators. The believer knows that it was an instruction from God that led Prophet Muhammad to "Call Ali" when he faced an insurmountable obstacle. In describing the origins of this prayer, a popular *zakira* once explained to me why this form of seeking aid is especially powerful. She noted that Ali was not only a companion to the Prophet, fighting alongside him and carrying the battle standard of the Muslims; he was also the key to at least one major victory: solving the intractable problem of reaching an enemy barricaded in an impenetrable fort. Using an authoritative *hadith* to tell the story of how the Prophet came literally to call on Ali, the *zakira* identified God as the source of knowledge, for it was divine intervention that led to this first "*Nadi-Ali.*" This oft-repeated fact assures and reminds the believer that asking for the imam's help is a divinely sanctioned action of great power. Ali is the remover of difficulties (*mushkil kusha*), the performer of great things, and will effectively bring one's needs before God (interview, Hyderabad, 28 January 2000).

Revealed scripture is the second popular conduit for supplication when performing an *amal.* Part of the power of a litany of Quranic verses resides in their meaning: they may uphold divine power or offer a reminder of the merciful intervention of God. For example, a popular *amal* is *ayat-e-Karimat* ("merciful verse," 21:87) which expresses the words taken from the mouth of prophet Yunus (Jonah) who is overcome by hardships and has been swallowed by a whale. In humble repentance he seeks divine intervention from the one he affirms as the only true God: "There is no god but Thou (O my Lord!), Glory be to Thee, verily I was of the unjust ones!" The Quran records God's reaction to this sincere appeal: "Then responded We [God] unto him and delivered him from the grief, thus do We deliver the believers" (21:88). This brief dialogue offers a divine promise: just as God delivered Yunus from his grief, God will deliver ordinary believers from theirs. Reciting *ayat-e-Karimat,* then, is a humble way for the believer to seek divine intervention, reminding God of a saving promise.

Other verses gain power because of their context. Torab (1998, 443) has recorded that women performing the *amal* known as the *khatm-e amman yujibu* know that its words—succinctly translated "Who will help me in my misfortune?" (27:62)—were recited by Zaynab when she came upon the body of her slain brother Husayn. Thus, reciting these words has multiple layers of significance, including literal meaning, the context surrounding their revelation, and how they have been used by beloved figures from religious history. Other passages that have gained particular popularity in Hyderabad include the first chapter of the Quran, *al-Fatiha,* sometimes called "the mother of the Quran" (*umm al-Quran*), which contains the humble supplication "and Thee alone we seek for help" (1:5). Or chapter *Ya Sin* (36), known as "the heart of the Quran." Its eighty-three verses make it one of the longest and most demanding recitations: when offered at Yadgar Husayni it requires the performance of forty women with clear fluency in reading and reciting Arabic. For many women, reciting *Ya Sin* is equivalent to reciting the full Quran—a ritual known as *khatm* (lit. "finished"). Although women sometimes use a full Quran recitation as a form of petition, many choose to recite a selected passage a fixed number of times, understanding that doing so is as powerful as reciting the full Quran. In this abbreviated form of reciting the revelation of God, *Ya Sin* reigns supreme, for as Allama Ghulam-e-Ali Haji Naji has noted in the popular devotional guide *Tuhfat al-Awam Maqbul* (n.d., 28), a single recitation of this chapter generates the same grace (*barakat*) as reciting the whole Quran twelve times. One can imagine, then, the abundant blessing believers link to an *amal* in which volunteers repeat *Ya Sin* thousands of times.

Yet, as we already have seen, for many Muslims the power of scripture is much greater than its linguistic content. The central focus in the ritual is not on the meaning of the words being recited, for a performer need not attend to every word or moment in her recitation. The importance lies in the correct utterance of the words; the fact that they are voiced is enough. As Azam Torab (2006, 238) and Emelie A. Olson (1994, 215) have noted in their studies of women's recitations in the Iranian Shia and Turkish Sunni contexts, meaning is conveyed unmediated through the senses rather than being based on deductive reasoning or exegesis. The Quran thus contains a powerful blessing simply because it is the holy word of God. We see this belief enacted by the devout in their very handling of the sacred book. Pious Muslims in Hyderabad keep the Quran separate from other books or, if they are dealing with a stack of books, put it on top of the pile. In the same vein people refrain from placing the scripture directly on the floor and touch it only when they are ritually pure. Belief in the holy book's *barakat* also underlies a wide range of practices, including displaying Quranic verses over one's doorstep or on the walls of the home; wearing talismans that display Quranic verses; using one's breath, sanctified by a recitation from the Quran, to blow on someone needing healing or blessing; writing verses from the Quran on a slate and then washing them off and giving the water to a sick person to drink. In all these practices—popular among Sunnis as well as Shias—the power lies not in the meaning of the revealed words themselves but the fact of their sacred origin.

This belief in the grace and power of the original words of revelation is one of the important reasons why people use Arabic to recite daily prayers or perform most other important rituals. While Urdu is the everyday mother tongue of most Muslim women in Hyderabad, Arabic is understood to be an incomparable language, indivisible from the blessing of the holy Quran. For the devout believer, then, using the sacred language and scripture to voice one's plea for divine intervention gives it a special power.

Dastarkhan: A Ritual of Celebration and Hope

Dastarkhan, which literally means "a cloth on which to place dishes [for a meal]," is a gathering of prayer and supplication that usually includes the remembrance of a member of the *Ahl-e-Bayt* and the consecration and sharing of food. It is known as a vow-making and honoring rite and is part of a rich and diverse constellation of food-connected intercessory rituals known as *niyaz* (although locals also use the term *nazr* to indicate some of these rites). The Persian term *niyaz* can be translated "petition," "supplication," and "prayer"; it also conveys a sense of dire need through its association with such words as *necessity* and *poverty.* While it is not clear when *niyaz* rituals developed, the practice of taking a vow before God, preparing food in the name of an intercessor, consecrating it by prayer, and sharing it has a long history in various religious traditions (Raj and Harman 2006, 3–11). Certainly *niyaz* was well established in India by the sixteenth century, when it first became part of rituals at shrines such as that of the sufi leader Shaykh Muinuddin Chishti in Ajmer. The practice remains popular among Sunnis as well as Shias. Perhaps the best-known *niyaz* is the one in honor of Jafar al-Sadiq called *kunde niyaz.* As part of a prayer of petition and celebration, Muslim women prepare a milk-based sweet pudding (*kir*) in small clay pots (*kunde*). The ritual food is blessed through the recitation of a special prayer of invocation (*Fatiha*) and then distributed and consumed.

While *niyaz* are performed by both men and women, the leadership in organizing these largely home-centered events is generally in female hands. Part of what makes *dastarkhan* distinct from other *niyaz* rituals is that women alone both lead and participate in it—even to the extent that pregnant women may decline to join the gathering on the chance that the unborn child is male. It differs from supplication rituals such as *amal* in that it carries a celebratory air, nurturing hope through stories of answered prayers. In Iran and certain parts of the Middle East and India (such as Mumbai), it is known as *sofreh* (Persian for "meal cloth") which appears to be the original term for the ritual (Omidslalar 2006).

In tracing the roots of the Iranian *sofreh,* Michael M. J. Fischer (1978) and Laal Jamzadeh and Margaret Mills (1986) have noted the ritual's existence in Zoroastrian as well as in Shia communities. Comparing the two, Jamzadeh and Mills conclude that the Shia form evolved from the older Zoroastrian form. The Prophet Zarathushtra preached a "joyful orientation to bodily life [and] a robust faith in living" (28). His followers, the majority faith community in Iran prior to the Muslim conquest (642 C.E.), saw a care for health and strength in body and mind as part of what furthered the presence of light and goodness in the world. The Zoroastrian religious calendar thus provided an abundant variety of joyous occasions for worship and food sharing, and it was one's duty to celebrate. The thanksgiving feasts (*goehambar*) were a bimonthly feature and involved the consecration and distribution of food to the community. They were often sponsored by an individual or family as a thanksgiving to commemorate a healing or other resolution of difficulty or in memory of someone who had died. A selection of food and other objects was displayed on a *sofreh,* the consecration cloth, with their number (seven) and symbol reflecting Zoroastrian cosmology. Among the most common items were fire for incense, a mirror, fresh bread, fruits, water and greens, and a mixture of seven kinds of dried fruits and nuts. Sugar, representing the sweetness of life, and scissors to ward off evil were additional ritual elements. Liturgy and prayers were then recited over the displayed items and steaming dishes of food, the fragrance of which was thought to please the departed souls or cosmic personages being honored. The consecrated food was then shared in the community.

The Iranian Muslim *sofreh* contains a remarkable number of elements common to the Zoroastrian form, starting with the meal cloth itself. Shias almost always use light in some form (usually candles), as well as fruits, water, flowers, grain derivatives (particularly wheat), sugar, dried fruit, and mirrors, but most are unaware of the links between these items and Zoroastrian cosmology. Muslim forms of the ritual incorporate such meaningful symbols as the Quran, *tasbih*, and other accoutrements of prayer, and Shia prayers and narratives replace the recitation of Zoroastrian ones. Jamzadeh and Mills suggest that using a *sofreh* as a votive ritual is a Muslim adaptation of the older Zoroastrian practice. Fischer (1978, 204) has argued that contemporary Zoroastrian and Muslim rituals are variations of a pattern, with supplication being an important part of women's religious lives generally and the ritual evolving through mutual borrowings between Muslims and Zoroastrians. Whether or not the Zoroastrian rite has been influenced by Muslim women's practices, it seems fairly certain that female innovation brought a formerly Zoroastrian ritual into Shia culture, substituting Muslim symbols for Zoroastrian ones, combining the joyous celebration with remembering the Karbala martyrs, and emphasizing an all-female feast of supplication rather than a communitywide festival.

Although it is tempting to speculate about the process through which Shia women adopted elements from an outside tradition, present scholarship does not allow us to piece it together from historical sources. As we have already noted, traditional research sources tend to be sparse in the information they yield about women's religious lives—even more so when rituals are home-based. We do know, however, that communities constantly shape their religious lives through the dynamic use of meaningful symbols and that the process of religious change stems in part from a flow of influences between local cultures. Juan Cole (2002, 138–60) has given an example of this dynamic at work in eighteenth- and nineteenth-century Lucknow, where Shia women's religious rituals included elements common in the wider Hindu community. Contrary to accusations from religious leaders, Shia women did not leave their faith; rather they supplemented it with religious discourse or practices appropriated from other traditions and modified for their own purposes.

As far as origins, then, it is possible only to surmise that the Muslim *dastarkhan* or *sofreh* ritual developed in Persia and, like other beliefs and practices, moved with Shias as they migrated. Today it is a popular and widely practiced female ritual. Iranian immigrants to whom Kathryn Spellman (2004, 71) spoke in London identified *sofreh* as their "primary way of practicing their religious faith." For some Hyderabad women it is a regular feature within the extended family, sometimes held on a monthly or weekly basis. Many more observe the ritual in shrines such as Yadgar Husayni; in 1996 alone women organized an average of two a week there (Anjuman Niswan Barkat-e-Aza 1996, 2).

A woman holds a *dastarkhan* for two main reasons. One is to celebrate the completion of a vow; the other is to create an opportunity for herself and others to make a vow. Often the two comingle, for every celebration of an answered prayer is an inspiration and opportunity for others to express their needs in a holy setting with renewed hope. Women seek healing for those who are sick, safety for those who are traveling, children for women who have not conceived or who desire a son; they pray for jobs for their husbands, brothers, and children; for marriage partners not yet found or being endured; for their children's studies; for the resolution of debt. The needs are largely personal but often involve health, protection, or the uplifting of others.

Dastarkhan, like many remembrance gatherings, are held to honor a particular member of the *Ahl-e-Bayt.* The difference is that since the ritual is one of petition, the purpose is not only to honor but also to ask the intercessory help of the blessed and remembered soul. In Hyderabad the most popular personages are Fatima, Abbas, Ali, and Imams Hasan, Zayn al-Abidin, and Musa al-Kazim (the second, fourth and seventh Imams, respectively). Women are influenced in their choice by tradition (for *dastarkhan* that are held regularly), a sense of interrelationship with a particular revered soul, their confidence in a specific *dastarkhan* formulation, or a soul's reputation for being helpful with a particular need. *Dastarkhan* is a communal ritual and is rarely performed by one individual alone, for it requires at least one person to tell and one other person to hear the narrated stories of the honored member of the *Ahl-e-Bayt.* There is a host (or a hosting family) and guests, including knowledgeable women who perform particular prayers, recitations, and narrations. The total number of participants invited is generally predetermined but differs from *dastarkhan* to *dastarkhan.* Women try to make the numbers meaningful: fourteen (or its multiples) is a popular choice; multiples of five and nine are also common.

Most *dastarkhan* have four main parts: a statement of intention, recitations including invocations and prayers, a vow opportunity, and the consumption of food. In discussing *amal* the importance of stating one's intention (*niyat*) before God has already been noted; this is, in fact, a part of every Muslim devotional act. In the *dastarkhan* the host sometimes performs this step just before she and others begin cleaning and preparing for the event, or she may express it verbally or silently as she begins the actual ritual. If she is holding the *dastarkhan* to complete a vow, she states this—out loud or to herself. If she is holding it as an act of supplicating and the beginning of a vow, she states this as well.

The body of the *dastarkhan* consists of prayers, recitations, and narrations. These are spoken in the presence of the food arrayed on the *dastarkhan* (meal cloth), for it is these prayers, poetry, and sacred stories that are the vehicle for transforming the food into a powerful receptacle of blessing (*barakat*). The recitations can consist of blessings on the Prophet and *Ahl-e-Bayt* (in prayer or poetry), selections from the Quran, *dua* and prayers of visitation (*ziyarat*), martyrdom stories, and accounts of the holy personality being honored. Each *dastarkhan* tends to be unique, although the reciting of miraculous accounts associated with the particular member of the

Ahl-e-Bayt is a common feature. For example, a *dastarkhan* held in the name of Imam Ali might feature elements such as celebratory poems (*qasidas*) that extol his virtues and strengths, narrations that portray his death and suffering, and/or a miracle story (*mujizat kahani*) in which he features.

At some point during the course of the *dastarkhan* there is an opportunity for participants to make a vow. Not all people do this, but when they do, their promise is almost always to repeat the ritual upon the fulfillment of their stated need. Sometimes the host or a ritual leader audibly invites the assembled women to take advantage of a particular special moment in the rite. At other times women know the ritual, and those who wish to make a vow proceed without a prompt.

The final element of a *dastarkhan* is the consumption of food. Like many of other elements in the ritual, the chosen food is usually influenced by the tradition of a given type of *dastarkhan* or the preference of the host. Most common are fruits and special sweet dishes (often made from wheat flour or bread); although bread and meat or other special preparations are sometimes featured. The main purpose of the chosen item is to serve as a tangible way to receive blessing, and women sometimes take the grace-filled food (*tabarruk*) home to share with others.

As already noted, a *dastarkhan* can be held in a home or in sacred spaces such as *ashurkhanas.* Many larger Shia shrines in Hyderabad have a designated room or outbuilding known as a *niyazkhana,* where women can hold a *dastarkhan* or other *niyaz* ritual in relative privacy. The *niyazkhana* at Yadgar Husayni requires booking in advance, and most women make a donation for use of the site. They can also pay a fixed amount there to have a team of volunteers do the preparations: purchasing and preparing the food, cleaning and purifying the ritual space, and coordinating or facilitating the *dastarkhan* itself. In such cases the hosts only have to invite the guests and come for the event. The following example took place in a believer's home and offers a glimpse of a typical *dastarkhan* as women observe it in Hyderabad.

Razia's house is only a short walking distance from Yadgar Husayni. Today the household is bustling: Razia's servant spent the previous day giving the main hall a thorough cleaning: all the furniture was moved out, the carpets removed, and the stone floor scrubbed. The ceiling fans, picture frames, and shelves have been dusted and the cushion covers changed. The large furniture has been pushed to the sides of the hall or temporarily stored in the adjoining bedrooms. The carpets have been rolled up, and a thick soft mat with fresh white sheets has been laid down. Two new brightly colored bed sheets have been spread out in different parts of the room as meal cloths. Razia's sister-in-law and a close friend are still working on final preparations in the kitchen along with two servant women. Another friend is setting out five large candles in the center of each meal cloth.

Razia's husband left to spend the day at a friend's house. She did not have to ask him to go, for he understood that this is a time when men are not welcome at home: Razia is arranging a women-only *dastarkhan,* a ritual she vowed to perform at a similar event held just over a year ago if her prayer to Fatima was answered. Her daughter who was diagnosed with cancer is now in total remission, and the doctors—puzzled by the strength of her recovery—say that all trace of the cancer cells is gone. Razia is ecstatic; it has been a horrendous year, with the chemotherapy, the pain of seeing her only daughter so sick, and her own fear and sense of helplessness. Through it all she has drawn heavily on a supportive circle of women and their leadership or assistance in performing rituals that carry her daughter's needs before God. At the *dastarkhan* she attended last year she lit a candle with a clear prayer for the complete recovery of her daughter. Now she feels the prayer has been answered and is honoring her vow to repeat the ritual.

Razia has invited twenty-seven women friends and relatives to join her on this happy occasion. They arrive singly or in small groups, taking off their sandals before entering the house to greet Razia and others. Those who wear chadors pause to remove the simple shawl-like cloths that they had wrapped casually around their heads and shoulders. The noise of conversation ebbs and flows as the main hall fills up. When all the women have arrived, Razia encourages them to take their places: fourteen around each meal cloth. The number carries special significance, for it is linked to the fourteen "pure ones" (*masumeen*) of Shia faith. Someone has lit incense, and a powerful floral smell fills the room. One of Razia's friends recites *Hadith-e-Kisa* and voices the intention of performing this *dastarkhan* to remember and honor Zahra ("the resplendent one"), Bibi (Lady) Fatima. On each meal cloth the five candles are lit with words of blessing; again the number is meaningful, representing the five persons believed to be closest to God: Prophet Muhammad, Fatima, Ali, Hasan, and Husayn. Also on the cloths are five different kinds of fruit, carefully cut, and bowls of a sweet (*malida*) made from bread, sugar, and clarified butter. In front of each woman is an unlit candle and a loop of prayer beads (*tasbih*). Razia lights her candle—the one she has saved from the last *dastarkhan*—using the flame of one of the five candles in the center of the cloth, then passes it around so that all can light their own candles from hers. If a woman wishes to put her need before God, she simply voices it silently within herself—stating a vow in the presence of Bibi Fatima—as she lights the candle. When she goes home later, she takes the candle with her, a reminder of her vow and a connection with Fatima.

The *dastarkhan* continues in the room with its twinkling of candle lights. The women recite prayers, including poetic greetings of praise (*salam*) to Bibi Fatima, and then begin a collective repetitive prayer. The women's voices are barely audible as each slides her loop of hundred beads through her fingers, one bead for each call of supplication, "Oh, Fatima, help me!" (*Ya Fatima adrikni*). The women follow their own rhythms, offering collective prayers numbering in the thousands. When they are finished, Razia's aunt narrates a story of the miraculous intervention of Fatima in the lives of poor but faithful people. The listeners occasionally call out blessings on the Prophet and his family (*salawat*). After the story is over, several women take turns leading the recitation of melodic poetry of praise known as *qasida.* Through most of the ritual Razia cries profusely. She later confesses that she was thinking of her daughter, of all she had gone through, of the difficulties of the situation and her own apprehensions. Some of the other women also are visibly moved, particularly during poetry which gives oblique references to the suffering which Fatima underwent in her life. The women conclude the ritual one hour and forty-five minutes after it started by blowing out their candles and partaking of the food. The informal conversation over the meal ranges widely, touching on Razia's daughter's recovery, news about different family members and friends, happenings at the local school, the escalating costs of food, and other details of the women's lives.

Ritual Components and Meanings

A woman who organizes a *dastarkhan* is usually quite clear about the steps that make it effective, starting with the cleanliness and purity of the venue. For Razia's *dastarkhan,* for example, preparations began with a thorough cleaning of her main hall—an essential step in creating a space where the holy can be present. Kitchen preparations were also carried out with extra care; only women who are ritually pure (not in their menses nor in the forty-day period following childbirth) can prepare the food that will be presented at the *dastarkhan.* The incense that is later lit has the same function of purification and preparation, its sweet smoke helping to define the space as sanctified.

In orchestrating a holy and powerful event, women make use of a wealth of meaning-filled symbols. In the *dastarkhan* described above, Razia used numbers that have deep meaning in the Shia context: fourteen women gathered around each meal cloth, five candle served as a centerpiece, five fruits as offerings. Reciting *Hadith-e-Kisa,* as we have seen, affirms the primacy of the Prophet's family and functions as a prayer to bless the gathering. Its symbolism is critical: at the very beginning of a ritual dedicated to Fatima is God's affirmation of the primary place of the immediate family of the Prophet. Fatima (and by implication, the ritual held in her name) replaces neither God nor the Prophet. Rather she stands in powerful and intimate connection with both. The presence of blessed food (*tabarruk*) is another element that contributes to the sense of holiness. Women invite blessing upon the fruits and sweets through their prayers and ritual actions. The food is no longer something prepared in the kitchen or bought in the market but nourishment touched by Fatima's presence. Just as with the *tabarruk* connected to a *majlis* or *jeshn,* women are careful either to fully consume these items or wrap carefully any that they wish to take home to share with their extended families.

Following the initial steps in the *dastarkhan* comes the opportunity to make a vow, which Razia signals using dramatic symbolism. As we have seen, light is a common feature in the original Zoroastrian ritual. In the Shia context, however, the theme of light is transformed. Through her lighting of candles, Razia communicates theology: she draws attention to the source of light in her life—the holy five—and the subtle truth that candles, like sacred souls, hold the light of the divine but are separate from it. In her *dastarkhan* the radiance of the candles is used not only to represent the *panjatan* but also to transmit grace. Each participant has her own unlit candle, just as last year Razia held an unlit candle at the *dastarkhan* she attended. Lighting hers from one of the central five candles, she passes this shorter taper around so that its flame can light the others, filling the room with light. The symbolism is rich: light comes through the holy five, and it is from them that others receive it—in this case, through the inspiring flame of one whose need has been met. It is a powerful enactment. There is no narration of the story of Razia's daughter's healing. There is no need, for all the women present already know of it through conversations related to their invitation to the event. Her story, her struggle, is familiar, because it is that of a relative or friend, a member of their own community. Razia's daughter is thus a woman very much like the women who attend. Yet she is also someone whose life has been transformed by supernatural intervention. Her tears and emotional response testify to joyful news: here lies a miracle gained through the grace and power of Fatima. And it is grace that is accessible to all who cry out in faith. It is in this moment of renewed hope that a vow can be made. Women sit, surrounded by reminders of power, presence, and answered prayer, and extend their candles to that of their fortunate friend and neighbor. It is no wonder that many seize the opportunity to make vows of their own. A woman has only to express her need, be faithful, and honor her vow when it is realized by hosting a *dastarkhan* dedicated to Fatima. Whether a woman makes a vow as she lights her candle is not known to others. It is only the candle that accompanies her home that becomes a witness to and a reminder of her hope that the miraculous is possible—if only she has faith.

The narrative elements that follow the votive ritual in Razia's *dastarkhan* are all ones featuring Fatima as their main subject. If the *dastarkhan* were dedicated to Abbas or Imam Ali, the content would shift accordingly. The melodic verses of praise poetry (*salam* and *qasida*) are ones that are also heard at joyful remembrance gatherings where their function is the same: to greet and eulogize this member of the *Ahl-e-Bayt.* The poems make passing references to personal qualities and events in Fatima's life that are familiar to those who have gathered. When one poem celebrates her courage, it also hints at the losses she will endure after her death, including the suffering and death of her children. Although the reference is only brief, it visibly touches some participants, including Razia, who later confesses that at that moment the pain and fear of almost losing her own child came rushing to the surface. The women offer a repetitive prayer (*tasbih*) that simply calls for Fatima's help, using the prayer beads to count thousands of utterances. Unlike the prayer that women offer in an *amal,* the collective recitation in Razia's *dastarkhan* is not a unified request for divine intervention in a specific crisis or issue. Instead the women unite in their call to have the Prophet's daughter respond to the individual requests represented by each lit candle. Finally, the women listen to an additional reminder of Fatima's sympathy and power when an elderly aunt reads a story of her miraculous intervention in people's lives.

One way to look at the *dastarkhan* is that it establishes or deepens a bond between the woman organizing the ritual and the holy personage in whose honor it is held. In the Persian society in which *dastarkhan* originated, reciprocity and hospitality are highly developed concepts; a person enters into an obligation of reciprocity by accepting another's hospitality. One effort in the ritual, then, is to cultivate a kind of reciprocal giving that strengthens partnerships with sacred souls of the *Ahl-e-Bayt.* Each *dastarkhan* also has its own performance structure and components, with a wide scope for variation. Fluctuating elements include recitations; prayers; types of food; participants, including the inclusion of special groups (such as unmarried young women); special items or ritual elements, such as the application of cosmetics (for example, henna), the hiding of a coin in a dish (the person receiving it gaining special blessing or the responsibility to hold another *dastarkhan*); and other variations. Abida Sultana, an Indian businesswoman who now lives in Canada, has given a sense of this variability in describing a *dastarkhan* that she regularly hosts:

> I continue the [annual] tradition of a *dastarkhan* which my own mother did. It commemorates the *Miraj* [the Prophet's "night journey" or mystical experience of Paradise], and we hold it on the twenty-seventh of Rajab—that's the month when most other people are taken up with Jafar al-Sadiq, may God bless him and grant him peace. I continue to do this because I think it is important to create unity between Sunnis and Shias, and to honor the Prophet in this way. To celebrate this event which Sunnis also revere causes them to say, "Oh. . . ." I invite neighbors and friends. . . . Before people come we do a recitation [of *Hadith-e-Kisa*]. The purpose of the [other] recitations [once people have come] is to educate. So we read the verses from the Quran which deal with the *Miraj,* and we read the Urdu translation, and

> we read from the biography of the Prophet and from the Imams. Then we read from the . . . [prayers of] the fourth Imam, and we pray for good guidance. It's not very structured. Not like [some] . . . *dastarkhan.* (Interview, Toronto, 6 April 2001)

In this instance a ritual known for making and honoring vows has been joined with a day of commemoration within the wider community of Muslims. Abida Sultana, whose family was a vital part of the Muslim intelligentsia in the early decades of Indian independence, sees in her *dastarkhan* the important goal of trying to build bridges between Sunnis and Shias. In the area of Canada where she lives, the Muslim community is relatively small, the Shia community even smaller. In this environment she values the ties with neighbors and friends from the wider Muslim community. By carefully choosing scriptural readings, biographical traditions, and other elements that celebrate the Prophet's miraculous journey to heaven, she creates a faith-based event in which her Sunni friends can join. Framing the ritual in this way is important to her, and the resulting *dastarkhan* both differs from and is contiguous with the tradition her mother began.

The Power of Stories

One of the most characteristic parts of a *dastarkhan* is the miracle story (*mujizat kahani*) that emphasizes divine intervention through the medium of a revered figure, whether it be Fatima, Ali, Abbas, or one of the imams. According to Vernon Schubel (1993, 37–38), miracle stories are the most ubiquitous narrative genre in the South Asian Muslim world; for Shia women, their recitation is the most common household ritual after the *majlis.* Attributing miracles to the *Ahl-e-Bayt* started as early as the twelfth century C.E. / sixth century A.H., with poetry and narratives praising Ali (Mahdjoub 1988, 55–60). This was part of an effort to demonstrate the superiority of Shias over Sunnis by showing that the family of the Prophet had the power to work miracles, a power generally perceived as belonging to prophets alone. The genre eventually expanded to include miracle stories about the imams, Fatima, and other members of the Prophet's family, and developed further in the cult of saints. The popular stories used in the *dastarkhan* have much in common with narratives from Shia and Sunni communities across the world (Spellman 2004, 74–76; Kandiyoti and Azimova 2004, 341–42).

The common plot of a miracle story is that a person finds a difficult situation miraculously resolved through the intervention of a holy soul. Sometimes there is an interesting twist, the happy resolution being horrifically reversed because of the forgetfulness or ignorant action of a protagonist. However, once the main characters realize their mistake and make amends, things are miraculously restored, and the tale is over. There is a range of occasions during which such stories are recited in Hyderabad, including when a person is making a vow. For example, a young woman might lose a valuable piece of jewelry and call on the help of a member of the *Ahl-e-Bayt,* vowing to recite the member's "story" if the jewelry is found. At other times the stories are used to commemorate a special occasion or to honor a certain personality or as part of a regular weekly or monthly family gathering.

Many Shia homes in Hyderabad have at least one or two of the small inexpensive booklets containing miracle stories, for they are easy to obtain at local shops or during celebratory events at certain shrines. It is from just such a book that Razia's aunt read during her niece's *dastarkhan.* What follows is a version of the popular story as it is presented in *Tuhfat al-Awam Maqbul* (Naji n.d., 207–16). the text is quoted directly to give a sense of the recitation's rhythm and style, including the call for blessings on the Prophet and his family (*salawat*) that commonly elicits a responsive recitation from the audience.

> This event is of an Arab goldsmith widow who had a young child. As usual one day in the morning she went to the well near her house to fetch water with her child. She left the child near the well to play while she proceeded to the well to draw water. Having filled her vessel, she looked for her child—who having noticed a potter's kiln nearby which was aglow, was attracted by it and had wandered off towards it—and not finding the child she presumed that the child must have toddled off home. But when she did not find the child at home, she was worried and again came to the well to look for him all-around. Not finding him there she became more worried and started weeping, moaning and yet roamed all over searching for him until evening time.
>
> By this time, everyone in the vicinity was informed of her son's disappearance without any clue and shortly by evening time there was a rumour that the child being attracted by the potter's kiln-fire had gone there and had fallen in the kiln and died. When she heard this news, she was very much shocked. Due to the shock and worry she fell unconscious in her house after weeping for a long time.
>
> While she was in the state of unconsciousness, she had a vision. She saw a highly dignified masked lady approaching to console her. She told her to be calm and patient and that her son would return to her safe and sound provided she take a vow that if her son returned safely to her she would call someone to tell her the Narration of *Janab-e-Sayyidah* [Lady of the Prophet's family], peace be upon her. The widow was very much impressed and felt joy at the assurance that her son would come back to her alive jumping from the kiln. In her unconsciousness she vowed to act as instructed.

> Thereafter when she opened her eyes, she was astonished to see her son coming towards her smiling. With the blessings and as promised by *Janab-e-Sayyidah,* the child was completely safe and sound. *Allahumma salla ala Muhammad wa-Ala Muhammad* [O God! Bless Muhammad and the family of Muhammad!].
>
> The widow was overjoyed. She immediately prostrated to thank Allah for the favour, picked up her child and rushed to the shop to buy some sweets to fulfill the promise she had made. After spending the two coins for the sweets, she went to her neighbours to request them to narrate the Event of *Janab-e-Sayyidah.* All the seven houses of neighbours she visited with the request, everyone had some or the other excuse. Some saying they did not remember the event, others saying they were not interested in such imaginary tales.
>
> She was very much disappointed on the reactions of her neighbours in spite of the fact that all were aware and saw that her loving child had returned to her safe and sound. Not knowing what to do next, since she herself did not know the Event of *Janab-e-Sayyidah,* which she very much wanted to hear and remember, she unconsciously in the state of worry was walking towards the outskirts of town to the forest. All of a sudden, the same dignified masked lady whom she had seen in her vision met her in the desert [deserted place] and again consoled her saying: "Do not grieve Khatoon. Spread your sheet and sit down attentively and remember it. *Allahumma salla ala Muhammad wa-Ala Muhammad.*"

The story continues with the masked lady narrating two "events." The first is about a Jewish family's wish for the honor of having the Prophet's daughter Fatima present at the wedding of their daughter. The father made the proper requests (first through the Prophet, then Ali) and left Fatima with the invitation. She worried whether to accept, aware that her presence might be perceived as an insult because she had no fine clothes or jewels to wear like the other women who would be attending. She voiced her worry to the Prophet, who encouraged her by saying, "You attend dressed with what you have according to the will of God." As Fatima was about to leave for the event her appearance miraculously transformed and, with dazzling light (*nur*), a heavenly fragrance, and an accompanying retinue of fairies, she proceeded to the site of the wedding. When she entered the home, the women were so dazzled that most fainted. The bride, however, did not recover from her faint for "her soul had departed from her." It was then that Fatima, feeling grief and concerned that people would blame her for the death, petitioned God with two *rakats* of prayer to "fulfill my reassurance given to these people" and restore the bride to life "for the sake of the Prophet and my own honor." Before Fatima had risen from her prayer mat, the bride opened her eyes and, blessing the

Prophet and the family of the Prophet, affirmed her belief in Islam and requested Fatima to purify her and teach her the religion. On witnessing this miracle, five hundred men, women, and children embraced Islam.

The second "event" narrated by the masked lady concerned two young women—a princess and the daughter of one of the king's ministers—who were separated from the king's hunting party because of a violent wind storm. Finding themselves alone deep in the forest, they wept with such emotion that they fell unconscious. Each then saw a vision of a dignified masked lady who suggested that they take a vow to arrange and listen to the "Event of *Janab-e-Sayyidah*" when they were once again home safely. Both girls took the vow, woke up, and shared with each other what had happened. At that moment, a minister of another king whose party was also hunting in the region approached the young women, heard their story, and told the king. The women returned with the second king to his kingdom, and their parents were informed. When the first king's minister came to pick the women up, the second king suggested a double marriage uniting the two kingdoms: the minister's daughter and his own minister's son, and his son and the princess. After some consultation the match was agreed upon, and both kingdoms became busy with the preparations for the weddings. In all the excitement the young women forgot their vow. A series of unfortunate events then took place that caused the king to doubt the brides and order their deaths for sorcery. Thrown into prison, the women again fell unconscious and saw the vision of the masked lady, who reminded them of their failure to fulfill their vow. She advised that it was not too late and, in response to their pleas of helplessness at not having the necessary ritual items, miraculously gave them two coins to obtain whatever was necessary. Somehow collecting sugar, fruit, flowers, and incense, they sat down for the narration of the "event." When the young women appeared before the king the next day, they requested him to verify the events for which they were accused, and it transpired that all was well once again. The women then explained what had taken place, and the king promised to repeat the ritual aithfully himself from that time onward.

> After narrating both the Events, the masked lady disappeared. The widow when she returned back to her house found that all her neighbour women who had refused to participate were inflicted with various afflictions.
>
> May the Almighty Allah, for the sake of *Janab-e-Sayyidah* . . . fulfill your wishes as he fulfilled the widow's wishes. Amen.

Almost every miracle tale has as its basis the story of a person struck by hardship or tragedy who feels helpless to solve the problem. In the story above it is a struggling single parent who suddenly loses her child. The theme of powerlessness is one with which many women can identify. Indeed, many of the stories (but not all) have a woman as the protagonist. She is usually beleaguered by issues well known to women—home or children at risk, a mother-in-law unfairly treating a new bride, a person at the mercy of the forces of the state. The miraculous intervention of a compassionate and powerful holy person, in this case Fatima, saves the situation. The stories demonstrate that a person is not powerless: she can call for divine aid, and, if she is a faithful and sincere believer and performs the right ritual acts, she can succeed in averting tragedy, if it is God's will.

A second theme that is a regular feature of these accounts is the contrast between unfaithful believers and people of good faith. A look at the widow who almost loses her child yields at least three things that characterize her as a woman of true faith. First, she is grateful. When her son returns home, her first act is to prostrate herself and thank God. Second, she honors her word. Her second act is immediately to rush out and purchase what is necessary to fulfill her vow. Finally, she is innocent in her ignorance. She herself does not know the story of Fatima but is earnest in wanting to learn. In contrast, we are presented with the unfaithful believer, who in this story is portrayed by the widow's female neighbors. When the grateful and relieved widow goes to each of her neighbors to ask them to narrate the "Events" of Fatima, the women have either forgotten or are not interested in "imaginary tales." Those who have forgotten are not innocent like the widow in their lack of knowing. Rather they have heard the accounts but have failed to value them, and by implication Fatima, by seeing that they continue to be told. The women who dismissed the events as imaginary stories echo actual voices from the Shia community: people who discredit recitations and rituals based on the miracles of the *Ahl-e-Bayt*. The miracle story addresses this situation directly, upholding the rightness of the faithful believer and promising punishment for the unfaithful, who must endure "various afflictions" for their refusal to respect and honor the *Ahl-e-Bayt*.

A third theme typical of this narrative genre and well demonstrated in the story above is instruction about the ritual itself. When the widow cannot find someone to narrate the Events of Fatima, the mysterious lady comes herself to perform this task. Be attentive, she tells the widow, and remember the story. The injunction is to keep the story of the power and grace of Fatima alive, not just in one's individual consciousness but in the community's collective memory as well. The believer is told that people will dismiss the tales or be uninterested in remembering them, but that they will reap the consequences of their unbelief. The listener also learns the importance of honoring a vow, even if it is made (as was the widow's) while one is unconscious. There are dire results for failing to do what one has promised, as the two young women who were imprisoned by the king discover. Even in such a situation, however, there is a window of mercy for those who repent with sincere hearts.

Interestingly, the details of ritual performance are assumed to be known to the listener. For example, the widow vows to "call someone to tell her the Narration of *Janab-e-Sayyidah.*" When her son returns, she immediately rushes out to purchase some sweets as her first act in fulfilling the promise. The connection between the sweets and the storytelling is assumed to be known by the listener. In the account of the two rescued women, when the two are in prison and decide to perform the ritual, they purchase sugar, fruit, flowers, and incense. Again, the details of what they do with these items is not part of the story. It is assumed that the listener already knows how one recites such a story: in a devout way (incense and flowers contributing to the sanctifying of the space), with the narrative consecrating the proffered sweets, fruits, or other edible items that are later consumed or shared by the listeners. A related point that almost every miracle story communicates is that the protagonist is able to obtain all she needs to conduct the ritual with very little money—"two coins" being the commonly specified amount. The implication is that anyone can perform the ritual, for it is simple, affordable, and accessible to all.

Telling the story in a ritual such as the *dastarkhan* also offers what Jamzadeh and Mills (1986, 35) call a "sacred origin legend." In other words, placing the story of Fatima's intervention within the context of religious history helps to establish the authority of this particular ritual. In the narratives detailed above, it is the two substories that define the ritual's origins: the first narrates the miracles of Fatima, the living daughter of the Prophet, and the second demonstrates how the otherworldly Fatima comes to Earth to help faithful believers. In the first account a worried Fatima is uncertain about attending a wedding because she lacks clothing worthy of the occasion. The miraculous transformation of her garments reflects her great favor with God. But the heart of the story comes later when Fatima petitions God to restore the life of the dead bride, and as a result more than five hundred Jews convert to Islam. Here, then, is the theology of petition and intercession: calling on the righteous Fatima enlists her help in petitioning God, through which all power comes, and brings great blessing to the community.

The second story of the young women lost in the forest helps to place Fatima's intervention in a larger context, for it demonstrates that the departed Fatima continues to be present in the world. The veil is a powerful symbol that signals the earthly presence of this otherworldly Fatima. All the saintly characters in miracle stories are veiled—even when they are men. The veil does not function as a symbol of modesty as it does in human society; if it did, Fatima would have no need to veil when she appeared to a woman in a dream, for men are absent. Rather, the veil conveys a respectful boundary that divides the believer from the mysterious sacred. It symbolizes the otherworldliness of the *Ahl-e-Bayt* who are not of this life, even though they have the power and authority to enter it. Moreover, the veil conveys a sense of mystery, reminding the believer that the figure must be discovered and known. Not everyone will recognize the intercessor's presence. The veil also hints at the fact that the world has not always been a safe place for the family of the Prophet. Shias know that each imam died as a martyr and that the world continues to be filled with many who reject the authority of the *Ahl-e-Bayt*. Only on the Last Day will all be revealed. For now, simply being able to recognize the soul behind the veil is a mark of faithfulness, for it is the true believer alone who recognizes the blessed chosen of God.

The miracle story, then, functions on many levels within the *dastarkhan*. It transmits important theological ideas about the sovereignty of God, the roles of the Prophet and *Ahl-e-Bayt*, the nature of intercession, and the concept of mercy. It provides reassurance and the promise of empathy: one is not alone in facing hardships, for there are others have suffered, including the family of the Prophet. It also reminds women of their agency in situations of overwhelming trouble, for they can achieve change by seeking the intervention of powerful sacred souls. In the *dastarkhan* the miracle tale is a reminder that through ritual a true believer has access to saving grace.

Not all women are comfortable with the miracle story tradition. Some Shias equate them with backward, less-educated religious practice. For example, Jamzadeh and Mills (1986, 42) have clarified that in Iran these stories often seem to be part of ritual in rural areas, with urban women tending to substitute texts that are more accepted by the religiously orthodox, such as martyrdom accounts. Torab (1998, 133) has noted that in the wake of the Iranian revolution, more conservative female gatherings of religious teaching and prayer (*jalaseh*) have sidelined to some degree the once popular *dastarkhan* (*sofreh*) rituals. Some Shias regard the stories as spurious and ignore them. For instance, in his brief essay on "ritual practices in Shi'ism," Seyyed Hossein Nasr ([1975] 1981b: 231–33) failed to mention the reciting of these popular tales in an otherwise comprehensive list of acts of faith that includes remembrance gatherings, reenactments of the events of Karbala, almsgiving, petitioning God for special needs, reciting the Quran, and the offering of litanies and prayers. In Hyderabad during the period of my research, the recitation of miracle stories related to the family of the Prophet seemed to be accepted across class and education levels. Perhaps this is because the narration is only one small part of the *dastarkhan*, with women having great latitude to incorporate other testimonies to faith, including Quranic readings, traditional prayers, and recitations of martyrdom stories. Women's openness to these tales may also reflect the fact that at its root, the miracle story simply upholds the notion that the *Ahl-e-Bayt* has the power to intervene miraculously in people's lives—a belief that few Shia choose to dispute.

Summary

Two ways in which devout women seek divine intervention in their lives are *amal* and *dastarkhan,* which differ in form but share ideas of blessing, intercession, and a transcendent power that aids in solving worldly problems. The emphasis on transforming the here and now is important, for it counters a dominant ideology that gives priority to worldly restraint and heavenly reward. Azam Torab (2005, 214) has pointed out that the Shia hierarchy in Iran generally denounces attention to what it sees as selfish, materialistic concerns in favor of desires directed toward the world to come. Yet a theology that gives primacy to the hereafter, with its imagined ideals of equality and justice, denies the reality of an existing world where social and material exclusions prevail—especially for those without privilege or authority. Intercessory rituals implicitly reject this hereafter ideology. As one devout woman succinctly put it, "There is no divide between religion [*din*] and the world [*duniya*]" (interview, Toronto, 6 April 2001). Such a here-and-now theology is not necessarily gender specific, as confirmed by studies on male religious behavior among rural or otherwise marginalized Muslims, such as Reinhold Loeffler's (1988) classic study of an Iranian village. What it does illuminate is a difference between those who see "pure faith" as separate from the cares of this world and those who see it as deeply embedded in actual human existence. Women are more often among the latter, for several reasons.

It is the challenges of life, according to the religious orator Jamila Jafri, that lie at the very heart of faith. To clarify her point the Hyderabad *zakira* relates the story of her pilgrimage to the grave of the eighth imam. In describing the scene she points out that there is always a crowd of people at the tomb. Women are among the most frequent visitors and come with tremendous devotion all through the day: at prayer times, between prayer times, early in the morning, and through the night.

> We say that since Imam-e-Raza died in exile, God promised that his tomb would always be full of pilgrims. Whether that is the reason for it or not, you find that whenever you visit, the place is packed. It is only with great difficulty that you can get to the latticework wall [*jali*] immediately surrounding the grave. . . . Anyway, when I was there I went early in the morning. There were crowds but somehow I managed to make it to the wall. Near me was this big [she uses her arms to show mammoth proportions] Iranian woman. She was clinging to the latticework, praying, praying. I

> know a bit of Persian, and it is close enough to Urdu that I could understand what she was saying. I was trying to go around the tomb and she blocked my way. I just couldn't get past her [to do the traditional rituals of visitation]. And what was she saying? "Oh, Imam-e-Raza, I've lost my sheep! Find my sheep!" [Jamila's face is animated and she begins to laugh vigorously]. Find my sheep! I come all the way from India and I cannot go around the tomb of my Imam because this woman has lost one sheep! *This* is devotion! (Interview, Hyderabad, 28 January 2000)

Finally taking a much anticipated pilgrimage to Iran, Jamila cannot perform the accepted ritual of circumambulating the tomb of a beloved imam because a local woman clings to it, sharing her current trial and plea with a sacred soul in whom she has absolute faith. As a female ritual leader, Jamila sees in the pleading pilgrim a powerful example of devotion, for the woman trusts completely in the intercessory power of the family of the Prophet. As Jamila implies, however, sharing one's struggles, challenges, and joys is just one side of a lively mutual relationship. Faithful believers also remember and honor the joyous and painful episodes in the lives of the *Ahl-e-Bayt*. Jamila points out that the crowd of pilgrims who regularly flock to the imam's tomb fulfills God's promise that, despite dying far away from home and family, this revered leader will never be alone. Thus, in the eyes of this religious leader, faith is deeply embedded in a web of interdependent relationships.

This relational framework is not confined to connections between the believer and transcendent souls. It also extends to the needs that women bring before God and the *Ahl-e-Bayt*. More than men, women seem to use ritual to seek divine help on issues faced by children, spouses, parents, and others (Betteridge 1993, 239–45; Fischer 1978, 202–13)—a finding that cuts across religious affiliation. For example, in her book on Hindu women's fasting ceremonies (*vrats*), Anne Mackenzie Pearson (1996) documents how Indian women perform votive fasts as a duty to maintain the well-being of their families as well as to gain personal social, physical, psychological, and spiritual benefits. The work of Susan Starr Sered (1999, [1992] 1996) shows how elderly devout Jewish women use symbols, myths, rites, and theological principles to safeguard the well-being of those with whom they are interdependently linked. This gendering of the human nurturing role is further validated by the community development field. Research in South Asia has revealed that a loan given to a female householder results in positive changes affecting the whole family, whereas a loan given to a male head of the house is most often used outside the home to advance projects to increase capital—which may or may not benefit family members (Jazairy et al. 1992, 293). This finding has shaped development policy, with loans given preferentially to females in order to improve the well-being of families. It is clear that women are relatively more socialized than men to meet not only their own needs but also those of a wider group, and they will use all available resources—prayer, monetary loans, and other means—to do so.

The issue of power adds further complexity to ties between nurture, ritual, and gender. Women's religious leadership is linked with gender separation, with female remembrance gatherings giving women opportunities for autonomy, influence, and ritual authority. Supplication rituals offer something more, since men cannot participate in events such as the *dastarkhan.* In this genre of ritual action, then, women alone have religious authority, their power arising from ritual competency, the *barakat* associated with the family of the Prophet, and tangible signs of answered prayers. This means that men who want to access the power of these supplication rituals must generally request women to perform them on their behalf. This happens not infrequently. For example, one mother told me how, when her oldest daughter became very ill, it was her adult son who asked her to perform an *amal* for her recovery. Torab (1998, 184) has recorded how a mother sponsored a *sofreh* at the request of her two sons, one of whom had gone to the Iran-Iraq front as a medical helper during the war and wanted the rite performed for his safe return. Kathryn Spellman (2004, 59) describes the "relief" expressed by an Iranian immigrant in Britain when he found out that women were offering a *sofreh* for him to pass his university exams. As Andrew Rippin (1993, 117) has noted in his survey of Muslim religious expressions, women's intervention rituals are "powerful tools in the relationship between men and women."

Most of the women with whom I spoke in Hyderabad saw male family members—husbands, brothers, and sons—as supportive of female-led intercessory rites. Although I did not personally encounter male antipathy about women-led rituals (indeed, I did not encounter overt female disapproval of such rituals either), some Shia religious authorities contest these rites of supplication. According to Laal Jamzadeh and Margaret Mills (1986, 56), for example, the religious orthodoxy in Iran is critical of female attempts "to initiate an individual, personal relationship with the sacred, on the analogy of earthly personal relationships." For these male leaders the *dastarkhan* or *sofreh* is a misperception of piety, a "pseudo-religious excuse for a party," and an un-Islamic invention.

It is possible that support for the *dastarkhan* or *amal* may decline as women engage more actively with the views of a critical multinational orthodoxy, whether through study and exchange or via information gained from the Internet and other electronic sources. In Uzbekistan, for example, religiously trained women in the late 1990s pressed for more orthodox ritual observances (Kandiyoti and Azimova 2004, 341–45), and female religious leaders have critiqued popular female practices in Tehran and Britain (Torab 2006, 134–36; Spellman 2004). However, given the dynamics of segregation and women's capacity for independent thought and action, there is no guarantee that women will choose to curtail their popular religious behaviors in response to criticism from the religious establishment. As Sabine Kalinock (2003, 546) observed in Tehran, the rejection of women's votive practices by the male hierarchy has only increased the popularity of such rites, especially among women critical of the escalating conservatism of that society.

With supplication rituals being a source of power for women, it is interesting to speculate why men have not tried to appropriate them. The powerful rituals of women's bereavement ultimately metamorphosized into commemoration gatherings led by men—at least in mixed-gender environments. Why have these rituals been gendered so differently? If we look at history, we find that the Shia community was severely persecuted in the decades following the death of Imam Husayn. Uniting for mourning gatherings was one of the few ways the community could legitimately meet, and the emotive narratives of the developing ritual offered a powerful means for building and solidifying Shia identity. Given male dominance in the society and male investment in promoting and shaping the ritual, it is not surprising that men ultimately assumed leadership with regard to this effective tool. Supplication rites, in contrast, are an expression of personal devotion that seeks to feed cosmic relationships and institute change in individual circumstances. On their own, *amal* or *dastarkhan* do not offer a strong means for building or mobilizing a communal identity and are therefore less attractive to people seeking ways to consolidate societal power. Should circumstances shift and the rituals become more useful in increasing some aspect of power, this situation could change. This shift seems to have taken place in some Indian Sunni shrines where men are in charge of organizing intercessory rituals involving food (*nazr*) on behalf of petitioners. At those sites male administrators have succeeded in turning extremely popular female rituals into income-producing activities for the shrine and, in the process, have shifted the gendering of the ritual.

What can we conclude about why collective supplication rituals remain so popular among devout women? Personal agency is certainly a strong factor, with women using *amal* and *dastarkhan* as tangible ways to address overwhelming difficulties, shed feelings of helplessness, and gain a sense of power and control. Equally powerful is the opportunity women gain to share their stories and challenges with others. Over the last decade, research has revealed a gendered link between positive social relationships and the human stress response. More specifically, as psychophysiologist Shelley E. Taylor has argued in her book *The Tending Instinct* (2002, 23–24), the pull to engage in mutually empowering relationships seems actively to mitigate the mental and physiological effects of stress among women. Taylor and her colleagues reviewed thirty North American studies that tested people's responses to situations such as unemployment, cancer, death in the family, sadness, and fear of crime. The research revealed that men tend to use a coping strategy of "putting their worries behind them," while women talked with friends, shared their problems, and tried to clear their concerns by airing them with others. In what is astounding unanimity for any scientific investigation, all thirty studies found women's responses to be "profoundly more social" than men's. Taylor concluded that turning to the social group during times of stress ranks alongside giving birth as one of the most reliable sex differences there is. She also argues that the female tendency to react to threatening situations by connecting with others has a very tangible impact on mental and physical health. Human stress systems react less strongly or recover more quickly when a person engages in positive social behaviors including sharing information, talking about fear or other feelings, giving or receiving practical help, and even experiencing the "invisible social support" of people's company.

Although Taylor's work is based on North American studies, her findings are intriguing. The innate response to "tend and befriend" during times of stress can help explain women's tendency to seek out the company and support of others when facing a crisis. It also may suggest why men and women often see the social benefit of ritual activity so differently, with men critiquing women's socializing at religious rituals as "wasting the whole day," while women identify forming and sustaining relationships as an important part of ritual gatherings. Elizabeth Warnock Fernea and Basima Q. Bezirgan (2005, 237) have posited an alternative explanation of this gender difference. They argue that men's economic productivity tends to place them in public social situations on a daily basis, whereas women's home-centered economic productivity limits direct contact with other women. This gendering of work means that men's needs for socializing are met through regular daily activity, while women must construct opportunities to meet similar needs of interacting with people outside the family. Whether one accepts the sociological explanations of Fernea and Bezirgan or the physiological ones offered by Taylor, there is no doubt that the social benefit of gathering with others is an important part of why *amal* and *dastarkhan* remain popular activites among religious women.

Conclusion

To document and explore the religious lives of Ithna Ashari Shia women a gendered approach is crucial, for most research and writing on Shia faith implicitly or explicitly reflects male expressions and beliefs. Thus this book has set out to answer three main questions. The first—how do pious Shia women nurture and sustain their devotional lives?—finds its answer in the exploration of female piety in terms of religious narrative, sacred space, ritual performance, female leadership, and iconic symbols. Such an exploration moves one beyond the common portrayal of Muslim women as part of a shallow backdrop to male-centered events and affords glimpses of female leadership in a variety of settings: narratives of Fatima, Zaynab, and Hind; contemporary remembrance gatherings and supplication rituals; and the founding and running of a unique women-only public shrine. Women use ritual to accompany, nurture, and take strength from others, whether the relationships exist within social or family circles or span the cosmos through ties to the family of the Prophet. These and other observations of women's rich religious lives have demonstrated how women actively construct rituals and spaces that powerfully express Shia devotion.

The second question—what new insights into Shia faith are gained through an understanding of the gendering of religious practice?—yields several fascinating findings. Female voices within Shia founding stories enlarge one's sense of how those events have meaning for believers. The struggle for succession to the Prophet becomes a story of loyalty and faithfulness rather than of winning or losing leadership; the events at Karbala give insight into what bravery means in the face of tragedy, moving beyond a focus on martyrdom as the sole expression of faith and commitment. Particularly illuminating is the high value placed on witnessing to the truth, an emphasis that defines not only the historical actions of Fatima and Zaynab but also a crucial female ritual role in shaping male religious identities. Uncovering the female origins of widely popular Shia rituals offers intriguing insights into gender and power in the community. Also enlightening is the exploration of male and female collaboration in rituals having distinct gender-dictated areas of authority or at religious sites managed by women or by men. Clearly, along with a broad shared universe of meaning and action, there are gendered streams of ritual and belief that profoundly influence how believers see, understand, and shape the tenets of Shia faith.

The third and final question asks what alternatives to conceptualizing religious behavior in terms of normative and popular categories might be considered. This scholarly habit, as we have seen, has isolated and devalued women's religious expressions, weakening our understanding of religion as a whole. Normative (or alternative) Islam is best described as a product of a dominant social group; popular Islam is that which is associated with people having only limited ability to define norms authoritatively. Thus the dichotomy most accurately portrays power and privilege in a given society. As we have seen, female visions, authority, and sources of knowledge are often expressed outside recognized religious establishments. While one might argue that this limits the power or resonance of female visions, it would be more accurate to say that this circumstance actually limits our ability to see and acknowledge them. Normative and popular, then, are largely categories that reflect our own visions of dominance and subordination. If we believe that a presumed normative Islam is beneficial in helping us understand what Muslims believe and practice, what shape might it take if the religious lives of marginalized believers such as Shia women were placed at the center?

Scholars have wrestled with the challenges presented by dichotomizing Muslim religious behavior, among them Jacques D. J. Waardenburg (1979) and Abdul Hamid el-Zein (1977). Arguably the most promising concept in more recent discourse is the idea of vernacular religion. Leonard Norman Primiano (1995) first proposed this term to signify religion as humans understand, interpret, and practice it. In part, the new expression was designed to replace *folk religion,* side-stepping the latter term's devalued meaning in comparison with orthodox or normative religion. The concept has drawn upon conceptual models from the fields of linguistics and architecture in which a given language is recognized as having forms that are inextricably tied to local society and geography. Primiano argues that all religion is vernacular at the level of everyday expression; even religious elites who frame doctrines and define boundaries believe and practice vernacularly. This way of seeing religion attempts to level the playing field of power and privilege by emphasizing that religious practices and doctrines gain meaning only when they are articulated and performed by believers.

The challenge of vernacular Islam, however, is that a universal is still assumed. In the worst case, *universal* is equated with a presumed standard Islam, bringing one right back to the problem of an essentialized ideal. When Margaret Mills (2003, 294) notes that there are "grounding principles" of Islam that consist of a universal set of basic requirements for practice and belief, she lists them as the five pillars of faith and the five of practice that are taught in any Sunni religious primer: belief in one God, in angels, in the revealed books, in the prophets, and in the Day of Judgment; and profession of faith, daily prayers, giving alms, fasting during the month of Ramzan, and pilgrimage to Mecca. Local Islamic practice, she asserts, is undertaken and debated in reference to these grounding principles. Yet, while these elements are certainly part of what constitutes the overarching language of Islam, it is a mistake to assume they are the touchstone for all religious experience. Projecting a shallow universal abandons the nuance, however limited, that Waardenburg (1979) expressed in asserting that alternative visions of normative Islam simultaneously exist.

To give an example, while all Muslims might accept the Quran as a source of authority, they differ in their ideas about what its words mean and in their access to those words. Muslims also see as authoritative the words and actions of the Prophet, although here again they may have different opinions on what those are and what they mean. These are not, however, the only sources of religious guidance and authority. Some Muslims draw upon the written reflections of the imams or the stories of their lives, or the guidance of religious leaders, or the inspiration gained through Sufi rituals, or the legal guidelines of a moral and religious code (*sharia*). Furthermore, even when people agree on sources of knowledge, they may disagree about the emphasis each should receive.

The second problem with identifying universal principles is that we assume they are imposed from above rather than constructed from below. In other words, they narrow the scope of religious vision, making it more difficult to hear the priorities and visions of actual believers. When Reinhold Loeffler (1988) studied the religious lives of an Iranian peasant community, he noted that the reality of men's lives—their hard physical labor and their shaky economic position—made it difficult to accommodate the Islamic core rituals of fasting, daily prayers, pilgrimage, and almsgiving. Responding to their specific existential situation, the men made use of vows, shrines, saints, written prayers, invocations, offerings, almsgiving, mysticism, and the maintenance of virtuous and charitable conduct to face the tangible realities of their existence. For these men Islam was not about fulfilling formalized rituals but about being guided by principles that they saw as intrinsic to being Muslim: a belief in a compassionate God and the resulting human obligation to act compassionately in relationships with all God's creatures.

Loeffler's experience reminds me of an encounter a friend of mine had in Hyderabad. Joyce Burkhalter Flueckiger was conducting the research for her book *In Amma's Healing Room* (2006), the fascinating study of a Muslim female spiritual healer in the city. Having a background in anthropology of religion rather than in Islamic studies, and working for months at a time in a context of Muslim ritual and cosmology, Flueckiger was always seeking to deepen her knowledge of what Muslims believed. One day she asked one of the followers of the healer and the follower's husband, themselves Sufis, "Who is a Muslim?" Flueckiger was surprised at the answer she received from the man, a lower-income working-class person with only moderate education. She expected him to name the five pillars of Islamic practice, or someone who went to a mosque, or even a follower of Prophet Muhammad. But after thinking for a moment, he said, "A Muslim is someone who, when someone is lying sick on the side of a road, stops and helps him. That's a Muslim." Flueckiger found the answer unexpected because she anticipated a more "normative" response. Yet, like the Iranian village men whom Loeffler studied, this urban Sufi-inspired Muslim saw the principle of acting compassionately as intrinsic to Muslim identity. If Flueckiger had assumed that she knew what Islam was, rather than asking for a person's own definition, she would have completely missed this core theological belief which had fundamental importance to this devout believer.

In the present study we have seen that women's ritual activities express central theological ideas of their own. In addition to well-recognized fundamentals of Shia faith, the rituals express a number of other overarching beliefs and values: that there are powerful cosmic personalities who are willing and able to intervene in people's lives; that sacred power expressed through rituals has the ability to transform situations, objects, and persons; and that blessing or grace (*barakat*) is a tangible quality gained through association with holy people, actions, or things. At their core these ideas express a belief in the connection between people and the divine or holy. Strengthened through the collective performance of ritual, these relational principles provide a basis for people's faith in the possibility of influencing worldly events with the help of powerful cosmic friends who are beloved by God.

Part of the reason we do not tend to see these ideas as central to Muslim belief is our own propensity to devalue the religious systems from which they emerge—or at least to privilege as a source of knowledge theological discourse in its formal, systematic form. Susan Starr Sered ([1992] 1996, 33) has challenged us on this point in her captivating study of Jewish women's religious expertise. She suggests that our tendency to favor formal discourse is ethnocentrism of the worst kind, for our underlying assumption is that the experience of the holy is more real and accessible to a religiously trained authority than it is to a devout believer engaged in a meaning-filled ritual—whether lighting candles to protect her family, or reciting revealed words to transform food into a channel for healing. Carol Gilligan (1982) made a similar observation in her seminal research on gender differences in the field of moral development. When Gilligan first entered the moral-development field, traditional measures of moral reasoning drew upon principles of justice as the orienting framework. By working with women Gilligan saw that females often used principles of relationship and care to define and solve moral dilemmas. Because the conceptual model was designed without sensitivity to its male bias, however, it rated these guiding principles lower in moral reasoning than principles of justice. Women thus consistently scored less morally developed than men. Gilligan's great contribution was to point out that the way we construct categories privileges certain perspectives, especially along gender lines, and that this hierarchy has led us to devalue the thoughts and actions of those who are marginal to definition making. Her research also eventually demonstrated that it is not only women whose moral reasoning draws on principles of relationship and care; men access this way of thinking and acting in the world as well.

In striving to place female religious perspectives at the center rather than at the periphery of Shia faith, I have found useful the way in which one renowned Muslim scholar worked through a somewhat similar challenge in a different context. In his preface to the pioneering book *Shia Islam* ([1975] 1981a), Seyyed Hossein Nasr pointed to the denigration and misrepresentation of Shia faith prevalent at the time within the Western study of religion. He noted that Sunni polemical attacks and the theological assumptions of Christian orientalists had heavily colored the Western academic encounter with Shia Islam. Nasr argued that correcting this distorted image of Shia beliefs and practices required that believers explain for themselves the parameters and expressions of their faith. To this end he collaborated with the respected religious authority Allamah Sayyid Muhammad Husayn Tabataba'i to give English readers what was arguably one of the earliest sympathetic guides to Shia beliefs.

There are two points in Nasr's analysis that I find particularly useful. First, he stresses the importance of presenting Shia beliefs and practices on their own terms, that is, "in all their fullness" from within their own traditional foundations and specific viewpoint (7). Shia religiosity, like that of the Sunni, he says, must remain faithful to itself and to its place as an essential aspect of the religion of Islam, even when its viewpoints contradict other perspectives. Second, Nasr affirms that Islam is a "multidimensional reality" (8) which, throughout its history, has lent itself to a multiplicity of interpretations. He calls this a sign of "Divine compassion," for religion's purpose is to convey "the message of heaven" to people having different spiritual and psychological needs and qualities. The affirmation of distinct, differing dimensions of Islam has enriched the religion overall, even while such diversity has also ignited controversy. Nasr argues that Shia Islam is "yet another dimension of the Islamic tradition" (3) and that Islam's essential multiplicity has not compromised its basic unity, but that unity can be understood solely through the prism of esoteric or mystical thought.

Like Waardenburg, Nasr is careful to compare Sunni and Shia "orthodoxies" and to use "authentic Shi'ite representatives" as sources of authority to explicate Shia faith. He would therefore probably disagree with extending his argument to worldviews rooted outside the bounds of Sunni, Shia, or Sufi religious hierarchies.

Still, his approach can be usefully applied to the present work. Scholars have tended to misunderstand and marginalize female religious behaviors at least as much as they once did Shia beliefs and practices. As was required then to correct mistaken information and assumptions, here also is needed a sympathetic, respectful presentation and analysis of a group's religiosity. In chronicling the ritual expressions of a particular female community, the present studies has led to several observations: that women find powerful meaning in religious rituals that they shape and perform; that such activities are grounded in a strong, coherent understanding of what it means to be a faithful Shia; and that such rituals address a range of important spiritual, psychological, and emotional needs. These findings counter simplistic assumptions, including those voiced by some Shia spokesmen, that women's religious behaviors are the result of limited education, lack of sophistication, and a less developed female nature.

When it comes to accounting for diversity in practices and beliefs, Nasr's theological explanation of Islam's essential multiplicity seems a useful alternative to making dichotomized categories. As we have seen, part of the impetus for preserving the normative/popular distinction comes from attempts to convey the unified vision of Islam expressed by many Muslims. Ronald A. Lukens-Bull (1999, 10) was correct in succinctly implying that a significant part of the solution involves separating the theoretical question "What is Islam?" from the theological question "What is Islam?" For Nasr, who draws upon a Shia tendency to distinguish exoteric from esoteric knowledge, Islam's unity is the deeper mystical reality lying behind its overt diversity. Islam is both diverse *and* united, and attempts to compromise the one for the other amount to a betrayal of the worst kind (6).

Implicit in Nasr's view is the acknowledgment of a few broad commonalities in Muslim belief, including the revealed word as a source of authority, and the centrality of narratives surrounding Prophet Muhammad. These common elements are augmented by other aspects to greater or lesser degrees according to the experiences, needs, histories, and priorities of particular individuals, groups, or communities. These may include love for the Prophet's family, acknowledgment of certain basic acts of faithful practice, or belief in God's justice and mercy. A particular emphasis or perspective gives rise to specific priorities and a range of practices and beliefs.

Using this framework in the present study to listen to women as they articulate what is important in their spiritual lives demonstrates that aspects of connection, relationship, and care are foundational. This foundation encompasses a twofold context of relationship: giving and receiving support among family, friends, and community and deepening a supportive relationship with God—particularly through those revered as God's beloved, the *Ahl-e-Bayt.* In other words, women's religious expressions are not a flawed approximation of male-defined norms and behaviors but a vigorous, authentic affirmation of Shia Muslim faith, having an emphasis on loyalty, connection, and saving grace.

I recently met with a cherished friend who had moved to the United States to live with her son. We talked about the shift and the connections she has been making with a new local community of Shias. I asked about the health of her daughter, who lives a long flight away on the opposite coast and had experienced a spontaneous remission from cancer several years earlier. "She is well," my friend beamed, and went on to describe her daughter's latest career advance. I remembered the anguish my friend had felt at the initial diagnosis, her hurried flight to the United States, and the regular phone calls to female ritual leaders and friends requesting *amal* and other prayerful rites for healing. My well-educated friend credits her daughter's miraculous recovery to the intervention of the *Ahl-e-Bayt* and the will of God and knows that, if a crisis should again arise, she can count on the family of the Prophet and a strong, faithful community of women. She continues her rich ritual life, although she now travels further to attend or lead a *majlis* or *jeshn.* Her son is helping her use the Internet to avail herself of other opportunities for connection: video clips of remembrance gatherings in Hyderabad, melodic poetry in audio or written forms, prayers in Urdu, English, and Arabic, sermons and stories about the *Ahl-e-Bayt,* photographs of holy sites, pilgrimages, and processions. My friend acknowledges with a sigh that she lives in a whole new world and admits that this world will enlarge the resources available to her granddaughter, should she decide to become a *zakira.* But it does not change the basics of what is important: giving and receiving support among family, friends and community, and deepening a supportive relationship with God—particularly, through the revered and beloved *Ahl-e-Bayt.*

APPENDIX

Sacred Dates in the Shia Muslim Calendar

The following listing of dates in the Muslim (lunar) year has been adapted from a popularly circulated pocket calendar printed in Hyderabad. The months are given in order.

Muharram

10 martyrdom of (third) Imam Husayn
25 martyrdom of (fourth) Imam Ali Zayn al-Abidin

Safar

7 birth of (seventh) Imam Musa al-Kazim
20 Arbain (fortieth day following the martyrdom of Husayn and his followers on the tenth of Muharram)
28 death of Prophet Muhammad
28 martyrdom of (second) Imam Hasan

Rabi-ul-Awwal

8 martyrdom of (eleventh) Imam Hasan al-Askari
17 birth of Prophet Muhammad
17 birth of (sixth) Imam Jafar al-Sadiq

Rabi-ul-Sani

10 birth of (eleventh) Imam Hasan al-Askari

Jumadi-ul-Awwal

13 death of Fatima (also observed on third Jamadi-ul-Sani)
15 birth of (fourth) Imam Ali Zain al-Abidin (also observed on 5th Shaban)

Jamadi-ul-Sani

20 birth of Fatima

Rajab

1 birth of (fifth) Imam Muhammad al-Baqir (also observed on 6th Rajab)
3 martyrdom of (tenth) Imam Ali al-Naqi

5 birth of (tenth) Imam Ali al-Naqi (also observed on 15th Zu'l-hijja and 2nd Rajab)
10 birth of (ninth) Imam Muhammad al-Taqi
13 birth of (first) Imam Ali
25 martyrdom of (seventh) Imam Musa al-Kazim
27 Shab-e-Miraj (night of the Prophet's journey to heaven)

Shaban

3 birth of (third) Imam Husayn
4 birth of Abbas
6 birth of Zaynab
14 Shab-e-Barat ("The night of mercy"; see Diane D'Souza [2004])
15 birth of (twelfth) Imam Muhammad al-Mahdi

Ramzan

15 birth of (second) Imam Hasan
19–21 martyrdom of (first) Imam Ali

Shawwal

1 Eid-ul-Fitr (feast which celebrates the ending of the fasting month of Ramzan)
25 martyrdom of (sixth) Imam Jafar al-Sadiq (also observed on fifteenth Rajab and fifteenth Shawwal)

Zi-qad

11 birth of (eighth) Imam Ali al-Reza
23 martyrdom of (eighth) Imam Ali al-Reza (also observed on 17th Safar)
Twenty-ninth martyrdom of (ninth) Imam Muhammad al-Taqi

Zul-hijja

1 marriage of Ali and Fatima
7 martyrdom of (fifth) Imam Muhammad al-Baqir
9 martyrdom of Muslim ibn Aqil
10 Eid-ul-Azha (feast of sacrifice, which commemorates the faithfulness of Abraham and his willingness to sacrifice his son)
18 Eid-ul-Ghadir-e-Khumm (occasion on which the Prophet nominated Ali as his successor)
24 Eid-ul-Mubahila (occasion on which the Prophet and his immediate family won a spiritual contest with the Christians, thus testifying to the superiority of Islam)

GLOSSARY

Ahl-e-Bayt (lit. "people of the house"): the family of the Prophet

alam: a symbolic standard of the Prophet's family consisting of an emblematic crest; when displayed by a faithful believer, it is usually attached upright to the end of a pole.

amal (lit. "practice"): a faithful action; usually a litany of prayer said in times of need or crisis and taking the form of a repeated powerful phrase or Quranic verse

anjuman: association; usually a religious association

Arbain: also known as *Chhelum*; the fortieth day after the martyrdom of Husayn and his (male) family and followers on Ashura

Ashura: the tenth day of the Muslim month of Muharram. Although the day had significance from before the time of the Prophet, it has assumed particular significance in the Shia community because it is the day on which Husayn and his followers were killed in Karbala.

ashurkhana (lit. "the house of Ashura"): anything from a lavishly designed building of grand proportions to a shelf in a cupboard or a temporarily transformed room in one's house; most often a building set aside for the housing of sacred icons and a meeting place for the community

ayat (lit. signs): verse from the Quran

barakat: blessing or grace

chador: outer cloak that women wear to conform with ideas of modesty

Chhelum: the fortieth day of mourning and an important remembrance day, often marking the end of the main period of mourning a person's death; for Shias it is also the name of the fortieth day after the tenth of Muharram, that is, an important remembrance day for Husayn and other martyrs of Karbala.

Dar al-Shifa (lit. "House of Healing"): a hospital constructed in the Old City during the time of Hyderabad's Qutb Shah kings. It is now a main Shia center that houses, among other things, a *madrasa,* a library, and several *ashurkhanas.* The neighborhood surrounding the structure is also known as *Dar al-Shifa.*

dastarkhan (lit. "meal cloth"): originally, the tablecloth spread on the ground for a meal; used ritually, a shared ritual meal dedicated in the name of a saint or one of the *Ahl-e-Bayt*

dua: a prayer of petition or supplication

Fatiha (lit. "opener"): a ritual of recited prayers, including *sura Fatiha,* the opening chapter of the Quran, which is generally used to invoke blessings on a person or thing

Fatima: the daughter of Prophet Muhammad and the wife of Ali, the cousin of the Prophet; she is the mother of Hasan and Husayn.

Ghadir-e-Khumm: the oasis at which the Prophet stopped to deliver his "farewell sermon" shortly before his death. In the Shia context it is the place where he formally nominated Ali as his successor before the Muslim community.

hadith: a formally preserved "report" or "account"; in the Shia context, a record of things said or done by the Prophet, the imams, or the *Ahl-e-Bayt*

Hadith-e-Kisa: an account that conveys the unique and holy place of the *panjatan*

hajj: pilgrimage to Mecca during the month of pilgrimage (Zul-hijja), the once-in-a-lifetime Muslim faith practice that includes the performance of certain specified religious rituals and the offering of prayers

hidayat: a "gift" or "present," usually of money. The term is used in religious circumstances when people feel the word *price* or *fee* is inappropriate; for example, when one purchases a Quran or gives recompense to a religious leader or ritual performer.

imam: divinely designated leader and sinless successor to the Prophet; the Ithna Ashari Shia believe there are twelve imams, the twelfth of whom is still alive but in concealment.

Ithna Ashari Shias: Shia Muslims believing in the twelve imams; the majority group among the minority Shias

jeshn: a celebration; normally a birthday or commemoration of a happy event in the lives of the *Ahl-e-Bayt*

jula: cradle; when used in a Shia performative context it is an icon representing the baby killed at Karbala.

Kaba: the most sacred structure in the Grand Mosque at Mecca. It is toward the Kaba that Muslims orient themselves in daily ritual prayer.

khatm (lit. "finished"): in the Hyderabad context, a shorthand term to refer to the ritual of reciting the full Quran in one sitting or during a specified period of time

majlis (lit. "sitting"): a mourning assembly

marsiya: an elegiac poem with a six-line verse form having from eight to more than one hundred verses; it is distinguished by a rhyming scheme of *aaaabb.*

masumeen: the fourteen pure ones—Muhammad, Fatima, and the twelve imams *matam:* an action of mourning consisting of the rhythmic striking of one's body, most often using one's hand on the chest

Mawla: "Master" or "Lord"; a title commonly used for Ali

minbar: a pulpit, usually consisting of stairs, on which the *zakir(a)* sits to deliver a sermon during a Shia assembly

mujizat kahani: miracle story, usually detailing the remarkable intervention of the *Ahl-e-Bayt*

mumin (pl. *mumineen*): a true or faithful believer, that is, a Shia

Nadi-Ali (lit. "call on Ali"): a prayer praising the first imam and calling for his intercession and help

namaz (Urdu, Persian; *salat* in Arabic): the ritualized form of prayer that most Muslims understand the Quran enjoins them to offer five times a day

nauha: a dirge in couplet form that narrates the tragedy of one or more members of the *Ahl-e-Bayt;* usually chanted at a *majlis* to the accompaniment of *matam*

nazr (noun form of *nzr,* "to vow"): a vow or an offering promised or given in response to a fulfilled vow; *nazr karna:* to vow, to make an offering; *nazr-o-niyaz* (lit. "vow and petition"): gifts and offerings

niyaz (lit. "petition," "supplication," "prayer"): an offering of food or alms in the name of a powerful figure such as the Prophet or member of his family, the imams, or other revered martyrs

niyazkhana: a room for performing votive rituals known as *niyaz*

panjatan (lit. "the five ones"): the central holy persons of the Prophet's family according to Shias—Muhammad, Fatima, Ali, Hasan, and Husayn

purdah (lit. "curtain"): a divide that segregates the women's section from that of the men; also can be used to signify the women's section or a woman's modest dress or outer cloak or covering

qasida: a poem in praise of a person

rakat: one cycle of prayer in the *namaz*

sajdaga: prayer tablet (usually made of earth from Karbala) on which a believer rests her head while performing a prostration during *namaz* or other prayers

salam: salutation, greeting, peace; also a genre of poetry of greeting that praises holy personalities, including members of the Prophet's family

salawat: as the plural of *salat* it means generally prayers or blessings or benedictions; for most Shias it refers to a specific blessing: *Allahumma salla ala Muhammad wa-Ala Muhammad* (O God! Bless Muhammad and the family of Muhammad).

sawab: the spiritual benefit or reward from God gained by performing a good deed or action

sayyid: descendent of Muhammad

sher nishin (lit. "the place where the lion [or tiger] is seated," *lion* being one of the euphemisms for Ali): the name of the room where the *alams* are kept at *ashurkhana* Yadgar Husayni

Shia: a term referring to those who support Ali as the immediate successor of Prophet Muhammad; in the context of this study, those who believe in the twelve imams

sura: one of the one hundred fourteen sections or chapters of the Quran

tabarruk: blessed food; blessing, benediction; "a portion of presents (or what is left of food presented to great men, etc.) given to their dependents" (Platts [1884] 1977)

tabut: the stylized replica of a corpse on a bier; used to represent the body of a slain martyr in Muharram rituals

tasbiḥ: string of prayer beads, usually numbering thirty-three; also sometimes refers to a repetitive litany of prayer

taziya: in the Hyderabad context, a tomb replica; in other places the term refers to a dramatic portrayal of the events at Karbala, sometimes called a passion play.

ulama (pl. of *alim,* "learned," "savant"): formally trained Muslim religious scholars

wuzu: ablutions before prayer

zakira (masc. *zakir*): "one who recites or remembers," a preacher, specifically during mourning or celebratory assemblies

zari: at one time used to refer to a railing or latticework screen surrounding a tomb or temple; in the Hyderabad Shia ritual context, the term refers to a sarcophagus and specifically to a replica of the latticework frame surrounding the tomb of one of the *Ahl-e-Bayt.*

zikr: "remembrance"; one of the terms used to refer to an oration delivered by a *zakir or zakira* at a religious assembly

ziyarat: the visitation or pilgrimage to the grave of one of the *Ahl-e-Bayt* or other revered souls; the term also refers to the ritualized visitation to graves that is accomplished through prayer at various times, including at the end of each *majlis* and *jeshn.*

REFERENCES

Anonymous. 1996. "Hazrat Zainab (a.s.)." *Mahjubah* 15 (7; Safar): 28–29.

Anonymous. 1994. "The holy shrine of Zainab [A.S.] in Damascus." *Ja'fari Observer* 6 (4): 21–24.

Abisaab, Rula Jurdi. 2006. "The Cleric as Organic Intellectual: Revolutionary Shi'ism in the Lebanese *Hawzas*." In *Distant Relations: Iran and Lebanon in the Last 500 Years,* edited by H. E. Chehabi, 231–58. London: I. B. Tauris.

Abou Zahab, Mariam. 2008. "Madrasas de femmes entre le Pakistan et Qom." in *Les Mondes Chiites et l'Iran,* edited by Sabrina Mervin, 287–300. Paris: Karthala.

Abu Talib, Ali ibn. 1990. *Nahjul Balagha.* Translated by Sayed Ali Reza. Areekode, Kerala: Islamic Foundation Press.

Aghaie, Kamran Scot, ed. 2005. *The Women of Karbala: Ritual Performance and Symbolic Discourses in Modern Shi'i Islam.* Austin: University of Texas Press.

——. 2004. *The Martyrs of Karbala: Shi'i Symbols and Rituals in Modern Iran.* Seattle: University of Washington Press.

Agraharkar, Vishal. 2005. "Political Incentives and Hindu-Muslim Violence: A Study of Hyderabad, India." Bachelor of Arts honors thesis, Williams College.

Ahmed, Akbar S. 1988. *Discovering Islam: Making Sense of Muslim History and Society.* London: Routledge.

Ali, Abdullah Yusuf. 1999. *The Meaning of the Holy Qur'an.* Revised edition. Beltsville, Md.: Amana Publications.

Ali, B. Meer Hasan. [1832] 1917. *Observations of the Mussulmans of India. Descriptive of their Manners, Customs, Habits and Religious Opinions.* 2nd edition. Notes and introduction by W. Crooke. London: Oxford University Press.

Ali, Maulana Muhammad. 1944. *A Manual of Hadith.* Lahore: Ahmadiyya Anjuman Ishaat-i-Islam.

Ali, Maulvi Mirza Bahadur. 1996. *Light of Guidance (Chiragh-e-Hidayat).* Hyderabad: Al-Shaheed Publications.

Ali, S. V. Mir Ahmed. 1997. *The Holy Qur'an: With English Translation of the Arabic Text and Commentary according to the Version of the Holy Ahlul-Bait.* Bombay: Al Iman Publication.

Alladin, Bilkiz. N.d. *Prayers for All Occasions.* Hyderabad: N.p.

Anjuman Niswan Barkat-e-Aza. 1996. *Report Salanah.* Hyderabad: Markazi Anjuman Niswan Barkat-e-Aza.

——. 1984. *Al-Husayn.* Hyderabad: Markazi Anjuman Niswan Barkat-e-Aza.

——. 1981. *Qawaid-o-Dawabit.* Hyderabad: Markazi Anjuman Niswan Barkat-e-Aza.

Asifi, Shaykh Muhammad Mahdi-al. N.d. *Supplication in the Eyes of the Ahl al-Bayt.* Translated by Jabir Chandoo. Tehran: Ahlul Bayt World Assembly. www.al-islam.org/supplication-in-the-eyes-of-ahlalbayt-muhammad-mahdi-al-asifi/ (accessed 24 April 2012).

Ayoub, Mahmud. 2000. "*'Asura.*'" In *Encyclopaedia Iranica,* edited by Ehsan Yarshater, 874–76. New York: Bibliotheca Persica Press.

——. 1978. *Redemptive Suffering in Islam: A Study of the Devotional Aspects of "Ashura" in Twelver Shi'ism.* The Hague: Mouton Publications.

Azad, Maulana Abul Kalam. 1985. *The Martyrdom of Husain.* Translated by Muhammad Iqbal Siddiqi. Delhi: Noor Publishing House.

Bamdad, Badr ol-Moluk. 1977. *From Darkness into Light: Women's Emancipation in Iran.* Edited and translated by F. R. C. Bagley. Hicksville, N.Y.: Exposition Press.

Banu, Miryam. 1984. "Tarikh Markazi Anjuman Niswan Barkat-e-Aza." In *Al-Husayn,* edited by Anjuman Niswan Barkat-e-Aza, 12–14. Hyderabad: Markazi Anjuman Niswan Barkat-e-Aza.

Baqri, Mir Hadi Ali. 1978. "*Hydarabad ke qadim ashurkhane.*" In *Jafariya Sade Hydarabad ki Azadari,* edited by Sayyid Taqi Hasan Wafa, 57–77. Hyderabad: N.p.

Bar-Asher, Meir M. 1999. *Scripture and Exegesis in Early Imami Shiism.* Leiden: E. J. Brill.

Bard, Amy. 2005. "'No power of speech remains': Tears and Transformation in South Asian *Majlis* Poetry." In *Holy Tears: Weeping in the Religious Imagination,* edited by Kimberly Christine Patton and John Stratton Hawley, 145–64. Princeton: Princeton University Press.

Barlas, Asma. 2002. *"Believing Women" in Islam: Unreading Patriarchal Interpretations of the Qur'an.* Austin: University of Texas Press.

Betteridge, Anne H. 1993. "Women and shrines in Shiraz." In *Everyday Life in the Muslim Middle East,* edited by Donna Lee Bowen and Evelyn A. Early, 239–47. Bloomington: Indiana University Press.

——. 1989. "The Controversial Vows of Urban Muslim Women in Iran." In *Unspoken Worlds: Women's Religious Lives,* edited by Nancy Auer Falk and Rita M. Gross, 102–11. Belmont, Calif.: Wadsworth Publishing.

——. 1986. "Domestic Observances: Muslim Practices." In *The Encyclopaedia of Religion,* edited by Mircea Eliade, 404–7. Chicago: University of Chicago Press.

Bigelow, Anna. 2004. "Sharing Saints, Shrines, and Stories: Practicing Pluralism in North India." Ph.D. diss., University of California at Santa Barbara.

Bilgrami, A. A. 1927. *Landmarks of the Deccan.* Hyderabad: Government of Hyderabad Printing Press.

Bilgrami, Tahseen Ahmed. 1995. "Contribution of the Bilgramis to Islamic Literature (Their *Ashur Khanas* and *Majalis*)." *Noor,* n.s., 1 (2): 29–39.

Brown, G. E. 1912. "Hyderabad." *Muslim World* 2 (1): 66–70.

Buitelaar, Marjo. 1993. *Fasting and Feasting in Morocco: Women's Participation in Ramadan.* Oxford: Berg Publishers.

Calmard, J., and J. W. Allan. 2000. "*'Alam va 'alamat.*" In *Encyclopaedia Iranica,* 785–91. New York: Bibliotheca Persica Press.

Chelkowski, Peter. 1995. "'Ashura.'" In *The Oxford Encyclopaedia of Modern Islam,* edited by John Esposito, 1:141–43. Oxford: Oxford University Press.

——. 1986. "Popular Shi'i Mourning Rituals." *Al-Serat* 12 (1): 209–26.

Chughtai, M. Abdulla. 1936. "The Deccan's Contribution to Indian Culture." *Islamic Culture* 10 (1): 40–62.

Cole, Juan R. I. 2002. *Sacred Space and Holy War: The Politics, Culture and History of Shi'ite Islam.* London: I.B. Tauris Publishers.

——. 1989. *Roots of North Indian Shi'ism in Iran and Iraq: Religion and State in Awadh, 1722–1859.* Berkeley: University of California Press.

Corbin, Henry. 1988. "The Meaning of the Imam for Shi'i Spirituality," translated by Charles Adams. In *Shi'ism: Doctrines, Thought and Spirituality,* edited by Seyyed Hossein. Nasr et al., 167–87. Albany: State University of New York Press.

Cornell, Rkia E. 1999. "Introduction." In *Early Sufi Women: Dhikr an-Niswa al-Muta'abbidat as-Sufiyyat by Abu 'Abd ar-Rahman as-Sulami,* 15–71. Louisville, Ky.: Fons Vitae.

Dakake, Maria Massi. 2007. *The Charismatic Community: Shi'ite Identity in Early Islam.* Albany: State University of New York Press.

David-Weill, J. 1960. "*'Alam.*" In *The Encyclopaedia of Islam,* new ed., edited by H. A. R. Gibb *et al.,* 1:349. Leiden: E. J. Brill.

Deeb, Lara. 2006. *An Enchanted Modern: Gender and Public Piety in Shi'i Lebanon.* Princeton: Princeton University Press.

Denny, Frederick M. 1985. "Islamic Ritual: Perspectives and Theories." In *Approaches to Islam in Religious Studies,* edited by Richard C. Martin, 63–77. Tucson: University of Arizona Press.

Doumato, Eleanor Abdella. 2000. *Getting God's Ear: Women, Islam, and Healing in Saudi Arabia and the Gulf.* New York: Columbia University Press.

D'Souza, Andreas. 1997. "'Zaynab, I am coming!' The Transformative Power of *Nawah,*" *Bulletin of the Henry Martyn Institute* 16 (3–4): 83–94.

D'Souza, Diane. 2004. "The Night of Mercy: Gender and Ritual in Indian Islam." *Journal of the Henry Martyn Institute* 23 (1): 3–27.

Eaton, Richard M. 1978. *Sufis of Bijapur: 1300–1700.* Princeton: Princeton University Press.

Eisenstein, Zillah. 1984. *Feminism and Sexual Equality: Crisis in Liberal America.* New York: Monthly Review Press.

Fadlullah, Sayyid Muhammad Husayn. 2002. *Fatimah al-Masumah (as): A Role Model for Men and Women* (London: Al-Bakir Cultural and Social Centre); http://al-islam.org/fatimahrolemodel (accessed 20 January 2004).

Fatima, Riaz. 1995. *Hyderabad main Risai Shaeri: 1857–1957.* Ph.D. diss., Osmania University, Hyderabad.

Fazel, Mohammed K. 1988. "The Politics of Passion: Growing up Shia." *Iranian Studies* 21 (3–4): 37–51.

Fernea, Elizabeth Warnock. [1965] 1989. *Guests of the Sheik: An Ethnography of an Iraqi Village.* New York: Doubleday.

Fernea, Elizabeth Warnock, and Basima Q. Bezirgan. 2005. "Women's Religious Rituals in Iraq." In *The Women of Karbala: Ritual Performance and Symbolic Discourses in Modern Shi'i Islam,* edited by Kamran Scot Aghaie, 229–39. Austin: University of Texas Press.

Fischer, Michael M. J. 1978. "On Changing the Concept and Position of Persian Women." In *Women in the Muslim World*, edited by Lois Beck and Nikki Keddie, 189–215. Cambridge: Harvard University Press.

Flaskerud, Ingvild. 2005. "'Oh, my heart is sad. It is Moharram, the month of Zaynab': The Role of Aesthetics and Women's Mourning ceremonies in Shiraz." In *The Women of Karbala: Ritual Performance and Symbolic Discourses in Modern Shi'i Islam*, edited by Kamran Scot Aghaie, 65–91. Austin: University of Texas Press.

Flueckiger, Joyce Burkhalter. 2006. *In Amma's Healing Room: Gender and Vernacular Islam in South India.* Bloomington: Indiana University Press.

Friedl, Erika. 1994. "Sources of Female Power in Iran." In *In the Eye of the Storm: Women in Post-revolutionary Iran*, edited by Mahnaz Afkhami and Erika Friedl, 151–67. Syracuse: Syracuse University Press.

Geetha, V. 2005. "Justice in the Name of God: Organising Muslim Women in Tamil Nadu." Paper presented at the conference "Negotiating Gender Justice," organized by the Centre for Global Feminist Studies, Gotenburg University, Sweden, 1–3 March.

Ghadially, Rehana. 2003. "A Hajari (Meal Tray) for 'Abbas Alam Dar: Women's Household Ritual in a South Asian Muslim Sect," *Muslim World* 93 (2): 309–22.

Gilligan, Carol. 1982. *In a Different Voice: Psychological Theory and Women's Development.* Cambridge: Harvard University Press.

Good, Mary-Jo DelVecchio. 1978. "A Comparative Perspective on Women in provincial Iran and Turkey." In *Women in the Muslim World*, edited by Lois Beck and Nikki Keddie, 482–500. Cambridge: Harvard University Press.

Gottschalk, Peter. 2000. *Beyond Hindu and Muslim: Multiple Identity in Narratives from Village India.* Oxford: Oxford University Press.

Greenfield, Kate. 1935. "The Chief Shi'a 'Alams of Hyderabad." *News and Notes* (Missionaries to Muslim League) 23 (June): 43–47.

Grimes, Ronald L. 1993. *Reading, Writing, and Ritualizing: Essays on Ritual in Fictive, Liturgical, and Public Places.* Washington D.C.: Pastoral Press.

Gross, Rita M. 2002. "Feminist Issues and the Methods in the Anthropology of Religion." In *Methodology in Religious Studies: The Interface with Women's Studies*, edited by Arvind Sharma, 41–66. Albany: State University of New York Press.

Grunebaum, Gustav von. [1951] 1981. *Muhammadan Festivals.* London: Curzon Press.

Guillaume, Alfred, ed. and trans. 1955. *The Life of Muhammad: A Translation of Ishaq's Sirat Rasul Allah.* London: Oxford University Press.

Hameem, Zahra and Zeinab Al. N.d. "Fatima Al-Zahra (p.b.u.h.)." Holy Karbala Net. http://holykarbala.net/english/fatima/ (accessed 16 May 2012).

Hashmi, Shabbir Ali, comp. 1999. *Selected Duaas for Many Occasions.* Hyderabad: Hawra Fatima Islamic Publications.

Heck, Paul L. 2004. "Vow." In *Encyclopedia of the Qur'an*, edited by Jane Dammen McAuliffe, 449–51. Leiden: E. J. Brill.

Hegland, Mary. 1998. "Flagellation and Fundamentalism: Transforming Meaning, Identity and Gender through Pakistani Women's Rituals of Mourning." *American Ethnologist* 25 (2): 240–66.

——. 1995a. "Shi'a Women of North-west Pakistan and Agency through Practice: Ritual, Resistance, Resilience." *Political and Legal Anthropology Review* 18 (2): 65–79.

——. 1995b. "Mixed Blessing: The *Majles*—Shi'a Women's Rituals of Mourning in North-west Pakistan." In *Mixed Blessings: Religious Fundamentalisms and Gender Cross-Culturally,* edited by Judy Brink and Joan Menchers, 179–96. New York: Routledge.

——. 1995c. "*Ahl al-Bayt.*" In *The Oxford Encyclopaedia of Modern Islam,* edited by John Esposito, 1:51–53. Oxford: Oxford University Press.

——. 1990. "Women and the Iranian rRevolution: A Village Case Study." *Dialectical Anthropology* 15 (2–3):183–92.

Hejaiej, Monia. 1997. "Women Storytellers in Tunis: A Living Tradition." Paper presented as part of the panel "Manipulating Tradition, Negotiating the Present in Oral Arabic Popular Literature" at the 31st Annual Meeting of the Middle East Studies Association of North America, San Francisco, 22–25 November.

Hjortshoj, Keith Guy. 1987. "Shi'i Identity and the sSignificance of Muharram in Lucknow India." In *Shi'ism Resistance and Revolution,* edited by Martin Kramer, 289–309. Boulder, Colo.: Westview Press.

——. 1977. "Kerbala in Context: A Study of Muharram in Lucknow, India." Ph.D. diss., Cornell University.

Hollister, John Norman. [1943] 1953. *Islam and Shia's Faith in India.* London: Luzac.

Hooker, Roger. 1994. "Rahi Masoom Raza's 'Half the Village.'" *Bulletin of the Henry Martyn Institute* 13 (3–4): 19–43.

Howarth, Toby M. 2005. *The Twelver Shi'a as a Muslim Minority in India: Pulpit of Tears.* London: Routledge.

——. 2001. *The Pulpit of Tears: Shi'i Muslim Preaching in India.* Amsterdam: Vrije Universiteit.

Hussain, Mir Moazzam. 1997. "Hazrat Zainab, the Incomparable." *Noor,* n.s., 1 (4): 6–10.

Hyder, Syed Akbar. 2006. *Reliving Karbala: Martyrdom in South Asian Memory.* Oxford: Oxford University Press.

Imamiyah Dinyat. 2001. 6 vols. Lucknow: Tanzim al-Makatib.

Imani, Ayatullah Sayyid Kamal Faghih, comp. 1999. *A Bundle of Flowers from the Garden of Traditions of the Prophet and Ahlul-Bayt (a.s.).* 4th edition. Translated by Sayyid Abbas Sadr-Ameli. Edited by Celeste Smith. Isfahan: Amir-ul-Mu'mineen Ali (a.s.) Library.

Jafri, S. Husain M. 1979. *The Origins and Early Development of Shi'a Islam.* New York: Longman.

Jamzadeh, Laal, and Margaret Mills. 1986. "Iranian *Sofreh:* From Collective to Female Ritual." In *Gender and Religion: On the Complexity of Symbols,* edited by C. W. Bynum, S. Harrell, and P. Richman, 23–66. Boston: Beacon Press.

Jazairy, Idriss, Mohiuddin Alamgir, and Theresa Panuccio. 1992. *The State of World Rural Poverty: An Inquiry into Its Causes and Consequences.* New York: New York University Press.

Jones, Justin. 2011. *Shi'a Islam in Colonial India: Religion, Community and Sectarianism.* Cambridge: Cambridge University Press.

Joseph, Suad, ed. 2003–2007. *Encyclopedia of Women & Islamic Cultures.* 6 vols. Leiden: E. J. Brill.

Kalinock, Sabine. 2003. "Supernatural Intercession to Earthly Problems: *Sofreh* Rituals among Shiite Muslims and Zoroastrians in Iran." In *Zoroastrian Rituals in Context,* edited by Michael Stausberg, 531–46. Leiden: E. J. Brill.

Kamalkhani, Zahra. 1993. "Women's Everyday Religious Discourse in Iran." In *Women in the Middle East: Perceptions, Realities and Struggles for Liberation,* edited by H. Afshar, 102–13. London: Macmillan.

Kandiyoti, Deniz, and Nadira Azimova. 2004. "The Communal and the Sacred: Women's Worlds of Ritual in Uzbekistan." *Journal of the Royal Anthropological Institute* 10 (2): 327–49.

Khalidi, Omar. 1992. "The Shi'ahs of the Deccan: An Introduction." *Hamdard Islamicus,* 15 (4): 31–52.

Khan Saheb, Nawab Mir Riasat Ali. 1972. "*Koh-i Mawla Ali.*" *Mahnama Mahe Kamil,* May–June: 3–9.

Khatoon, Zohra. 1990. *Muslim Saints and Their Shrines.* Jammu: Jaykay Book House.

King, Ursula, ed. 1995. *Religion and Gender.* Oxford: Blackwell.

Knighton, William. [1855] 1990. *Nawab Nasir-ud-Din Haider of Oudh: His Life and Pastimes.* New Delhi: Northern Book Centre.

Lalljee, Yousuf N., comp. 1977. *The Martyrdom of Imam Husain, Grandson of the Holy Prophet.* Bombay: Esquire Press Private Ltd.

——. N.d. *Janab-e-Zainab A.S.* Bombay: P. H. Hamid.

Leonard, Karen Isaksen. 2007. *Locating Home: India's Hyderabadis Abroad.* Stanford, Calif.: Stanford University Press.

Lewis, B., Ch. Pellat, and J. Schacht, eds. 1960–2002. *Encyclopaedia of Islam.* New edition. 11 vols. Leiden: E. J. Brill.

Livingston, James C. 1989. *Anatomy of the Sacred: An Introduction to Religion.* New York: Macmillan.

Loeffler, Reinhold. 1988. *Islam in Practice: Religious Beliefs in a Persian Village.* Albany: State University of New York Press.

Lukens-Bull, Ronald A. 1999. "Between Texts and Practice: Considerations in the Anthropology of Islam." *Marburg Journal of Religion* 4 (2): 1–10.

Mahdjoub, Mohammad-Djafar. 1988. "The Evolution of Popular Eulogy of the Imams among the Shi'a." Translated by John R. Perry in *Authority and Political Culture in Shi'ism,* edited by Said Amir Arjomand, 54–79. Albany: State University of New York Press.

Mahmood, Saba. 2005. *Politics of Piety: The Islamic Revival and the Feminist Subject.* Princeton: Princeton University Press.

Marcus, Julie. 1992. *A World of Difference: Islam and Gender Hierarchy in Turkey.* London: Zed Books.

McAuliffe, Jane Dammen, ed. 2001–2006. *Encyclopaedia of the Qur'an.* 5 vols. Leiden: E. J. Brill.

——. 1981. "Chosen of All Women: Mary and Fatima in Qur'anic Exegesis." *Islamochristiana* 7:19–28.

Mehdi, Syed Akbar. 2000. "Azadari of Hyderabad and Its Background." In *Hyderabad ki Azadari,* edited by Syed Taqi Hasan Wafa, translated by Syed Mohammed Taher Bigrami, 5–25. Hyderabad: Idara-e-Jaferia.

Miller, Jean Baker, and Irene Pierce Stiver. 1997. *The Healing Connection.* Boston: Beacon Press.

Mills, Margaret. 2003. "Islam" in *South Asian Folklore: An Encyclopedia,* edited by Margaret A. Mills, Peter J. Claus, and Sarah Diamond, 294–97. New York: Routledge.

Momen, Moojan. 1985. *An Introduction to Shi'i Islam.* New Haven: Yale University Press.

Morgan, David. 2005. *The Sacred Gaze: Religious Visual Culture in Theory and Practice.* Berkeley: University of California Press.

Mufid, Shaykh al-. N.d. *Kitab al-Irshad: The Book of Guidance into the Lives of the Twelve Imams,* translated I. K. A. Howard. Qum: Ansariyan.

Musvi, Rashid. 1989. *Dakkan men Marthiya aur Azadari 1857–1957.* New Delhi: Turqi Urdu Bivru.

Naidu, Ratna. 1990. *Old Cities, New Predicaments: A Study of Hyderabad.* New Delhi: Sage Publications.

Naji, Allama Ghulam-e-Ali Haji. N.d. *Tuhfat al-Awam Maqbul.* Lahore: Ansaf Press.

——. n.d. *Tohfat-ul-Awaam* (abridged and transliterated). Translated by Syed Alamdar Hussain Sajjad Agha. Karachi: Rahe Najat.

Naqvi, Sadiq. 1999. *Essays in Islam.* Hyderabad: Bab-ul Ilm Society.

——. 1993. *Muslim Religious Institutions and their Role under the Qutb Shahs.* Hyderabad: Bab-ul-Ilm Society.

——. 1984. "The Socio-Cultural Impact of Karbala." In *Red Sand,* edited by Mehdi Nazmi, 211–20. New Delhi: Abu Taleb Academy.

Nasr, Seyyed Hossein. 1988. "Shi'ism and Sufism." In *Shi'ism: Doctrines, Thought and Spirituality,* edited by Seyyed Hossein. Nasr et al., 101–8. Albany: State University of New York Press.

——. [1975] 1981a. "Preface." In *Shia,* Allamah Sayyid Muhammad Husayn Tabataba'i, translated by Seyyed Hossein. Nasr, 1–11. Qum: N.p.

——. [1975] 1981b. "Appendix III: Ritual Practices in Shi'ism." In *Shia,* Allamah Sayyid Muhammad Husayn Tabataba'i, translated by Seyyed Hossein. Nasr, 231–33. Qum: N.p.

Nasr, Seyyed Hossein, Hamid Dabashi, and Seyyed Vali Reza Nasr, eds. 1988. *Shi'ism: Doctrines, Thought and Spirituality.* Albany: State University of New York Press.

Nicholson, Reynold A. 1907. *A Literary History of the Arabs.* London: T. Fisher Unwin.

Nigam, M. L. 1984. "Indian Ashur Khanas: A Critical Appraisal." In *Red Sand,* edited by Mehdi Nazmi, 115–23. New Delhi: Abu Taleb Academy.

Noori, Mirza Najm ul Hassan. 2000. "The *Maatami* Groups of Hyderabad." In *Hyderabad ki Azadari,* edited by Syed Taqi Hasan Wafa, translated by Syed Mohammed Taher Bigrami, 101–4. Hyderabad: Idara-e-Jaferia.

——. 1978. "*Hydarabad ke Matam-e-Guruh.*" In *Jafariya Ada-e Hydarabad ki Azadari,* edited by Seyd Taqi Hasan Wafa, 133–37. Hyderabad: N.p.

Olson, Emelie A. 1994. "The Use of Religious Symbol Systems and Ritual in Turkey: Women's Activities at Muslim Saints' Shrines." *Muslim World* 84 (2–3): 202–16.

Omidslalar, Mahmoud. 2006. "Sofreh." In *Encyclopaedia Iranica.* Online edition. http://www.iranicaonline.org/articles/sofra (accessed 10 November 2006).

Padwick, Constance E. 1961. *Muslim Devotions: A Study of Prayer-Manuals in Common Use.* London: S.P.C.K.

Paper, Jordan. 1997. *Through the Earth Darkly: Female Spirituality in Comparative Perspective.* New York: Continuum.

——. 1994. "Slighted Grandmothers: The Need for Increased Study of Female Spirits and Spirituality in Native American Religions." *Annual Review of Women in Religion* 3:88–106.

Patel, Sayyidah Rabap Sultana Akbar. 1992. *Mere Jazbat.* Hyderabad: N.p.

Pearson, Anne Mackenzie. 1996. *"Because It Gives Me Peace of Mind": Ritual Fasts in the Religious Lives of Hindu Women.* Albany: State University of New York Press.

Pelly, Lewis. 1879. *The Miracle Play of Hasan and Husain.* London: W. H. Allen.

Pinault, David. 2001. *Horse of Karbala: Muslim Devotional Life in India.* New York: Palgrave.

——. 1997. "Shi'ism in South Asia." *Muslim World* 88 (3–4): 235–57.

——. 1992. *The Shiites.* New York: St. Martin's.

Platts, John T. [1884] 1977. *A Dictionary of Urdu Classical Hindi and English.* New Delhi: Oriental Books Reprint Corporation.

Pool, John J. 1892. *Studies in Mohammedanism.* Westminster: Archibald Constable.

Prabhudas, D. S. 1998. "Village Muharram Observances in Andhra Pradesh." Master of Theology thesis, Henry Martyn Institute / College of Serampore.

Prasad, Dharmendra. 1986. *Social and Cultural Geography of Hyderabad City: A Historical Perspective.* New Delhi: Inter-India Publications.

Primiano, Leonard Norman. 1995. "Vernacular Religion and the Search for Method in Religious Folk-life." *Western Folklore* 54:37–56.

Qibla, Mawlana Syed Sulaiman Hyder Saht. 1995. "Hazrat Zaynab (a.s.)." *Hashmi Mizan* 1 (7): 7–13.

Qureshi, Regula B. 1996. "Transcending Space: Recitation and Community among South Asian Muslims in Canada." In *Making Muslim Space in North America and Europe,* edited by Barbara Daly Metcalf, 46–64. Berkeley: University of California Press.

Rabinow, Paul. 1975. *Symbolic Domination. Cultural Form and Historical Change in Morocco.* Chicago: University of Chicago Press.

Rahman, Fazlur. 1985. "Approaches to Islam in Religious Studies: Review Essay." In *Approaches to Islam in Religious Studies,* edited by Richard C. Martin, 189–202. Tucson: University of Arizona Press.

Raj, Selva J., and William P. Harman, eds. 2006. *Dealing with Deities: The Ritual Vow in South Asia.* Albany: State University of New York Press.

Rippin, Andrew, ed. 2007. *Defining Islam: A Reader.* Equinox Publishing.

——. 1993. *Muslims: Their Religious Beliefs and Practices.* Vol. 2, *The Contemporary Period.* London: Routledge.

Rizvi, Saiyid Athar Abbas. 1986. *A Socio-Intellectual History of the Isna 'Ashari Shi'is in India.* 2 vols. Canberra: Ma'rifat Publishing House.

Rizvi, Sayyid Muhammad, ed. 1984. *Imam Husayn: The Savior of Islam.* Richmond, British Columbia: N.p.

Rizvi, Yaqoob Hasan. 1996. *Ali—The Miracle of Mohammad (S.A.W.).* Mumbai: Baitul Hamd Publications.

Ross, Denison E. 1914. *An Alphabetical List of the Feasts and Holidays of the Hindus and Muhammadans.* Calcutta: Superintendent Government Printing, India.

Ruffle, Karen G. 2011. *Gender, Sainthood & Everyday Practice in South Asian Shi'ism.* Chapel Hill: University of North Carolina Press.

Sachar, Rajinder, Saiyid Hamid, T. K. Oommen, M. A. Basith, Rakesh Basant, Akhtar Majeed, and Abusaleh Shariff. 2006. "Report on Social, Economic and Educational Status of the Muslim Community of India." Report of the Government of India's High Level Committee on the Status of Muslims in India. http://www.minorityaffairs.gov.in/sachar (accessed 14 October 2011).

Safrani, Shebhaz H. 1992. "Golconda Alums—Shimmering Standards." In *Golconda and Hyderabad,* edited by Shebhaz H. Safrani, 69–80. Bombay: Marg Publications.

Sarma, Rani. 2008. *The Deodis of Hyderabad: A Lost Heritage.* Delhi: Rupa.

Sayyid, Haadee Husayn. 1981. *Biography of Faatimah Zahraa.* Karachi: Peermahomed Ebrahim Trust.

Schimmel, Annemarie. 1987. "Islamic Religious Year." In *Encyclopedia of Religion,* edited by Mircea Eliade, 7:454–57. New York: Macmillan.

Schubel, Vernon. 1993. *Religious Performance in Contemporary Islam: Shi'i Devotional Rituals in South Asia.* Columbia: University of South Carolina Press.

Sered, Susan Starr. [1988] 1999. "The Domestication of Religion: The Spiritual Guardianship of Elderly Jewish Women." In *Across the Boundaries of Belief: Contemporary Issues in the Anthropology of Religion,* edited by Morton Klass and Maxine Weisgrau, 96–112. Boulder, Colo.: Westview Press.

[1992] 1996. *Women as Ritual Experts: The Religious Lives of Elderly Jewish Women in Jerusalem.* New York: Oxford University Press.

——. 1988. "Food and Holiness: Cooking as a Sacred Act among Middle-Eastern Jewish Women." *Anthropological Quarterly* 61 (3): 129–39.

Shaheed, Farida. 1995. "Networking for Change: The Role of Women's Groups in Initiating Dialogue on Women's Issues." In *Faith and Freedom: Women's Human Rights in the Muslim World,* edited by Mahnaz Afkhami, 78–103. Syracuse: Syracuse University Press.

Shams al-Din, Shaykh Muhammad Mehdi. 1985. *The Rising of al-Husayn: Its Impact on the Consciousness of Muslim Society.* Translated by I. K. A. Howard. London: Muhammadi Trust.

Sherwani, Haroon Khan. 1976. "Town Planning and Architecture of Haidarabad under the Qutb Shahis." *Islamic Culture* 50 (2): 61–80.

——. 1974. *History of the Qutb Shahi Dynasty.* New Delhi: Munshiram.

Sherwani, H. K., and P. M. Joshi, eds. 1973. *History of Medieval Deccan 1295–1724.* 2 vols. Hyderabad: Government of Andhra Pradesh Press.

Shureef, Jaffar. 1832. *Qanoon-e-Islam. Customs of the Musulmans of India.* London: Parbury, Allen.

Smith, Wilfred Cantwell. 1991. *The Meaning and End of Religion.* Minneapolis: Fortress Press.

Spellman, Kathryn. 2004. *Religion and Nation: Iranian Local and Transnational Networks in Britain.* New York: Berghahn Books.

Sperl, Stefan, and Christopher Shackle, eds. 1996. *Qasida Poetry in Islamic Asia and Africa: Eulogy's Bounty, Meaning's Abundance.* Leiden: E. J. Brill.

Stetkevych, Suzanne Pinckney. 2010. *The Mantle Odes: Arabic Praise Poems to the Prophet Muhammad.* Bloomington: Indiana University Press.

Stowasser, Barbara Freyer. 1994. *Women in the Qur'an, Traditions and Interpretations.* Oxford: Oxford University Press.

Sulami, Abu 'Abd ar-Rahman as-. 1999. *Early Sufi Women: Dhikr an-Niswa al-Muta 'abbidat as Sufiyyat.* Translated by Rkia E. Cornell. Louisville, Ky.: Fons Vitae.

Tabai, Aqa Sayyid Nasir Mashidi Taba, comp. 1990. *Ibn al-Zahra Wawayla.* Hyderabad: Sadar Markazi Anjuman Matami Guruha Ajmi.

Tabari, Abu Ja'far Muhammad ibn Jarir al-. 1997. *The History of al-Tabari: An Annotated Translation.* Vol. 8, *The Victory of Islam.* Translated and annotated by Michael Fishbein. Albany: State University of New York Press.

——. 1990. *The History of al-Tabari: An Annotated Translation.* Vol. 19, *The Caliphate of Yazid B. Mu'awiyah.* Translated and annotated by I. K. A. Howard. Albany: State University of New York Press.

Tabataba'i, Allamah Sayyid Muhammad Husayn. [1975] 1981. *Shia.* Translated and edited by Seyyed Hossein Nasr. Qum: N.p.

Tapper, Nancy. 1990. "Ziyaret: Gender, Movement, and Exchange in a Turkish Community." In *Muslim Travellers: Pilgrimage, Migration and the Religious Imagination,* edited by Dale F. Eickelman and James Piscatori, 236–55. London: Routledge.

——. 1983. "Gender and Religion in a Turkish Town: A Comparison of Two Types of Formal Women's Gatherings." In *Women's Religious Experience,* edited by Pat Holden, 71–88. London: Croom Helm.

——. 1978. "The Women's Subsociety among the Shahsevan Nomads of Iran." In *Women in the Muslim World,* edited by Lois Beck and Nikki Keddie, 374–98. Cambridge: Harvard University Press.

Tapper, Nancy, and Richard Tapper. 1987. "The Birth of the Prophet: Ritual and Gender in Turkish Islam," *Man,* n.s. 22 (1): 69–92.

Tassy, Garcin de. [1831] 1995. *Muslim Festivals in India and Other Essays.* Translated and edited by M. Waseem. Delhi: Oxford University Press.

Taylor, Shelley E. 2002. *The Tending Instinct.* New York: Times Books.

Thaiss, Gustav. 1995. "*Husayniyah.*" In *The Oxford Encyclopaedia of the Modern Islamic World,* edited by John Esposito, 2:153–55. Oxford: Oxford University Press.

——. 1972. "Religious Symbolism and Social Change: The Drama of Husain." In *Scholars, Saints and Sufis: Muslim Religious Institutions in the Middle East since 1500,* edited by Nikki R. Keddie, 349–66. Berkeley: University of California Press.

Thurlkill, Mary F. 2007. *Chosen among Women: Mary and Fatima in Medieval Christianity and Shi'ite Islam.* Notre Dame, Ind.: University of Notre Dame Press.

Torab, Azam. 2006. *Performing Islam: Gender and Ritual in Islam.* Leiden: E. J. Brill.

——. 2005. "Vows Mediumship and Gender: Women's Votive Meals in Iran." In *Gender, Religion and Change in the Middle East: Two Hundred Years of History,* edited by Inger Marie Okkenhaug and Ingvild Flaskerud, 207–22. Oxford: Berg Publishers.

——. 1998. "The Neighborhoods of Piety: Gender and Ritual in South Teheran." Ph.D. diss., University of London.

Trimingham, J. Spencer. [1959] 1970. *Islam in West Africa.* Oxford: Oxford University Press.

Varshney, Ashutosh. 2002. *Ethnic Conflict and Civic Life: Hindus and Muslims in India.* New Haven: Yale University Press.

Vedantam, T., ed. 1975. *Muharram in Hyderabad City: A Monograph of the Census of India, 1971.* New Delhi: Government of India.

Waardenburg, Jacques D. J. 2002. *Islam: Historical, Social and Political Perspectives.* Berlin: Walter de Gruyter.

——. 1979. "Official and Popular Religion as a Problem in Islamic Studies." In *Official and Popular Religion: Analysis of a Theme for Religious Studies,* edited by Pieter H. Vrijhof and Jacques Waardenburg, 340–86. The Hague: Mouton.

Wafa, Sayyid Taqi Hasan, ed. 2000. *Hyderabad ki Azadari.* Translated by Syed Mohammed Taher Bigrami. Hyderabad: Idara-e-Jaferia.

——. 1978. *Jafariya Ada-e Hydarabad ki Azadari.* Hyderabad: N.p.

Walbridge, Linda S. 1997. *Without Forgetting the Imam: Lebanese Shi'ism in an American Community.* Detroit: Wayne State University Press.

Wiley, Joyce. 2001. "'Alima Bint al-Huda, Women's Advocate." In *The Most Learned of the Shi'a: The Institution of the Marja' Taqlid,* edited by Linda S. Walbridge, 149–60. Oxford: Oxford University Press.

Wink, André. 1993. "Islamic Society and Culture in the Deccan." In *Islam and Indian Regions,* vol. 1, *Texts,* edited by Anna Libera Dallapiccola and Stephanie Zingel-Avé Lallemant, 217–28. Stuttgart: Franz Steiner Verlag.

Winkelmann, Mareike Jule. 2007. *Reaching the Minds of Young Muslim Women: Girls Madrasas in India.* Gurgaon: Hope India Publications.

——. 2005a. "Everyday Life in a Girls' Madrasah in Delhi." In *Educational Regimes in India,* edited by Radhika Chopra and Patricia Jeffery, 160–77. New Delhi: Sage Publications.

——. 2005b. *From Behind a Curtain: A Study of a Girls' Madrasah in India.* Amsterdam: Amsterdam University Press.

Yarshater, Ehsan, ed. 2000–2004. *Encyclopaedia Iranica.* 15 vols. New York: Bibliotheca Persica Press.

Yel, Ali Murat. 1993. "The Great and Little Traditions." *Hamdard Islamicus* 16:89–121.

Young, William C. 1993. "The Ka'ba, Gender and the Rituals of Pilgrimage." *International Journal of Middle East Studies* 25 (2):285–300.

Zakir. 1980. *Tears and Tributes.* 5th revised edition. Hyderabad: Shaheed Associates.

Zein, Abdul Hamid el-. 1977. "Beyond Ideology and Theology: The Search for the Anthropology of Islam." *Annual Review of Anthropology* 6:227–54.

INDEX

ABOUT THE AUTHOR

DIANE D'SOUZA is director of continuing education and of the Mission Institute at the Episcopal Divinity School in Cambridge, Massachusetts. She is widely published in the fields of gender, religion, interreligious dialogue, and peace building. D'Souza lived and worked in India for nearly twenty years, where she taught Islam and Christian-Muslim relations and conducted research on Muslim women's religious practices. She earned her doctorate in religious studies from Vrije University in Amsterdam, the Netherlands.